P

THE POLITICS OF SEX

THE POLITICS OF SEX

Prostitution and Pornography in Australia Since 1945

BARBARA SULLIVAN

Department of Government
University of Queensland

CAMBRIDGE
UNIVERSITY PRESS

PUBLISHED BY THE PRESS SYNDICATE OF THE UNIVERSITY OF CAMBRIDGE
The Pitt Building, Trumpington Street, Cambridge CB2 1RP, United Kingdom

CAMBRIDGE UNIVERSITY PRESS
The Edinburgh Building, Cambridge CB2 2RU, United Kingdom
40 West 20th Street, New York, NY 10011–4211, USA
10 Stamford Road, Oakleigh, Melbourne 3166, Australia

First Published 1997

Printed in Australia by Brown Prior Anderson

Typeset in Baskerville 10/12 pt

National Library of Australia Cataloguing in Publication data

Sullivan, Barbara Ann, 1952–.
The politics of sex: prostitution and pornography in
Australia since 1945.
Bibliography.
Includes index.
ISBN 0 521 55408 X.
ISBN 0 521 55630 9 (pbk).
1. Prostitution – Government policy – Australia – 20th
century. 2. Prostitution – Australia – History – 20th
century. 3. Pornopgraphy – Government policy – Australia –
20th century. 4. Pornography – Australia – History – 20th
century. 5. Sex oriented businesses – Australia – History –
20th century. 6. Sex oriented businesses – Government
policy – Australia –. I. Title.

A catalogue record for this book is available from the British Library

ISBN 0 521 55408 X hardback
ISBN 0 521 55630 9 paperback

Contents

Acknowledgements

Most books have a long and turbulent gestation; this one is no exception. It began as a PhD dissertation in the Department of Government, University of Queensland. My thanks to this department – and to Don Fletcher in particular – for the generous support which they extended to me during my time as a postgraduate student and junior colleague. In 1994–96 I was a Postdoctoral Fellow in the Political Science Program, Research School of Social Sciences, Australian National University. During this period I had the time to re-think, revise and extend the dissertation material into this book. I would like to thank the RSSS and, in particular, Barry Hindess, for making this possible.

There are many friends and colleagues who have sustained me in this work over the years. I owe a special debt of gratitude to Judith Allen who was there at the beginning with love, encouragement and enthusiasm. If this book is an 'end', it would not have been achieved without the friendship of Frances Bonner, Julie James Bailey, Michael Bittman, Chilla Bulbeck, Ian Cook, Elizabeth Grosz, Peter McCarthy, Marcia Neave, Rosemary Pringle, Gail Reekie, Sophie Watson, Elizabeth Wilson, Elizabeth Wood, Anna Yeatman, Christine Helliwell, Judy Wajcman, Kathy Daly and, in particular, Felicity Grace. My thanks too to several postgraduate students who have talked to me about their work, adding pleasure and interest to my life and work – Kylie Stephen, Heather Brook, Helen Keane, Jennifer Curtin, Rebecca Stringer and Bridget Gilmour-Walsh. I am grateful to Fiona Patton, Alison Murray, various members of SQWISI, WISE and the PCV, and fellow members of the Mae West Foundation (ACT branch) for their talk. Also to Warwick, Avinashi, and Ziji for their various gifts and skills. Finally, I would like to thank Gail Reekie and two anonymous readers for their many useful comments and suggestions on the manuscript; and Phillipa McGuinness at CUP for her consistent encouragement to make this book as good as I could.

BARBARA SULLIVAN

Abbreviations

ACTLAD	Australian Capital Territory Legislative Assembly, *Debates.*
CJC	Criminal Justice Commission (Queensland)
Fitzgerald Report	Queensland 1989, *Report of a Commission of Inquiry Pursuant to Orders in Council (Chairperson G. E. Fitzgerald)*
Fitzgerald Transcript	Queensland 1987–88, Unpublished Transcript of Proceedings. Commission of Inquiry Pursuant to Orders in Council (Chairperson G. E. Fitzgerald)
HofR	Commonwealth of Australia, House of Representatives, *Debates.*
JSCVM	Commonwealth of Australia 1988, *Report of the Joint Select Committee on Video Material.*
Neave Report	Victoria, 1985, *Inquiry into Prostitution: Final Report.*
NSWPD	New South Wales, Parliament, *Debates.*
NSWSCP	New South Wales 1986, *Select Committee of the Legislative Assembly Upon Prostitution: Final Report.*
NTLAPR	Northern Territory, Legislative Assembly, *Parliamentary Record.*
QFBR	Queensland, Films Board of Review, *Annual Report.*
QHAR	Queensland, Department of Health, *Annual Report.*
QLBR	Queensland, Literature Board of Review, *Annual Report.*
QPAR	Queensland, Police Department, *Annual Report.*
QPD	Queensland, Parliament, *Debates.*
SAPD	South Australia, Parliament, *Debates.*

Senate	Commonwealth of Australia, Senate, *Debates.*
SMH	*Sydney Morning Herald.*
VPD	Victoria, Parliament, *Debates.*
WAPD	Western Australia, Parliament, *Debates.*
Wolfenden Report	Great Britain, 1957, *Report of the Committee on Homosexual Offences and Prostitution.*

Introduction

The sex industries have undergone a significant expansion and diversification in Australia since the end of World War II. New forms of prostitution – such as massage parlours, escort agencies, fantasy phone-in services, and overseas sex tourism – have emerged alongside the more traditional brothel and street prostitution. Since the early 1970s a vigorous pornography industry has also been established and the public display and private consumption of sexually explicit material has become an important feature of Australian culture. Sex shops selling pornography and sex toys can be found in all capital cities, while a flourishing mail order industry in X-rated videos now operates out of the national capital. Soft-core men's magazines such as *Playboy* and *Penthouse* – as well as more recent additions such as *Australian Women's Forum* (designed for female readers) – are openly displayed in local newsagents. In the 1980s and 1990s, the growth of computer-based information technologies has led to the development of new avenues for distributing pornography.

This book is about the growth of the sex industries since 1945 and about the approaches adopted by Australian law-makers in relation to both 'prostitution' and 'pornography' (in whatever way these terms have been understood by their users). I look at some of the major changes in prostitution and pornography over the last four decades and at how Australian governments have responded to (or, in some cases, helped produce) these changes. This aim of this book is *not* to make a substantial case for more 'freedom' or, alternatively, more government 'control' of commercial sexual practices. I want to step back a little from simply replaying one or the other side of what, at present, looks like a highly polarised debate between those who want more regulation of the sex industries and those who want less. The particular aim of this book is both more circumscribed and descriptive

1

(although in the conclusion I do discuss the legal and policy implications of my analysis). I want to look at how present political debates
about the regulation of pornography and prostitution have been
produced. That is, instead of asking what pornography and prostitution *are* and how they should be dealt with, I seek to establish the
conditions of their 'problematisation' (Foucault 1991). To this end I
look at how politicians and other authoritative public figures have
talked about prostitution and pornography over the last fifty years, the
problems they see to be connected to these practices, and the way
these matters have changed over time.

Today, any discussion of prostitution and pornography is usually
associated with intense controversy. There appear to be fundamental
divisions in the community and within political parties about both the
moral status of these sexual practices and the role that governments
should play in their control. Conservatives, liberals and feminists battle
over the meaning of prostitution and pornography and about the
shape of appropriate forms of regulation.

The nature of this battle has become particularly apparent over the
last two decades in Australia, with the deployment of a range of new
political and legal strategies addressed to the sex industries.[1] In the
1970s, for example, all Australian jurisdictions moved towards regulating – rather than simply prohibiting – the distribution of pornography. Since the 1980s, however, significant conflicts have erupted
about the regulation of sexually explicit material, particularly child
pornography and media that depict sexual violence and non-violent
erotica. A largely uniform approach to the regulation of sexually explicit material now exists across Australia, except in relation to X-rated
videos which can be sold only in the Australian Capital Territory and
the Northern Territory (and cannot include child pornography or
non-consensual sexual violence). Over the same period, significant
conflicts have also occurred about the decriminalisation or legalisation
of prostitution.[2] Some states and territories – notably New South Wales,
Victoria, the Australian Capital Territory and the Northern Territory –
have moved towards a partial decriminalisation of prostitution-related
activities, and Australia now has a more diverse set of prostitution laws
than any other country. Legal zones of prostitution exist in relation to
brothels in the Australian Capital Territory, Victoria and New South
Wales; in relation to street soliciting for the purposes of prostitution in
New South Wales; and in relation to escort agencies in the Northern
Territory and Victoria.

In this book I suggest that many of the conflicts surrounding
present attempts to improve control of prostitution and pornography
have arisen only in the last five decades. This has occurred as the sex

industries have expanded and diversified; as new norms of sexual behaviour have been deployed that emphasise the importance of privacy, sexual freedom and mutuality; and as discourses about the equality of men and women have assumed a new importance within mainstream political institutions. In the present day the sex industries have become an important focus for the negotiation of power. This means that political debates about the regulation of prostitution and pornography have become centrally implicated in broader social negotiations about 'good' or 'inappropriate' sexual behaviour, about 'proper' relations between men and women, and about equality, exploitation, women's citizenship and social justice. My aim in this book is to locate a specific discussion of the sex industries, and of changes in the politico-legal regulation of these, within the context of an examination of broader changes in the political and sexual culture.

The Field of Inquiry

Both *prostitution* and *pornography* are notoriously difficult concepts to define. Prostitution is usually understood as the exchange of money for sex. But, in practice, it is often difficult to establish a clear distinction between prostitution and other types of sexual-economic transactions. So, while most people agree that prostitution includes direct payment for sexual intercourse, there is less unanimity where payment takes the form of presents, accommodation or food. Moreover, as I show in Chapter 7, the legal definition of prostitution has recently expanded in many Australian jurisdictions to encompass voyeuristic practices (for example, strip shows and table-top dancing) as well as non-monetary exchanges.

Similar conceptual difficulties are also evident in the definition of pornography. Dictionaries usually define pornography as 'the explicit description or exhibition of sexual activity in literature, films, etc., intended to stimulate erotic rather than aesthetic feelings' (*Concise Oxford Dictionary of Current English*, 7th edn, 1984). The element of intention is obviously crucial here in terms of distinguishing pornography from other, more aesthetic, representations. But the intention of a text is never completely transparent and it is usually impossible to distinguish pornography objectively from other forms of representation (for example, advertising and non-pornographic erotica) that sexualise and objectify the human body. Moreover, a focus on the 'pornographic' intention of authors, photographers and film-makers tends to obviate the role of the audience, readers and spectators, in the creation of the meaning of a text.

In this book my use of *prostitution* and *pornography* is largely contextual. I examine the way that these terms have been deployed in various periods before, but primarily since, 1945. In particular, I am interested to see how law-makers and policy-makers have described prostitution and pornography, the social problems that are said to emerge from these practices, and changes in ideas about the most appropriate political responses. Thus, the search for definitive or essential meanings is displaced by an examination of how meanings change over time and for actors within specific political and cultural contexts.

Historically, there seem to be links between prostitution and pornography. Various dictionaries cite a historical usage of the term *pornography* as meaning 'the writing of prostitutes'. As I demonstrate in Chapter 1, legal measures designed to eliminate or control prostitution and pornography have often been enacted simultaneously. In the late nineteenth and early twentieth centuries, governments took the view that these and other 'social evils' (such as gambling and opium use) were destructive of the health of both individuals and whole populations. Consequently, all of these practices became subject to much wider criminal penalties.

In the present day, the link between prostitution and pornography is not nearly so visible; separate laws and regulations usually apply to these practices and most people regard them as conceptually distinct. But terms like *the sex industry* have also become widely accepted in governmental and public discourse over the last decade. This terminology is usually used to denote the owners and operators of various sex businesses (such as brothels and mail-order video outlets) as well as their workers and consumers. From this perspective, prostitution and pornography are linked by their status as commercial sexual practices; they both involve an explicit exchange of money for sexual products and/or services.

Some contemporary feminist scholars (Pateman 1988; Barry 1995) also link the practices of prostitution and pornography. Their analyses suggest that masculinist sexual practices – including rape, sexual harassment, prostitution, and the production and consumption of pornography – are instrumental in both creating and maintaining women's oppression. From this perspective, then, there are important conceptual and practical links between prostitution and pornography. While some writers in this camp use the term *sex industry* in their critiques (Pateman 1988), others reject it as a strategy designed to 'normalise' 'female sexual slavery' (Barry 1995).

In the original conceptualisation of this text I also adopted the view that prostitution and pornography existed on a continuum of sexual practice related to women's oppression. More recently, however, I have moved away from the influence of Carole Pateman's *The Sexual Contract* (1988) and sought to address some of the problems associated with this sort of feminist approach (Sullivan 1995). Consequently, in this book, I tend to refer quite specifically to the practices of prostitution or pornography (indicating links where these are apparent but not assuming a link is always present). I also use the terms *sex industries,* or *prostitution industry* and *pornography industry.* As indicated in Chapter 7, this terminology is increasingly used by law-makers and policy-makers in Australia. Its deployment has also brought some clear advantages – particularly, in terms of establishing new regimes of occupational health and safety – for workers in the sex industries.

The term *sexual culture* is used throughout this book to refer to the range of discourses about sex and sexuality which are circulating at any given time. I have been interested to look at what has been understood as 'normal' sexual practice – and how this has changed over time – within the dominant sexual culture. The changing conceptualisation of what is 'normal' – and, therefore, of what is 'abnormal' – appears to have had a significant impact on law and public policy addressed to prostitution and pornography in the post-war period. In each chapter, therefore, I spend some time discussing the constitution of 'normal' sex before going on to look at how law-makers and policy-makers talk about prostitution and pornography.

Existing Approaches

There is an enormous contemporary literature on pornography and prostitution. Some of this material has been written by workers in the sex industries (Pheterson 1989; Delacoste and Alexander 1988; Anderson 1992), by the owners of sex businesses (Richardson 1992), and by professional lobbyists for the industries (Swan 1992; Eros Foundation 1992). There is, of course, also a considerable academic literature on pornography and prostitution. Most of this has emerged from the disciplines of history, sociology, psychology, criminology, political science and English literature, and from interdisciplinary areas such as gender studies and cultural studies (Daniels 1984b; Day and Bloom 1988; Donnerstein *et al.* 1987; Elshtain 1990; Griffin 1981; Hebditch and Anning 1988; Hobson 1987; Horn and Pringle 1984; Kendrick 1987; Pateman 1988; Kimmel 1990; Bell 1994).

In the Australian context, little academic research has been done on the sex industries. In the 1960s and 1970s several authors investigated specific aspects of pornography and prostitution (Coleman 1974; Dunstan 1968; Turner 1975; Winter 1976). More recently, some important social science research on the prostitution industry has been

published (Perkins and Bennett 1985; Hatty 1989; Perkins 1991;
Perkins *et al.* 1994) and a significant feminist literature on the history
of prostitution has been created (Allen 1990; Arnot 1986; Daniels
1984b; Davidson 1984; Dixson 1976; Horan 1984; Summers 1975).
Australian feminists appear to have been less interested in pornography (exceptions include Gross 1981; Jones 1984; Pringle 1981).

Most of this Australian and international material addresses a
different range of concerns from the ones under investigation in this
book. In general, there has been remarkably little attention in the literature to the constitution of the sex industries as a social and political
problem – particularly in the post-war period – and to the role of the
'normal' sexual culture in this process. The available literatures tend
not to explore changes in the politico-legal context in which the sex
industries operate or to describe the legal regulation of prostitution
and pornography in relation to changes in 'normal' sexual culture.

A great deal of the contemporary Australian and international literature on prostitution and pornography is also flawed by a number of
significant conceptual problems. In the first place there is often an
explicit or latent sexual essentialism. There is, then, a tendency for all
sexual relations (including those which are enacted commercially) to
be represented as the product of natural drives and instincts rather
than as activities which, although corporeally located, are always situated in a particular cultural context. Male sexuality in particular is
often represented as an essential biological drive, relatively unaffected
by prevailing social and cultural mores. This is why prostitution is
commonly referred to as 'the oldest profession', and as both an
ancient and unchanging sexual practice which reflects male sexual
needs (see Bullough 1964; Winter 1976). Pornography is also often
represented in this way: a historical feature of all human societies
which is a 'natural' product of sexual drives and instincts (Hyde 1964;
Kendrick 1987; Marcus 1966).

It is likely, however, that the sexual practices today designated as
prostitution and pornography are specific to our own culture and
period. Several authors have recently argued that 'prostitution' has
varied across history and between cultures (Halperin 1989; Peters
1989; Ralston 1988; White 1986; Bell 1994). They have suggested that
the particular form of prostitution found in most contemporary
Western societies, including Australia, emerged only in the late nineteenth and early twentieth centuries (Walkowitz 1980a, b; Allen 1984;
Rosen 1982). Bell (1994) has recently written about prostitution in five
different 'discursive domains': in the texts of Plato; in medical
discourse of the nineteenth and early twentieth centuries; in contemporary feminist theory; in texts produced by prostitutes themselves

since the 1970s; and in prostitute performance art. Her analysis under-lines the very different ways that have been adopted of talking and writing about prostitution in human societies.

Similarly, the cultural meanings assigned to sexually explicit repre-sentations have not always been the same as they are in Western culture of the late twentieth century. Even within the last century of Western culture, there are distinct variations in the content of pornography which suggest changing cultural meanings. Weeks (1981: 84), for example, has noted that homosexual themes – which are an important part of the present-day pornographic genre – were absent from Victo-rian pornography. Similarly, contemporary pornography is not as concerned with flagellation and cross-class sexual encounters that were the basis of much late-nineteenth-century pornography. Even during the last twenty years new themes have emerged in pornography. Linda Williams has noted the appearance of a preoccupation with oral sex in the New Age pornographic films of the early 1970s – for example, in *Deep Throat* (Williams 1989). A perusal of the current catalogues of X-rated video distributors in Canberra suggests that new concerns with ritual bondage and with anal sex are emerging in the 1990s.

The use of sexual essentialist frameworks in the contemporary liter-ature on pornography and prostitution has frequently led to further conceptual problems. Some sociologists, for example, have argued that prostitution and pornography allow for the 'discharge' of anti-social (male) sexual drives in a process that is conducive to the good order of society (Davis 1937; Polsky 1967). This sort of functionalism means that cultural factors, particularly those relating to the acquisition of 'normal' masculinity and 'normal' male sexual drives, are rendered invisible and unimportant.

Another common problem in the literature on pornography and prostitution – one that is related to the adoption of a latent or explicit sex essentialism – is libertarianism. If all sexual relations are the product of natural drives and instincts, then legal, cultural or institu-tional factors which prohibit or otherwise regulate access to pornog-raphy and prostitution can be represented as instruments of 'sexual repression' (Thornton 1986; Winter 1976). This sort of approach – what Foucault (1981) calls the 'repression hypothesis' – has been substantially challenged over the last decade. Foucault argues that sexuality is one of the main conduits for power in modern Western cultures. In his view, power is transmitted via the 'deployment' of sexu-ality, that is, through the production of a range of discourses 'about sex' and the investment of these with various technologies of power and knowledge. Consequently, sexuality cannot be dealt with only in terms of a negative power or repression (Foucault 1981; see also Weeks

1981). Laws designed to curb sexual behaviour might be repressive, but they are also productive – of new pleasures, discourses, and political and cultural forms. Foucault, for example, has argued that nineteenth-century laws criminalising male homosexuality made possible the formation of a 'reverse discourse' by which 'homosexuality began to speak on its own behalf' (1978: 101). Similarly, Annette Kuhn (1988) has suggested that film censorship laws and practices in the early twentieth century were instrumental in the production of new cinematic forms and audiences in Britain.

Some useful work on prostitution has recently been published in the area of political economy (Reynolds 1986) and Marxist analyses have been applied to the contemporary pornography debate (Soble 1986). Within political theory, various authors have examined both prostitution and pornography as ethical issues of relevance to government (Shrage 1989; Ericsson 1980; Pateman 1983a, 1988; Clark 1983). However, these deliberations have tended to occur in isolation from any consideration of the constraints imposed by existing political arrangements. Moreover, the debate on prostitution and pornography within political theory has tended to focus on a narrow range of issues – censorship, freedom of speech, and the right to sexual freedom – without addressing the limitations of a liberal framework or, indeed, the ways in which liberal approaches already structure the debate on prostitution and pornography within political theory (Hunter *et al.* 1993; Brown 1981).

Within feminist scholarship the sex industries have occupied an important conceptual role. Feminist analyses of prostitution now extend back over a century in relation to prostitution and over two decades in relation to pornography (see Allen 1990; Daniels 1984a; Hobson 1987; Jeffreys 1984; Millett 1971; Rosen 1982; Sellen and Young 1987). There are, however, substantial disputes within feminism about the moral status of prostitution and pornography, and about the role which government should adopt towards the sex industries. Some feminists suggest that prostitution is the most blatant example of women's sexual oppression by men and thus has important political ramifications for all women. Carole Pateman, for example, argues that it is the general display and marketing of women's bodies by the sex industry that 'continually reminds men – and women – that men exercise the law of male sex-right, that they have patriarchal right of access to women's bodies' (1988: 199). In her view, it is the public assertion by the sex industry of women's sexual accessibility which enables men to constitute themselves as the dominant sex in both public and private life.

Other feminists, however, have been critical of this approach. Some, like Gayle Rubin (1984), argue that prostitution and pornography are harmless sexual activities. Others suggest that Pateman is constructing an essentialist feminist position on sex work which is unable to deal with important differences (over time, between cultures, and between different commercial sexual practices) and which substantially downplays the role of other public institutions – particularly marriage and the labour market – in the constitution of specific types of male dominance (Sullivan 1995).

Outline of the Argument

In this book I trace important shifts in politico-legal approaches to the sex industry and relate these to changes in the broader sexual culture. The main focus is at the point where new laws and policies are proposed and debated, rather than at the point where law and public policy are applied and have effects. This is an important distinction because – most obviously in relation to prostitution – there are often significant differences between what the law says and how it is applied (Allen 1990). I am, then, interested in the process by which public figures constitute authoritative meanings associated with the sex industry – how 'problems' are defined and 'appropriate' regulatory regimes established.

I examine a variety of different texts in this process. In order to identify dominant discourses in the sexual culture during different historical periods, I examine demographic statistics, newspaper stories, novels and films that have been particularly controversial, and academic and popular literature on changes in sexual attitudes and behaviour. My questions are varied: How have scientific, popular and literary sources described the very apparent changes in Australian sexual mores since 1945? How have changes in 'normal' relations between men and women been represented, and how have these representations impacted upon the cultural meanings assigned to specific sexual practices such as pornography and prostitution? Has the constitution in the post-war period of a dominant sexual culture which emphasises the importance of companionate and egalitarian relations between the sexes influenced men's resort to prostitution? Now that women are more sexually available outside marriage, do men go to prostitutes less frequently and/or for different reasons from their grandfathers? Why has pornography been represented as an ordinary feature of normal sexual relations since the 1960s and 1970s? What has been the influence of feminism on this process?

In order to identify important shifts in politico-legal regimes addressed to the sex industry, I have examined statutes, official documents produced by political actors, and the official records of authoritative 'speech acts', such as parliamentary debates. Most researchers regard parliamentary debates as a peripheral resource or as a flawed account of what was 'really' happening. But I regard them as a valuable text for the analysis of political discourse despite (or even because of) their ritual and performative aspects. When governments – or individual members of parliament – are proposing new legislation, they offer to the parliament some explanation of why they think this legislation is necessary. These comments, together with those of other members who participate in the debate on a new bill, are preserved verbatim in the official record of parliamentary proceedings. Significant interjections from the floor, the Speaker's comments while controlling debate and, often, comments about the general demeanour of the house (for example, 'Laughter') are also recorded. From parliamentary debates, then, it is possible to construct an account of the reasons for proposing the new legislation (that is, what new 'problems' have entered the political domain), and the main points of dispute between various political actors and to identify important 'intertexts' (that is, literary, scientific and political texts that parliamentarians use in their deliberations and that therefore become part of the parliamentary record). This analysis of political discourse is placed alongside the texts which are indicative of changes in the sexual culture.

In the first chapter of this book I undertake a brief examination of the sex industry in Australia before 1945. I argue that both prostitution and pornography were first constituted as public and political problems in the late nineteenth and early twentieth centuries. At this time shifts in Australian and Western sexual culture increasingly marked sexual behaviour as an important indicator of the moral health of individuals and populations.

In Chapter 2 I examine the decade following the end of World War II. While initially there was little official interest in the prostitution industry, new cultural concerns about sexual 'deviance' – notably homosexuality and prostitution – began to appear in the early 1950s. These were to have their main politico-legal impact in the period after 1955. However, in the early 1950s a range of popular publications – comics and 'salacious' magazines – came to be identified as politically problematic. Today, most of this material would be regarded as innocuous or as soft-core porn. New laws addressed to objectionable literature were enacted in most states during the mid-1950s. I argue that this was due to changes within the publishing industry (which meant that this sort of popular publication was more available) and, most importantly, to the deployment within the dominant sexual culture of discourses about the need to protect children and to encourage appropriate patterns of sexual behaviour.

In Chapters 3 and 4 I examine the period between 1955 and 1969, when commercial sexual practices became an important social and political issue in Australia. This is evident in the number of new anti-prostitution laws enacted from the late 1950s onwards and in the increasing intensity of debate about literary censorship and pornography in the 1960s. I argue that in this period Australian sexual culture increasingly began to constitute normal sexuality in terms of freedom, reciprocity and mutuality. Because prostitution was seen to be the antithesis of this, it was regarded as an increasingly problematic sexual practice. At the same time, the consumption of erotic novels and – as the 1960s progressed – of pornographic publications was increasingly designated as a sign of sexual and cultural freedom. A popular opposition to censorship began to emerge in this period as sexual libertarianism entered mainstream political discourse.

In Chapter 5 I show that the sex industries expanded significantly in the early 1970s; both the number and range of pornographic publications on the Australian market increased and massage-parlour prostitution proliferated. At the same time traditional and conservative approaches to the government control of the sex industries were being called into question by influential sections of the electorate. I suggest that an increasingly libertarian sexual culture had its maximum effect on law and public policy in this period. While this had less impact on prostitution, it produced a substantial reformulation of censorship procedures in all Australian states between 1973 and 1975.

Chapter 6 shows that, from the late 1970s onwards, commercial sexual practices were increasingly constituted as a site of social and political controversy. There were a large number of official inquiries into prostitution and pornography and several important attempts at law reform during the late 1970s and 1980s. In three states – New South Wales, Victoria and South Australia – legislation which aimed to decriminalise prostitution was debated in parliament. New laws were also enacted which, to some extent, limited the rights of adults to consume pornography (particularly child pornography and material that combined sex and violence). I argue that this trend was due to changes in the sexual culture and an increasing deployment of feminist discourses which problematised both the consumption of pornography and the existing laws against prostitution. Other important factors were the increased participation of women in mainstream politics and the emergence of new 'managerial' discourses which stressed the importance of reforming the legal and administrative context in which the sex industries operated.

In Chapter 7 I discuss the most recent changes in politico-legal approaches to the sex industries. These include a decriminalisation of prostitution in the Australian Capital Territory and the Northern Territory, new laws in Victoria and New South Wales, and a more extensive criminalisation of prostitution in Queensland. I argue that this continuing trend towards decriminalisation has been a consequence of the continuing (but now often contradictory) impact of feminist discourse; increasing numbers of women and feminist parliamentarians (of various political persuasions); the impact of HIV/AIDS on governmental concerns about public health; and new citizenship claims by sexual minority groups such as homosexuals and prostitutes. In almost all jurisdictions, decriminalisation has also involved the expansion of legal definitions of prostitution, the development of new bureaucratic machinery to extend official control of prostitution, and the elaboration of criminal law (most notably against illegal and street prostitution). As my examination of parliamentary debates shows, this has occurred as the normative status of prostitution transactions – their appropriateness and acceptability – has become highly contested.

In the 1990s new censorship laws have been developed to deal with computer games and, more generally, to extend governmental powers over publications, films and videos. These changes have been surprisingly uncontroversial, indicating perhaps the attainment of another (albeit temporary and contingent) political consensus about the regulation of pornography. In the wake of feminist and conservative critiques of pornography in the 1980s, there appears to be widespread acceptance of the need to prohibit certain sorts of pornography. Self-regulation – supplemented by codes of conduct and some new criminal law – is presently being proposed to deal with the transmission of pornography on the Internet and via computer bulletin boards.

In the conclusion I discuss the main findings of the investigation and make some speculative comments about the limitations and possibilities of legal reform at this point of time. As is clear from the preceding discussion, my investigation is not designed to produce evidence for normative claims about how the sex industries should or should not be regulated. However, as several readers of this text have commented, it is clear that I have developed some views on this matter. In the conclusion, therefore, I briefly indicate the basis of my support for the decriminalisation of prostitution, for ongoing public debate about the representation of sex and gender, and (with significantly more reservation) in favour of the present censorship system.

PART ONE

Forming the Sex Industries

CHAPTER 1

Marking Danger: Prostitution and Pornography Before 1945

Today, prostitution and pornography attract a great deal of public and political conflict. In the media, parliament and many other public arenas, heated debates occur about the moral status of prostitution and pornography and about the role which governments should play in their control. This has not always been the case. In the first section of this chapter I suggest that there was little official concern with prostitution in the first eighty years of European settlement in Australia. Prostitution was not constituted as an object of official concern until the second half of the nineteenth century, when a plethora of new laws were passed which sought to define, prohibit and regulate various aspects of the prostitution trade. Through an examination of parliamentary debates I identify some of the main sexual discourses which impacted on the official assessment of prostitution at this time.

In the second section of this chapter I examine the constitution of pornography as a specific 'social harm' in the nineteenth century. This led to the elaboration of new laws in relation to material which was deemed to be obscene and indecent. In addition, various regulations and practices were developed to deal with the censorship of films, novels and popular literature. These changes were not accompanied by any significant public or political debate, especially in comparison to the present day. In the period before World War II there appears to have been a high level of consensus about what was obscene and indecent and about what governments should do in relation to such material.

Prostitution

Prostitution is often said to have arrived in Australia with the First Fleet. Perkins (1991: 68) found no evidence that prostitution 'as we might recognise it' existed amongst Aboriginal peoples in Australia before European settlement. Some historians have concluded that a substantial proportion of the convict women transported to Australia between 1788 and 1867 were prostitutes in the 'mother country' (Robson 1963: 181) although others have argued against this view (Robinson 1979). Clearly, many of the male convicts transported during this period, as well as soldiers in the New South Wales Corps, participated in the prostitution trade in England. However, as clients, they belonged to a relatively invisible social group, one that has been of little concern to historians, social scientists and law-makers until very recently.

Anne Summers (1975: 270–4) suggests that, even if women convicts were not prostitutes before their transportation, they were left with few choices after their arrival. This was because the organisation of penal settlements in Australia subjected all women (particularly convict women but, at a later point, also free immigrant and Aboriginal women) to an 'enforced whoredom'. In order to survive, women were forced to trade sexual services for food, shelter and protection. Summers argues that, from its inception, Australian society has assumed and enforced the prostitution of women. This point is supported by Heney (1978: 5) and Dixson (1976: 139). However, both Kay Daniels and Deborah Oxley have been critical of this approach. Oxley (1996: 8) argues that both feminist and mainstream historians have 'worked within the dominant portrayal of female whoredom, seeking to reinterpret what it meant rather than to question its fundamental validity'. According to Daniels (1984a), a much more nuanced analysis of the role of women in the early penal settlements is necessary: it must take into account both the political effects of labelling convict women as prostitutes (as many contemporary historians have done) and the range of different sexual behaviours which were called prostitution in the eighteenth century. This latter point is also made by both Perkins (1991) and Walkowitz (1980a).

Perkins (1991: 69) argues that only a minority of convict women survived through formal prostitution. De facto relationships were the norm for working-class women – both in England and after transportation to the Australia colonies – and such women were often labelled 'whores' and 'sluts' by the middle-class authorities. But this is a view which clearly assumes that a sharp distinction *can* be drawn between formal prostitution and other sorts of sexual-economic relationships. Many feminist authors, such as Summers, conceptualise prostitution on a continuum of heterosexual relationships. So prostitution, like both marriage and de facto partnerships, is seen to involve an essential element of sexual-economic exchange (in which women have little choice but to trade sex for economic benefit). This continuum approach is clearly at odds with contemporary socio-sexual norms in which the commercial and temporary nature of prostitution is sharply distinguished from the romantic, loving relationships of marriage and cohabitation. In the eighteenth century, however, it is not clear that such sharp distinctions were always drawn. As Judith Walkowitz (1980a) has suggested, the line between normal sexual behaviour, promiscuity, and clandestine and casual prostitution may have been quite blurred for working-class women in the eighteenth century.

That some form of prostitution flourished during the penal and colonial periods has often been explained by reference to the dispro- portionate numbers of men and women in Australia during the late eighteenth and nineteenth centuries. In 1800 men constituted 80 per cent of the population over twelve years of age, while in 1861 there were still 38 per cent more males than females. This sex imbalance evoked all sorts of 'official anxiety and corrective plans' (Allen 1989: 222). As it was assumed that men had to have some sort of outlet for their biologically driven sexual needs, the shortage of women was frequently represented in official discourse as a threat to the mainte- nance of social order. The local and British authorities deemed it necessary to have a supply of women to keep the men, both convict and free, 'quiescent' (Allen 1989: 227).

In this context, prostitution could be regarded by the authorities as both inevitable *and* desirable; its inevitability proceeded in an uncom- plicated fashion from men's sexual needs, while its desirability was connected to the 'dangers' involved in leaving these needs unad- dressed. According to Daniels (1984a: 41), concerns about male homo- sexuality had assumed some significance in the Australian colonies by the 1840s. There were, then, additional reasons for the authorities to regard prostitution as desirable; any sort of heterosexual behaviour could be represented as a useful means of preventing the appearance of 'unnatural' sexual liaisons between men. According to Daniels (1984a: 23), this meant that: 'while the colonial authorities came to believe that in marriage lay the hope of creating an ordered and civilized society, encouragement of marriage and tacit recognition of the utility of prostitution were compatible, not alternative, policies'. For colonial administrators at this juncture in Australian history there were clear continuities between prostitution and 'normal' heterosexual relations such as marriage. This was the main reason why relatively little official attention was paid to the issue of prostitution in the early colonial period.

The Initial Constitution of Prostitution as a Problem

By the mid-nineteenth century, however, prostitution was beginning to be perceived as a social and political problem and as an appropriate object of new laws. Daniels (1984a: 49) suggests that this shift was an important marker of the transition from penal settlement to free colony. However, it is clear that the increasing problematisation of prostitution – and of other 'deviant' sexual behaviour in this period – was not confined to Australia.

Foucault (1976) and Weeks (1981) have identified a reorganisation of social life in all Western cultures during the eighteenth and nineteenth centuries. This involved a general realignment of morality around sexual behaviour and a proliferation of discourses about sexual proprieties and pleasures. According to Foucault, this 'deployment of sexuality' was related to the deployment of modern forms of power. In talking, writing and researching 'about sex', knowledge was produced which offered access to the life of the individual body and the life of the species. Such 'bio-power' became an effective means of disciplining both individual bodies and whole populations. In the nineteenth century, Foucault (1976: 146) suggests, sexuality became a specific theme of 'political operations, economic interventions ... and ideological campaigns for raising standards of morality and responsibility: [sexual behaviour] was put forward as the index of a society's strength, revealing of both its political energy and its biological vigour'. In a similar vein, Weeks (1981: 23) argues that attention to the ethics of sexual behaviour in the nineteenth century became an important means of managing a wide range of social problems associated with rapid industrialisation and urbanisation. He suggests that there was 'a continuous battle over the definition of acceptable sexual behaviour within the context of changing class and power relations'.

Some of the dimensions of this discursive battle are evident in a recent deconstructive analysis by Sharon Bell (1994) of key texts in the public debate about prostitution which occurred in the nineteenth and early twentieth centuries. Bell presents a reading of Parent-Duchalet's anthropological study of Parisian prostitutes (1836); William Acton's *Prostitution Considered in its Moral, Social and Sanitary Aspects in London and Other Large Cities and Garrison Towns* (1857); the British *Royal Commission on the Contagious Diseases Acts* (1871); Havelock Ellis's *Sex in Relation to Society* (1910); and two essays by Freud (1905 and 1910). Bell argues that these texts represent a bourgeois 'mapping' of the prostitute body. Prostitutes were 'analyzed and categorized in relation to the bourgeois female ideals: the good wife and the virtuous daughter'. As a result of this process, new norms of respectability were elaborated; 'the bourgeoisie formulated its own identity by producing the prostitute as other' (Bell 1994: 40–72).

Contagious Diseases Acts

It was the administration of the *Contagious Diseases Acts* – and their actual or attempted application to the Australian colonies – that provided the main discursive opportunity for public debates about sexuality to focus on the issue of prostitution in the nineteenth century. In Britain, several *Contagious Diseases Acts* were passed by the parliament between 1864 and 1869. These provided for the compulsory registration of prostitutes in several naval ports and garrison towns in the south of England. Their aim was not to prevent prostitution but to control venereal disease in the armed forces, although other evidence suggests that the incidence of venereal disease was actually declining after 1860 (Weeks 1981: 85). Registered prostitutes were required to report for periodic medical examinations; those identified as suffering from a venereal disease were detained in lock hospitals for periods up to six months or until a visible cure was effected.

As Bell and others argue, the *Contagious Diseases Acts* 'created prostitution as a distinct legal category'. Before this time, prostitutes were not legally delineated from other women or from other categories of individuals who were variously designated as 'vagrants'. The Acts 'identified sex as a public issue, differentiated male from female sexuality, marked certain types of sexual activity as dangerous, and produced the prostitute body as the site of disease and pollution' (Bell 1994: 55). According to Walkowitz, working-class women in Britain frequently resorted to casual prostitution during periods of (normal) seasonal unemployment. There was, then, some opposition to the implementation of the *Contagious Diseases Acts* from members of this class. Where previously it had been possible for prostitution to be a temporary and relatively anonymous stage in a woman's life, registration forced the assumption of a professional status. Moreover, by causing prostitutes and their neighbours to acknowledge publicly what had previously been tolerated informally, a new distinction was forged between the respectable and unrespectable poor. This meant that working-class women were presented with a new and difficult set of options. On the one hand, those who were forced to register as 'common prostitutes' also adopted a distinct social and professional identity, one which isolated them from the broader working-class community. On the other hand, women who sought to maintain their links with the community found that their opportunities for earning a living were considerably reduced. More generally, the fear of being identified and registered as a prostitute established significant new limitations on women's sexual behaviour (Walkowitz 1980a: 201; Weeks 1981: 90).

Walkowitz has suggested that the *Contagious Diseases Acts* in Britain were part of a broader legal effort to contain some of the dangers that the urban poor posed to an emerging bourgeoisie. Official intervention into the lives of prostitutes clearly offered police an opportunity for the general surveillance of working-class communities (Walkowitz 1980a: 203). As Weeks argues, however, the *Contagious Diseases Acts* seemed to be an *ad hoc* response to a perceived crisis (venereal disease in the armed forces) rather than the expression of a coherent program designed to bring about a 'bourgeois hegemony'. Moreover, it was the administration of the Acts, rather than their passage through parliament, that was instrumental in 'crystallising and shaping' a set of broader concerns around the issue of sexuality. As Weeks (1981: 85) argues: 'Only as the [*Contagious Diseases Acts*] were put into operation piecemeal, were their assumptions clarified, and their aims consciously formulated and defended by regulationists. And only as the operation of the Acts was perceived did a groundswell of opposition develop.' The public debate and opposition occasioned by the administration of the *Contagious Diseases Acts* were productive, particularly insofar as they led to the elaboration of both new discourses and new political positionings around prostitution. A scientific medical discourse on prostitution was clearly already in place. As Bell (1994: 51–5) argues, texts like William Acton's *Prostitution Considered in its Moral, Social and Sanitary Aspects* ... (1857) identified female prostitutes as vectors of disease and prostitution itself as ineradicable. Consequently, Acton argued strongly in favour of the regulation of prostitute women and in support of the *Contagious Diseases Acts*.

But declaring their opposition to the Acts and to scientific medical discourses on prostitution, feminists like Josephine Butler elaborated public critiques of prostitution and of male sexuality for the first time. They argued against the sexual double standard (which meant that women but not men were punished for the same sexual acts) and against the 'state regulation of vice'. The *Contagious Diseases Acts* were seen to degrade women and to encourage men in sexual depravity. Although this approach successfully focused debate on men and on the clients of prostitutes, Bell claims that feminists simply inverted the terms of the dominant (medical) discourse on prostitution and did not, therefore, substantially challenge the status quo. While feminists shifted the blame for the transmission of venereal disease from women to men, they also wrote the prostitute body as the victim of male pollution, a female body 'invaded by men's bodies and men's laws' (Bell 1994: 61–3). Thus, nineteenth-century feminist discourse participated in a general pathologisation of prostitution and prostitute women, although it is not clear to what extent other feminist speaking positions were possible at this time. It was, moreover, in the formation of new feminist discourses – and in the formation of new political alliances with Christians, social purity advocates and working-class men – that the campaign to repeal the *Contagious Diseases Acts* in Britain was won.

Contagious Diseases Acts, based on the British Acts, were passed in two Australian colonies – Queensland (1868) and Tasmania (1879). In both cases the need to maintain the fighting efficiency of the British Navy was cited as the main reason why legislation was required. In Queensland, members of parliament argued that a *Contagious Diseases Act* was necessary because of the arrival in the colony of a particularly malignant form of syphilis borne upon a

> tide of immigration that set to in this colony about 1864 and subsequent years ... [As a result] a large number of loose women were landed in Brisbane, whose gross conduct and behaviour in the public streets in broad daylight, betokened that they had not come to this colony to earn their livelihood by honest toil, but on the contrary, to lead lives of vice and prostitution [Queensland Parliament, Legislative Council Journals, 1879, 28: 1389–95].

Prostitutes and female immigrants were thus represented as women of poor character who resorted to prostitution out of a desire to avoid what was regarded as more honest toil. Moreover, it was these women who were regarded as wholly responsible for the transmission of venereal disease – a view that simply disregards the role of the male clients of prostitutes.

In Queensland (but not in Tasmania), the *Contagious Diseases Act* was applied to all major towns regardless of whether they were seaports or inland cities. An 1879 parliamentary investigation into the working of this Act argued that the scope of the legislation in Queensland meant that this state 'led the world' in its concern for the social effects of venereal disease (Legislative Council Journals 28: 1389). Evans (1984: 159), however, has argued that the Queensland *Contagious Diseases Act* was never applied to all, or even a majority, of the prostitutes in gazetted towns: 'The Act was enforced at various times, only in Brisbane and a number of its shires, Rockhampton, Cooktown and Maryborough. In Cooktown, the Act soon lapsed for want of a "lock hospital" and in Maryborough, seemingly for want of sufficient prostitutes to supervise'. But for those women who were subjected to medical examinations and to periods of incarceration in a lock hospital, the Acts were a significant threat. Moreover, as Evans (1984: 145) argues, the official register of common prostitutes 'defined absolutely the membership of those named as being among a fixed debased category of women' while also endangering any woman who sought sexual experience outside of marriage. Evans (1984: 146) cites a Dr Turner who, in 1911, suggested that: 'The Act is intended to apply to prostitutes; if applied to any woman who is not a prostitute already, it makes her into one.'

Contemporary feminist historians have argued that the Australian *Contagious Diseases Acts* were part of an ongoing process 'in which the state gave its recognition to what it saw as the necessary existence of prostitution in the community and marked out certain women for that function by designating them as prostitutes and treating them differently before the law'(Daniels 1984a: 58).

Contagious Diseases Acts remained in force until 1903 in Tasmania and until 1911 in Queensland (the Queensland Act was not actually repealed until 1971). In the other Australian colonies the efforts of an organised and articulate lobby group – largely composed of feminists and social purity advocates – either prevented the passage of venereal diseases legislation, as in South Australia in 1869, or prevented its implementation, as in Victoria (Murnane and Daniels 1979: 8; Arnot 1986: 15).

Why, then, was there no effective campaign against the state regulation of prostitution and the repeal of the *Contagious Diseases Acts* in Queensland and Tasmania? Daniels offers several possibilities that point to the importance of socio-economic factors as well as to particular regional and political differences. She argues that the absence of an effective campaign in Tasmania may have been due to the lack of a registration clause in the relevant *Contagious Diseases Act* (this was also absent from the Queensland legislation) and to the relatively small number of women incarcerated under the provisions of this law. She also suggests that the particular configuration of political forces which led to the repeal of the *Contagious Diseases Acts* in Britain was not a feature of nineteenth-century Tasmanian society. The political alliance of middle-class women and working-class men 'who opposed what they saw as a villainous aristocratic alliance of government, doctors and military men, was absent in Tasmania'. As doctors enjoyed a considerably greater social status in the colonies than they did in Britain, there was also more public support in Tasmania for the scientific medical discourse on prostitution that favoured legislation on contagious diseases (Daniels 1984a: 77–9). While Daniels's argument specifically addresses Tasmania, it also applies to Queensland. Barclay (1974) has drawn attention to the importance of the medical lobby in Queensland; debate on the *Contagious Diseases Act* was dominated by medical men both inside and outside parliament.

Perhaps the most significant difference that Daniels identifies between Tasmania and Britain was the historical importance that had already accrued in the ex-convict colony to the category 'whore'. She suggests that in the late nineteenth century Tasmania was 'a society more anxious than most to draw a dividing line between prostitutes and "respectable" women' (1984a: 77–9). This is compatible with the argument of Dixson and Summers that Australian culture has been deeply marked by the 'enforced whoredom' of women in the penal settlements and by the rigid distinctions drawn later between women who were 'damned whores' and women who were bourgeois wives and 'God's police'. If, as both Daniels and Summers suggest, the dividing line between prostitutes and respectable women has been of particular historical importance in Australia, then specific configurations of sexual politics around the issue of prostitution might be expected to emerge in Australia. In later chapters I demonstrate that this did indeed occur.

New Laws Against Prostitution

In the last decade of the nineteenth century and first decades of the twentieth century there was an unprecedented range of legislative activity on the issue of prostitution by Australian parliaments. In New South Wales, the most populated and urban state, sweeping changes to the prostitution laws took place in 1908. This was accompanied by a plethora of other new legislation designed to suppress the use of opium, alcohol and tobacco, and to curtail gambling, abortion and the distribution of indecent literature.

The 1908 *Police Offences Act* in New South Wales outlawed soliciting for the purposes of prostitution and introduced new penalties for the landlords of brothels as well as for male persons who lived on the earnings of prostitution. In order to facilitate prosecutions, brothel-keeping was changed from an indictable to a summary offence. In 1909 a *Prisoners Detention Act* was also introduced in New South Wales to provide for the compulsory detention beyond their original term of all prisoners (male and female) who were found to be suffering from a venereal disease. Originally this legislation was to apply only to female prisoners, most of whom would have been serving sentences for prostitution-related activities. It attracted strong opposition from feminists like Rose Scott (see Allen 1995), who regarded the measure as both discriminatory and tantamount to the 'state regulation of vice'. The bill was eventually renamed and redrafted to include male as well as female prisoners.

Allen has argued that the legal reforms in New South Wales in 1908 reduced the public visibility of prostitution without undertaking its wholesale suppression. She has shown that the policing of the prostitution trade actually declined in New South Wales after 1908 (1990: 73, 91). However, it appears that the capacity for women to practise independently also declined as pressures increased on street prostitutes and the trade moved indoors. Previously, prostitutes had been able to come to individual arrangements (with police, bludgers, landlords, etc.) to achieve the protection and/or accommodation that was necessary for the practice of their trade. After 1908 they were often forced to negotiate with criminal networks 'because only such networks could afford the large fines or less conspicuous financial arrangements' that were necessary to avoid, or minimise, arrests (Allen 1990: 75). In this process the prostitute workforce became both professionalised (that is, locked into a professional working identity) and proletarianised: 'Structurally, [the prostitute] retained less of her earnings and became more like an employee of her "protectors"'(Allen 1990: 96). It is likely that these organisational changes also had effects on the prostitution transaction itself. As both Rosen (1982: 96–8) and Allen (1990: 75) suggest, the relationship between prostitutes and their clients probably became cooler and more businesslike as the trade became professionalised. This signals the possibility that a shift in the legal and cultural meaning of prostitution in the early twentieth century may have changed the actual experience of prostitution transactions for both workers and their clients.

New anti-prostitution measures similar to the New South Wales provisions were enacted in all the other Australian states, except Queensland. In Western Australia, for example, the 1892 *Police Act* outlawed soliciting for the purposes of prostitution, while amendments in 1902 made brothel-keepers, landlords and owners liable to summary conviction. These amendments also established new penalties for men found to be living on the earnings of prostitution. Despite a successful campaign in Western Australia against the introduction of a *Contagious Diseases Act* in the late nineteenth century, prostitutes were apparently required to undergo medical examinations in the 1890s (Davidson 1984: 176). By 1904 the Western Australian *Police Act* was being used – with the cooperation of certain magistrates – both to examine and to imprison prostitutes who were suffering from, or were suspected to be suffering from, a venereal disease. As a direct result of police activity (that is, selective policing and prosecution), tolerated zones of prostitution were established in both Perth and Kalgoorlie between 1905 and

1920 (Davidson 1984: 165). Thus, despite formal public and parliamentary opposition to what was perceived to be the 'state regulation of vice', state functionaries were directly implicated in the organisation of the prostitution trade in Western Australia.

In Victoria, the 1891 *Police Offences Act* prohibited soliciting for the purposes of prostitution. Amendments to this Act in 1907 provided penalties for owning, keeping or letting premises that were to be used for the purposes of prostitution, as well as for male persons living on the earnings. Although the Victorian parliament had passed health legislation in 1878 which provided for the examination and incarceration of prostitutes with venereal disease, public opposition to these measures meant that the legislation was never gazetted (Arnot 1986: 15). As in Western Australia, police developed their own methods for removing diseased prostitutes from the trade. The *Police Offences Act* and an unofficial arrangement with selected magistrates was used to ensure that prostitutes suspected of having a venereal disease were sentenced to maximum gaol terms (Arnot 1986: 15). Arnot suggests, however, that regular purges of the police force in Victoria prevented police and criminal networks from assuming the significant role in the organisation of the prostitution trade that they played in New South Wales. Thus, any trend towards the segregation and centralisation of prostitution in Melbourne (such as occurred in Sydney, Perth and Kalgoorlie) was subject to both disruption and dispersion during the early 1900s.

In South Australia new laws were passed in 1907 to prohibit soliciting and to suppress the 'public annoyance' associated with the presence of brothels in residential areas (Horan 1984: 112). As in Victoria and Western Australia, a successful campaign was waged in South Australia during the late nineteenth and early twentieth centuries against any measures which could be viewed as the 'state regulation of vice'. Venereal diseases legislation and the examination of prostitutes was opposed by a coalition of feminists, social purity advocates and senior police (Murnane and Daniels 1979: 9). The participation of police in this particular political alliance indicates that there were some significant differences between the states in police culture. It is likely that the police in South Australia did not participate overtly in the organisation of the prostitution industry (as they did in Queensland and Western Australia).

In Queensland, soliciting for the purposes of prostitution and being a male person living on the earnings of prostitution was prohibited under the terms of the 1911 *Health Act*. While this Act also established a system for the free and anonymous treatment of all people suffering from venereal disease, it maintained a distinction between prostitutes and the general population that had been initiated under the 1868 *Contagious Diseases Act* (Evans 1984: 149). Separate institutional arrangements for the detention and treatment of prostitutes with venereal disease were established at the lock hospital in the grounds of Boggo Road gaol. The *Health Act* also provided for the detention – beyond the term of their sentence – of all prisoners found to be suffering from a venereal disease.

Although brothel-keeping became an indictable offence under the Queensland Criminal Code in 1897, owning, letting or keeping premises for the purposes of prostitution did not become a summary offence until 1931 when the *Vagrants, Gaming and Other Offences Act* brought Queensland prostitution law into a position of some parity with that of the other states (Carter 1982: 67–93; Evans 1984: 148). Evans has shown, however, that police harassment affected street prostitution and forced the closure of some brothels from the mid-nineteenth century onwards. Thus, it would appear that the absence of formal legal arrangements for the ready policing of brothels did not deter the Queensland police from adopting a major role in the organisation of the prostitution trade. As a consequence of the wider powers of arrest granted under the 1911 *Health Act*, 'police were circularised to suppress street walking vigorously and to prosecute "bludgers" who ran brothels' (Evans 1984: 147, 149). The overall aim, though, was the containment and control of prostitution rather than its elimination. Recent evidence presented to the Fitzgerald Commission of Inquiry indicates that some houses of prostitution in Brisbane were in continuous existence from before the turn of the century to the late 1950s (Fitzgerald Inquiry, Exhibit 22).

It is notable that Queensland – unlike all the other Australian states in the first decade of the twentieth century – did not pass an anti-prostitution Act similar to the New South Wales *Police Offences Act*. There are several likely reasons for this, but perhaps the most important was the historical continuity of health regulations aimed at prostitutes in Queensland (in particular, the continuity of arrangements for the examination and incarceration of prostitutes under the 1868 *Contagious Diseases Act* and the 1911 *Health Act*) and the informal police surveillance established via these. Another possible reason for the late passage of wide-ranging prostitution laws in Queensland was the strong position held by the Labor Party. In all state parliaments during the early decades of the twentieth century, the Labor Party opposed the passage of police offences legislation; it argued that such laws would be used to curtail the freedom and harmless pleasures of working class men. In Queensland, the 1931 *Vagrants, Gaming and Other Offences Act* was passed in a brief interlude of non-Labor government (1929–31) in the midst of a long period of Labor rule (1915–57). Labor members of parliament opposed the Act and defended the established system of 'tolerated houses' of prostitution (QPD 159: 1430, 1746, 1748). To a significant extent this approach was premised on a defence of the interests of male clients of prostitutes. In 1916, for example, a Vagrants, Gaming and Other Offences Bill (aiming to tighten the law in regard to brothel prostitution) was debated in the Queensland parliament. Although this bill failed to pass beyond its first reading, the member for Aubigney indicated that Queensland parliamentarians had a clear interest – as clients – in the prostitution trade:

> I am pleased to see ... the provision with regard to disorderly persons – not that it affects me personally at all (Laughter). Some ladies are of spurious character, and if all these disorderly persons of suspicious character are to be wiped out, it would be a very good thing for some of us when we go home at the end of the week (Renewed Laughter) [QPD 124: 2060].

Such an open and jocular acknowledgement that parliamentarians were clients of prostitutes would have been less likely in other Australian states by 1916 and would not occur at all (at least in the same terms) in the present day.[1] Similarly, the defence by Queensland parliamentarians of the system of tolerated houses of prostitution – a defence which was very apparent during debate on the 1931 legislation – would have been most improbable in South Australia, Victoria or New South Wales in the same period. It seems that regional political cultures have had a direct bearing on the form and timing of a general trend towards the criminalisation of prostitution. In Queensland, prostitution was designated as a social and political problem at a much later date than in the other Australian states.

Politicians Debate Prostitution

While prostitution probably became more professional and less visible in the late nineteenth and early twentieth centuries, it also became more clearly the object of legal and political discourse. An examination of parliamentary debates about prostitution in this period provides some indication of the cultural meanings attached to the legal changes just described. As new laws were proposed and evaluated by parliamentarians, prominent cultural discourses – about sexuality and prostitution – were deployed.

Perhaps the most prominent characteristic of parliamentary debates in the early twentieth century was the very different ways that prostitutes and their clients were represented. It was the figure of the prostitute – rather than the client – that was the object of official scrutiny and of a pathologising discourse. Bell argues that the stereo-typical – and often contradictory – images that we have of prostitutes today were first formulated in scientific and medical texts in the nine-teenth and early twentieth centuries. These represented 'the prostitute body' as diseased and immoral, as sexually deviant, as criminal, as working-class, as a suffering victim (Bell 1994: 71).

Prostitutes were certainly represented in these ways in Australian parliamentary debates during the early twentieth century. They were described as 'purveyors of disease' and as a 'menace to the morals of the people'. But they were also described as practitioners of 'the grue-some and tragic trade of the public harlot', 'unfortunate women' who were victims of men's lust and 'ruined by men'. While several members of the New South Wales parliament argued that women resorted to prostitution out of economic necessity, others contended that prostitu-tion was merely a means of avoiding real work and achieving an easy life (NSWPD 30: 570, 588; 31: 2186, 1713, 2233, 1675–8; QPD 159: 897).

In all states the Labor Party opposed the passage of new anti-prosti-tution laws. In the New South Wales parliament, for example, Labor members argued that the *Police Offences Act* involved an unwarranted increase in police powers and presented a significant threat to the freedom of working-class men and women. One member went so far as to suggest that the anti-prostitution measures were 'in restraint of trade'. Others, however, argued that the bill was aimed at the 'wives, sisters and daughters of the workers' while the 'toff prostitutes' remained free to service middle-class men and 'the deep-seated, respectable immorality' that was the privilege of the upper classes (NSWPD 30: 469; 31: 1675–713).

This did not mean that prostitute women were regarded as workers, and parliamentarians clearly saw their role as defending the rights of working-class men to (affordable) prostitution. Even among Labor members the suggestion that the prostitute was a woman of 'abnormal sexual desires' could not readily be dismissed although, for some, the origin of these desires was seen to be the conditions generated by capi-talism: 'The unhealthy surroundings of factories … the perpetual strain of working amongst machinery, the vitiated atmosphere … generates forms of sexual hysteria and in a great number of cases leads to the ulti-mate downfall of women' (NSWPD 31: 692). In the early twentieth century, therefore, the prostitute was constituted as an ambivalent figure within legal and parliamentary discourse. On the one hand, she was a victim; on the other hand, she was an abnormal and deviant woman. It was this latter discourse which tended to dominate.

In general, the roles which men played as clients in prostitution transactions were not commented on in parliamentary debates before World War II. As suggested above, a feminist anti-prostitution discourse was elaborated in the late nineteenth century and tended to focus attention away from prostitute women and onto their male clients. But this sort of feminist discourse was not deployed in Australian parliamentary debates in the first half of the twentieth century. An increased scrutiny of prostitutes' clients was threatened by the level of public attention which came to be focused on venereal disease, particularly during and immediately after World War I. However, it appears that 'promiscuous amateurs' – women who were not professional prostitutes – were often blamed for the dissemination of venereal disease in this period. The official focus on prostitutes and promiscuous amateurs tended to deflect attention from the role of men in prostitution transactions and in the spread of venereal disease.

It is notable too that the appearance during World War I of discourses about 'promiscuous amateurs' marked an important reformulation of the category of 'bad' women. Promiscuous amateurs – women who engaged in extra-marital sex for pleasure alone (and perhaps the 'normal' heterosexual rewards) – were an innovation. The amateurs were increasingly distinguished from women who plied the trade of 'common prostitute'. However, in this process the deviance and marginality of prostitutes were both reformulated and intensified.

While parliaments paid little attention to the role of men in prostitution transactions, they were not altogether absent from the debate. Clients were sometimes represented by parliamentarians as the victims of seduction (by prostitutes). Young men were seen to be most vulnerable to the wiles of women soliciting on the streets. As one speaker in the Victorian parliament argued in 1928, 'many lads are being led astray by these women' (VPD 178: 3755). More commonly, however, clients were represented simply as ordinary men acting under the impetus of their normal biological drives. The resort to prostitutes was regarded as both natural and inevitable for men whose sexual needs could not be accommodated 'in the ordinary way', that is by a wife (QPD 159: 1749). Thus, bushworkers, workers on the goldfields, unmarried men and – particularly in times of war – soldiers and sailors were seen to have specific needs for sex without intimacy and responsibility (Horan 1984: 100; Davidson 1984: 169). In Queensland, the Northern Territory and Western Australia, Aboriginal women and Japanese prostitutes were often regarded as providing a 'solution' to the sexual needs of Chinese immigrants and 'coloured' male labourers indentured upon sugar plantations and pearl luggers. Indeed, white prostitutes who serviced this clientele were regarded as particularly 'revolting and degraded' and suffered harsher criminal penalties when brought before the law (Evans 1984: 139; Sissons 1977; Arnot 1986).

For men without other sexual outlets, prostitution was usually considered to be the lesser of two evils, for 'when nature calls men must go somewhere'. If deprived of easy access to prostitutes, men were regarded as more likely to rape innocent women and children. This representation of male sexuality as an unstoppable force, as a drive that demanded an outlet or, if blocked, produced significant social consequences, meant that prostitution could continue in the twentieth century to be regarded as both inevitable and necessary. In the eyes of Australia's legislators, prostitution was both an 'ineradicable social vice' *and* a desirable means of addressing the specific sexual needs of certain groups of men (QPD 159: 1788, 1451).

While clients were not regarded as pathological in the period before World War II, there was one category of men who were. This was the bludger or, in American parlance, the pimp, a man who lived on the earnings of prostitution. He was often the husband or boyfriend of a prostitute and could be actively involved in protecting or touting for the prostitute. Parliamentarians described the bludger as 'the most detestable wretch on the face of the earth' and as a man 'worthy of no respect whatsoever' (NSWPD 31: 1675). While Allen (1990: 93) has shown that men were rarely arrested for living on the earnings of prostitution, their constitution within parliamentary discourse as particularly evil and deviant men is a notable feature of debate in this period. It is not completely clear why this should be so, although the work of Carol Pateman suggests some possibilities.

Pateman (1988: 189–218) argues that prostitution is a fundamentally sexed transaction and a means whereby men purchase sex-right over women. In her view, sex-right is both sexual – 'in the sense of establishing orderly access by men to women's bodies' – and more broadly political because it establishes men's power over women (1988: 2). From this perspective, it might be suggested that the bludger is reviled because he is a man whose life transgresses the fraternal social bonds which bind all men in a political alliance with each other; he is a traitor to his sex because he disrupts the sexed boundaries between the seller and purchaser of prostitution services. That is, the bludger can be represented as a man who is involved on the wrong side of the prostitution contract (or, at least, wrong for men). It is notable that, during the recent Fitzgerald Inquiry in Queensland, several senior police suggested that they had always acted against men who were involved in managing brothels and who lived on the earnings of prostitution. However, the management of brothels by women (who presumably also lived on the earnings) was regarded as 'quite an acceptable standard' (Fitzgerald Transcript: 277). As the twentieth century has progressed, laws against living on earnings have been extended to cover women (see Chapters 3 and 4). However, it is the male bludger who remains most prominently in public discourse.

Pornography

Most authors suggest that modern forms of pornography first appeared in the seventeenth century. They argue that this was a reaction against the increasing repression of sexuality in Western culture, a trend which was most prominent in the Victorian period (Hyde 1964; Marcus 1966; Kendrick 1987). However, as suggested in the introduction, Foucault (1978) has offered a convincing case against this 'repressive hypothesis'. Following this lead, Hunter, Saunders and Williamson (1993) trace the origins of pornography in a 'Christian technology of the flesh' – that is, in confessional techniques designed to elicit 'a minute mapping of the sexual body'. This mapping process was a means of instilling an ever more detailed sense of the erotic and, therefore, was also a way of locating sin, directing the conscience and intensifying spirituality. Hunter *et al.* argue that these techniques then migrated beyond the religious institutions, 'through the agency of print and print literacy', to produce 'effects of desire in other milieus'. Thus, 'biblio-erotics', or the use of books to achieve sexual pleasure, should be regarded as the profane and secular manifestation of an ethical practice of the body developed within religious institutions.

The migration of this practice was dependent on the acquisition of certain 'cultural competencies'. Most notable here was the ability to read and, because the majority of pornography was produced in France, the ability to read in a foreign language. As a result, the use of sexually explicit material was initially confined to 'a small sector of the literate public: aristocratic and middle-class men, predisposed to self-cultivation and possessing sophisticated literate abilities' (Hunter *et al.* 1993: 31–40).

Hunter *et al.* also suggest that pornography was not constituted as a public problem until the early eighteenth century when the first conviction for obscene libel was recorded in a major British court. Notably, this involved a book which had been freely available in London since 1683.[2] This conviction marked an expansion of the governmental sphere, with the court accepting 'a new disposition of public morality, one which cut across the existing division of jurisdiction between the civil and the ecclesiastical courts'. Thus, a specific type of immorality was transposed from sin to crime, and its regulation shifted from the religious to the legal domain. What provoked this shift was 'the formation of a public for pornography' in the late seventeenth and early eighteenth centuries. In the wake of a rapid expansion of print literacy and of the book trade, pornographic texts became available in the English language and could be marketed to a wider audience (Hunter *et al.* 1993: 49–51). This created a potentially new group of (male) pornography consumers, as well as new governmental problems in regard to controlling the dissemination of pornography. As Hunter *et al.* point out, the law at this time entered a field already 'dense' with specific forms of social, ethical and religious regulation. The objective of the new laws was not a complete suppression of biblio-erotics but a governing of the distribution of pornography so that it was available only to readers with specific (and highly developed) 'ethical-legal competencies'.

In the mid-nineteenth century pornography, like prostitution, became identified as a specific social harm: one which threatened the moral and medical health of both individuals and populations. As Hunter *et al.* argue: 'Identified with the problem of precocious sexuality and made a target of the great anti-masturbation campaigns undertaken by nineteenth-century sexual medicine and pedagogy in home and school, pornography became pathologised as a secret cause of the vice that robbed youth of its physical and mental health and threatened the future of the family and the race' (1993: 45).

Weeks (1981: 20) describes a major increase in the market and supply of pornography in Europe by the mid-nineteenth century. The policing of pornography also intensified in this period. In Britain two key changes occurred in this period – the 1857 *Obscene Publications Act* and the Hicklin judgement of 1868. The *Obscene Publications Act* did not, in fact, create any new offences or establish a statutory definition of obscenity (Hunter *et al.* 1993: 63). It was concerned only with facilitating the seizure and destruction of publications which were deemed to be obscene.

The first legal definition of obscenity occurred in 1868 when what came to be known as the Hicklin test entered British common law. According to this: 'the test of obscenity is ... whether the tendency of the matter so charged as obscenity is to deprave and corrupt those whose minds are open to such immoral influences, and into whose hands a publication of this sort may fall' (*R v. Hicklin* LR 3 QB 360). However, Hunter et al. argue that the legal determination of obscenity was quite straightforward in the nineteenth century, 'reflecting a certainty that informed the law about the nature of obscenity and its detrimental effects'. A direct (and uncontroversial) relationship was assumed to exist between exposure to obscene publications and moral harm – and between individual moral harm and harm to the community – for those who did not have the necessary 'cultural competencies' to deal with this material: that is, for the majority of the population.

In the twentieth century the Hicklin test has remained as an important (if more controversial) feature of obscenity law in Britain, the United States and Australia.

Australian Laws Against Obscene and Indecent Material

Between 1876 (Victoria) and 1902 (Western Australia) each state or colony in Australia passed obscenity legislation modelled on the British Act of 1857 and incorporating the Hicklin test. A range of new legislation, designed to suppress the dissemination of literature and film that was merely 'indecent' rather than wholly 'obscene', was also enacted in most Australian colonies in this period. This frequently occurred alongside legal measures that were meant to suppress other social vices such as gambling and prostitution. In New South Wales, for example, the *Obscene and Indecent Publications Act* of 1901 was significantly amended in 1908 by changes to the *Police Offences Act*. As suggested above, this Act also prohibited a range of new prostitution-related offences. Thus, the legislative control of pornography – and of other social-sexual problems such as prostitution – was clearly linked within the Australian body politic by the early twentieth century.

After federation in 1901, state laws against obscene and indecent material were supplemented by a range of new federal laws and regulations which aimed to prevent the importation of 'questionable' material and to establish censorship regimes. Under the terms of the Australian Constitution, unlimited powers to censor material inhere in each state government.[3] However, in practice, it has been the Commonwealth government – under its power to make laws with respect to trade and commerce – which has been responsible for censorship decisions. Particularly in the period since 1945, censorship has frequently been a source of contention between state and federal levels of government. The resolution of censorship problems, and the definition of new censorship concerns, has often been implicated in wider disputes about the proper limits of Commonwealth power.

Censorship

One characteristic of the censorship regimes developed in Australia during the early twentieth century was that art, literature, popular publications and film were treated as distinct objects of governmental concern. In general, film has attracted more stringent censorship provisions than printed publications while, within this latter category, 'high art' literary publications have been dealt with much more leniently than popular publications such as magazines.

In the early twentieth century, literature was seen to be the province of the educated middle classes. Parliamentarians argued that literary censorship was unnecessary, for deciding what was good to read was 'a matter of education, development of the critical faculties and the higher forms of culture'. Moreover, literature that was in any way doubtful in terms of these criteria was 'certainly not purchased by poor people, because they are not in a position to make such purchases'. Some Labor members of parliament did object, on class grounds, to the practice of prohibiting cheap editions of some novels while expensively bound copies were exempt. However, there appears to have been broad agreement among parliamentarians that the censorship of obscene postcards and photographs was 'essential' (QPD 159: 1427, 1745–50). The political certainty in this area was also evident in lower court decisions in cases which involved the possession or exhibition of obscene photographs and publications. For example, two cases were reported in the *Sydney Morning Herald* during the 1930s; in the first of these a man was charged with occupying rooms containing indecent publications, while, in the second case, a choirmaster was fined £20 for exhibiting indecent photographs (6 February 1934; 12 March 1937).

Coleman (1974: 10) reports that between 1902 and 1928 Australian federal customs prohibited only three works of literature. These were Balzac's *Droll Stories*, Boccacio's *Decameron*, and paperbound editions of the works of Rabelais. However, several other publications were on the banned list – *Photo Fun*, *Photo Bits*, some French books titled *La Bibliothèque Curieux* and a book of nudes called *Academical Studies*. While Coleman draws a clear distinction between items of literature and the other prohibited publications, it is not apparent that the federal censorship authorities shared this view at this time.

In 1929 federal censorship practices took a sudden change of direction. James Joyce's *Ulysses* was banned and a new test for indecency was introduced. This was the 'average householder test' which was concerned with 'whether the average householder would accept the book in question as reading matter for his family'. By 1936 there were 5000 books on the prohibited list, a change which denotes increasing governmental concern with the category of obscene and indecent publications.

Organised public opposition to the processes of government censorship was also becoming manifest by the mid-1930s. Initially, this opposition was directed at 'political censorship' and at official attempts to both censor and contain political unrest. Bertrand claims that, while the debate over censorship was not widespread before World War II, it was the issue of political censorship in the 1930s which caused left-wing politics to become identified with an anti-censorship position (1978: 60). In 1936, for example, *Ten Days That Shook the World*, an account of the Russian revolution, was banned in Australia. This move was condemned by communists and left-wing supporters.

Opposition to the censorship of literature led to the formation of the Book Censorship Abolition League in 1937 (*SMH*, 4 February 1937). Largely as a result of the political activities undertaken by this group and by the Writers League, the Commonwealth government reorganised its censorship apparatus in 1937 and established a Literature Censorship Board with formal powers to review the censorship of material that claimed some artistic integrity (*SMH*, 16 June 1937).

One important reason why public attention came to focus on the issue of literature censorship in the 1930s was the first appearance of mass-produced American comics. These began to enter Australia 'on an unprecedented scale' in the early 1930s (Coleman 1974: 106–9). They met widespread opposition – particularly from church and women's groups – and there were calls for a total prohibition. The problems associated with these magazines seemed to be many. They frequently contained advertisements for patent medicines and for sex literature with titles like 'Learn the Art of Turkish Love' and 'Have a Second Honeymoon'. New government regulations were passed in order to ensure the erasure of such advertisements prior to the comics' sale. However, they were still seen as both morally and educationally harmful, particularly as their representation of 'Negro and Italian influences' was seen to be undermining 'Australian racial characteristics' and an Australian national identity (Coleman 1963: 109).

Coleman says that the American comics could be divided into several different cat-egories – romantic, detective, scientific, and the deliberately pornographic (1974: 109). Titles like *American Film Fun* and *Merry Go Round* fell into the category of deliberately pornographic and were subject to an immediate Customs ban. However, the detective and romance magazines were regarded more ambivalently, as a new problem which could not be conclusively addressed under the existing regulations. Romance magazines such as *True Confessions* contained stories like 'My Strange Honeymoon Experiences', 'Has Every Girl a Price?' and 'My Own Desire (Defiantly She Loved, Dearly She Paid)'. These were not legally obscene or indecent, but they were widely regarded as unsuitable, particularly for the teenage girls who were their main consumers. Thus, the dividing line between magazines that were 'deliberately and obviously pornographic' and those which were not, was becoming less confidently discernible.

The concern with American comics in the 1930s also brought into sharper political focus the issue of literature censorship. It was by reference to, and comparison with, popular commercial publications that new claims for the de-censorship of literature became possible. In the period after the formation of the Literature Censorship Board in 1937 the list of prohibited books was severely culled. This resulted in the release of some literary works, for example *Ulysses*. At the same time, and as a direct result of concerns about American comics, the Commonwealth moved to tighten censorship regulations in relation to material that was deemed to be 'non-literature'. New regulations were passed which prohibited all literature that, 'in the opinion of the Minister, and whether by words or pictures ... (a) unduly emphasises matters of sex or crime; or (b) is calculated to encourage depravity'. Within two months, forty-eight magazines had been classified as prohibited imports by the federal Customs authorities. These included magazines with titles like *Candid Confessions, Intimate Romances, Facts of Life, Horror Stories*, and *Current Psychology and Psychoanalysis* (Coleman 1963: 110). Thus, the de-censorship of (some) literature was achieved by the establishment of a new dichotomy between artistic and popular publications, with popular literature marked out for increased surveillance and prohibition.

There were some clear differences between the states in their approach to popular magazines and comics. Apart from the American product, Australian glossy magazines such as *Man, Pix* and *Health and Sunshine* (which were published in Australia but contained material syndicated from American sources) were also regarded as pornographic by sections of the Australian community. As these magazines were published in New South Wales they were not subject to the new federal Customs regulations gazetted in 1938. However, both the government and the police in New South Wales adopted a permissive attitude towards these publications. In other states (such as Queensland and Victoria in 1938) moves were made to amend summary offences legislation and extend the definition of 'obscene' to include all publications that unduly emphasised matters of sex, crime and violence, or that were calculated to encourage depravity. In Victoria at least one of the Sydney glossies – *Man* – was immediately seized and destroyed by police (Coleman 1963: 116).

National trends in relation to the censorship of literature and popular magazines were not fixed by the late 1930s and early 1940s. In 1941, for example, the Minister for Customs – acting against the advice of the Literature Censorship Board – again placed *Ulysses* on the list of prohibited imports. This decision was widely applauded by the churches, but attacked by the Australian Fellowship of Writers, the

NSW Workers Educational Association, the Rationalist Association, the Australian English Association, the Civil Rights Defence League, and the St Kilda branch of the Labor Party (Coleman 1963: 19). This again demonstrates the role of censorship decisions in the formation of new political configurations and alliances. It also suggests that the censorship of publications deemed to be 'literature' was increasingly becoming a political issue. In this case the decision to ban *Ulysses* pitted traditional moral institutions, such as the church, against an emerging alliance of writers and civil libertarians. The formation of this particular anti-censorship position was to be of some significance after the war.

Conclusion

Both prostitution and sexually explicit publications came to be identified as social and political problems for the first time in the late nineteenth and early twentieth centuries. This was probably a local indicator of a wider trend within Western culture whereby the moral health of individuals and populations came to be measured in terms of sexual behaviour. A range of new anti-prostitution measures was enacted by Australian state governments in this period. But, in this process, it was only certain categories of persons associated with the prostitution trade – prostitutes in particular – who were identified as problematic in a legal sense. The activities of clients and the prostitution transaction itself were not regarded as important by parliamentarians. I have suggested that this was because politicians and the prevailing sexual culture regarded men's use of prostitutes as natural and inevitable, as well as conducive to the good order of society.

Pornography was also constituted as a social and political problem in the late nineteenth and early twentieth centuries. Laws prohibiting obscene and indecent publications were passed in all states in this period and later supplemented by a range of censorship regulations and practices. All of these measures remained relatively uncontroversial until at least the late 1930s. At this time a new alliance of writers and civil libertarians began to challenge the existing political consensus around censorship. However, the challenge was confined to material which was deemed to have literary merit. General agreement remained that overt obscenity should be prosecuted to the full extent of the law, and that strict censorship regulations should apply to both popular publications and film.

CHAPTER 2

A New Moral Economy?
The Immediate Post-War Years, 1945–55

In the decade following the end of World War II Australia entered a period of significant prosperity. This was fuelled by a flood of foreign investment, an inflow of labour in the form of immigration, and the development of new forms of domestic consumption (Rowley 1972; Connell and Irving 1980: 298). Alongside these economic changes a new sexual culture began to emerge, one that emphasised quite different patterns of normal sexual interaction. Initially, this new sexual culture did not have a significant impact on political attitudes towards the sex industry, although by the mid-1950s some effects were becoming evident. In the decades that followed, the re-orientation of normal sexual behaviour produced a significant shift in the ways that Australian parliaments addressed the sex industry.

In the first section of this chapter I explore some of the main features of this emerging post-war sexual culture and, in particular, the development of new companionate forms of heterosexuality. I show that marriage became more popular in this period and the pursuit of sexual pleasure (both inside and outside marriage) more explicit. This change was facilitated by the increased availability of abortion and contraception and by the increasing deployment of sexual themes in popular literature.

In the second section of this chapter I examine changes in the political regulation of prostitution in Australia during 1945–55. While several minor legislative initiatives were enacted in this period, the prostitution industry in general attracted relatively little political attention. I argue that this was due to a range of factors: a natural decline in the industry at war's end, the impact of new antibiotic treatments in the control of venereal disease, and the stability of existing extra-legal arrangements for the organisation of the prostitution trade. Thus, there was little need or public demand for political attention to focus on the prostitution industry. An examination of parliamentary debates shows significant continuity between political attitudes towards prostitution before and after the war.

In the third section of this chapter I show that new cultural and political concerns about 'sexual deviance' – notably male homosexuality and prostitution – began to emerge in the early 1950s. I argue that the appearance of these concerns was directly related to the development of a companionate sexual culture. As a result, prostitution was increasingly conceptualised within political discourse as an undesirable sexual practice that deserved more legal surveillance. These political concerns were to have their main impact on the law in the period after 1955 (see Chapter 4).

In the fourth section of this chapter I examine the issue of pornography and literary censorship in the period. I show that in the early 1950s certain types of popular literature designed for children and adolescents were marked out for official intervention. A range of new state laws was applied to comics and to 'salacious' magazines (some of which would today be regarded as soft-core pornography) while, in Queensland, an additional censorship body – the Literature Board of Review – was established. I argue that the formation of tougher legal controls on popular literature was directly related to changes in the publishing industry and to the appearance of new political concerns about the need for governments to protect children and teenagers and to encourage the development of 'appropriate' patterns of behaviour (including sexual behaviour). An examination of parliamentary debates shows that the child reader was clearly identified within political discourse as vulnerable to a range of modern social dangers, many of which were sexual.

Post-war Sexual Culture

The period 1945–55 is usually represented as a time in which there was a general reassertion of traditional life and traditional sex roles (Reynolds 1991: 195; Summers 1975). While the desire for this was undoubtedly an important component of post-war Australian culture, Marilyn Lake (1990) argues for a different interpretation of this period. She suggests that new forms of femininity were already emerging in Australia during the 1930s – forms which revolved around sexuality, sexual attractiveness and youthfulness – and that these were reinforced, rather than undermined, by Australian women's experience of World War II. The stationing of foreign troops on Australian soil was a particularly important factor in this process for, in Lake's terms, it had the effect of sexualising the local female population. In her view the war was an important 'gendering activity', one which reconstituted gender relations in ways that could not be ignored: 'There could be no return to the old order at the end of the war. Indeed by the 1950s it was becoming clear that the tensions generated by the changing structure of femininity and by the concomitant wartime stimulation of female desire had created havoc with "traditional roles"' (Lake 1990: 283). As a result of the war, women established new public roles in the paid work-force and, to a lesser extent, in politics. There was a small but significant increase in the number of women in state and federal parliaments from 1938 onwards.[1] In the immediate aftermath of World War II, however, there was a concerted campaign in Australia to encourage women out of the workforce. This was usually couched in terms of what would now be called an affirmative action for men. As one member of the South Australian parliament argued, 'any woman who is in a position which could be occupied by a man [should] be relieved in the interests of returned men' (SAPD 1946: 189, 273). Men's interest groups, such as the Returned Servicemen's League, actively participated in this process by mounting public protests over the number of women 'still working in the public service' (SMH, 24 June 1946). Newspaper articles encouraged women into domesticity as well as giving advice on how to integrate the returned serviceman back into family life (SMH, 24 February 1946; SMH, 28 June 1945).

Marriage rates, which had already climbed steeply during the war, continued to rise until 1955 (McDonald 1975: 192). A baby boom occurred, although this was largely due to the increased number of marriages rather than a return to the large family sizes common earlier in the twentieth century (Siedlecky and Wyndham 1990).[2] In the post-war period, then, an increasing percentage of the population embarked upon marriage; they also tended to marry younger and to have smaller families than their predecessors.

Women were also more actively seeking sexual pleasure both inside and outside marriage although, according to Fink (cited in Lake 1990: 283), the majority of young unmarried women in the early 1950s remained inexperienced in sexual intercourse. According to Lake, the popularity of marriage in the 1940s and 1950s and the 'triumph of domesticity' was not a conservative retreat into traditional sex roles but a path increasingly adopted by young women in their pursuit of sexual pleasure. Thus, 'in place of the adventure of economic independence' (during the war) women were offered, and took up, 'the adventure of sexual romance' in marriage (Lake 1990: 269).

These changes were seen to have clear implications for men. During a visit to Sydney in 1951 anthropologist Margaret Mead said that new patterns of family life had emerged since the war and, in particular, this meant that fathers were now expected to be more involved with their young children (*SMH*, 18 August 1951). But it might be surmised from Lake's article that men were also increasingly required to be companions and lovers to their wives in ways that were not likely fifty years before. By the 1940s the use of contraceptives (in particular condoms, pessaries and diaphragms) was becoming widespread (Siedlecky and Wyndham 1990), and there is evidence to suggest that abortion was widely practised. In 1946 the member for Clifton Hill, Mr Cremean, told the Victorian parliament that the practice of abortion had 'assumed wide dimensions throughout the allegedly civilized world'. He cited a 1936 New Zealand government inquiry which found that approximately 13 per cent of pregnancies ended in (criminal) abortion and suggested that the abortion rate in Australia was somewhat higher than this. Such practices were said to be related to 'the indiscriminate distribution of pornographic literature, sex appeal in films and advertising, the risqué joke and the general lowering of the standard of public conduct' (VPD 222: 2617–23).

Increasingly, then, it became possible for women, like men, to separate sex from reproduction and to engage in a search for sexual pleasure. This is not to suggest that contraceptives were readily available. Siedlecky and Wyndham (1990: 26–37) show that reliable contraception remained difficult to obtain until the introduction of the Pill in 1961. The issue of contraception and abortion remained controversial and enmeshed in a wider political debate about Australia's declining birth rate. In Victoria, for example, members of parliament argued that the availability of contraceptives was bringing about 'the defeat of natural increase' (VPD 225: 160–1); abortion was said to be 'slowly but surely sapping the body politic and destroying the moral, economic and social welfare of Australia' (VPD 222: 2623).

There is also evidence to suggest that there was an increase in the number and severity of sex offences in the immediate post-war period in Australia (Allen 1990: 224). The Premier of South Australia said he thought this was 'inevitable when the shorter week now being worked is taken into account' (SAPD 1947: 1585). It is not clear whether this increasing rate of sex crime was due to the demobilisation of servicemen, to a general 'readjustment' of society to post-war conditions, or to a rising level of sex antagonism (as traditional sex roles came under challenge). There were, however, some particular cases which caused major public debate and are indicative of general shifts in the sexual culture. For example, during the mid-1950s in New South Wales, four boys under the age of eighteen were sentenced to life imprisonment for the gang rape of a 19-year-old woman (at this time the penalty for adults convicted of rape in New South Wales was death by hanging). This sentence provoked a major public outcry. The editor of the *Sydney Morning Herald* argued that the penalty imposed on these 'mere lads' was 'archaic and barbarous' and called for a major review of the New South Wales *Crimes Act* (18 June 1954). These views were supported by various clergymen and by the Minister for Justice, who argued that society had failed these youth by not giving them adequate sex education and by permitting a variety of 'incitements to lust' – such as pictures of semi-nude women in newspapers and pornographic magazines at the newsagent. He said that sex offenders should receive 'psychotherapy until cured', not life sentences (*SMH*, 19 June 1954). Other members of the public argued that rape was a result of inadequate sex education, improper child raising practices, and the increased availability of salacious literature (*SMH*, 24, 22, 25 June 1954). Thus, sex offenders were psychologised; as well, new discursive links were forged between the perpetration of sex offences and the increased availability of soft-core pornography.

Several authors have argued that it was during World War II that sexually explicit literature moved from its place in a marginal underground world into mainstream American culture (D'Emilio and Freedman 1988: 280; Talese 1980: 58). This was encouraged by the United States military. The Navy, for example, officially sanctioned the use of female nudes in decorating the nose of fighter planes, and pin-ups were widely circulated 'to boost morale and encourage heterosexual fantasy in the sex-segregated military' (D'Emilio and Freedman 1988: 274–5).[3] A fortune was made during the war by New York publishers who produced magazines with titles like *Flirt, Titter, Wink,* and *Eyeful,* magazines that greatly appealed to lonely servicemen overseas (Talese 1980: 58).

There is evidence to suggest that some of these publications also found their way into the hands of Australian servicemen during the war. In *We Are the Rats* (1945), a semi-autobiographical novel by Lawson Glassop, one of the main characters is a member of the Australian Army in Tobruk during World War II. He returns from leave in Cairo with 'American pornography', a 'perv book' called *Saucy Stories,* and proceeds to read to his 'digger mates' some of the more sexually explicit passages. In 1946 *We Are the Rats* was prosecuted in New South Wales as an obscene publication (see below).

After the war the market in sexually explicit literature expanded significantly in the United States. D'Emilio and Freedman argue:

> fly-by-night producers and distributors of erotica, working out of basements and garages, churned out playing cards, slides, photos, homemade movies, and even records of pornographic content. The minimal capital that the

business required and the small size of the operations made it relatively easy to enter the field and virtually impossible for law-enforcement officials to suppress it. By the mid-1950's, estimates of the dollar volume of this sexual industry ranged from a few hundred million dollars to a billion dollars a year [1988: 280].

A new genre of popular publications also became available to cater for the taste acquired for soft-core porn during the war years. These included magazines such as *Peep* and *Stag*, the nudist publication *Health and Sunshine, Art and Photography* (which specialised in 'refined' nudes), and *Modern Man* (D'Emilio and Freedman 1988: 282; Talese 1980: 57), as well as a range of often luridly illustrated paperback novels. A 'paperback revolution', initiated in 1939 by the American publishing company Pocket Books, meant that books became both cheaper and more readily available. In the immediate post-war period publishers also began to explicitly use sex to boost paperback sales. D'Emilio and Freedman report:

> Bantam issued its first 'beefcake' cover in 1948, promoting *The African Queen* with a naked man emerging from the water. In the same year, Popular Library produced its famous 'nipple cover' to entice readers to purchase *The Private Life of Helen of Troy*. By the early 1950s lurid designs and suggestive copy dominated the paperback field [1988: 280].

The pin-up too remained popular after the war, suggesting that 'these filaments of fantasy had permanently infiltrated the erotic consciousness of the returning veteran' (Talese 1980: 59). This was confirmed by the dramatic success of *Playboy* magazine, launched by Hugh Hefner in 1953. Talese says:

> prior to *Playboy*, few men in America had ever seen a colour photograph of a nude woman … Although the Kinsey Report revealed that nearly all men masturbated, it was still a dark deed in the early 1950s, and there had been no indication of its association with pictures; but now the strong connection was obvious with the success of *Playboy*, a magazine that had climbed in circulation within its first two years from 60,000 copies sold per month to 400,000 [1980: 38].

Hefner offered a new type of magazine, one that presented sex as both wholesome and liberatory. He made sure that his centrefolds were 'the normal pretty girl that men saw each day in large cities and small towns' (Talese 1980: 104–5) rather than women who epitomised sex as a vice or scandal. Thus, Hefner was 'the first man to become rich by openly mass marketing masturbatory love through the illusion of an available alluring woman' (Talese 1980: 38–9, 90).

Some of these 'erotic' American magazines were available in Australia or were produced locally from syndicated American sources (*Playboy*, however, was not available in Australia until 1963). An example of the latter was *Man: The Australian Magazine for Men*, which published a mixture of serious articles, provocative cartoons, 'artistic' nudes and semi-nudes from the late 1930s through to the late 1950s. Women also were now said to be much more interested in reading 'sexy' novels and magazines (*SMH*, 3 July 1949); a range of new publications, like *Confidential* and *Keyhole*, were produced in this period specifically for female readers (D'Emilio and Freedman 1988: 280).

The findings of Kinsey *et al.*, reported in 1949, give some indication of changes in (American) sexual practices in this period, changes that are both indicative for Australia and relevant to the study of prostitution. In 1950 the Queensland Department of Health indicated that the Kinsey report was directly applicable to the Australian context. The Division of Enthetic Diseases (which dealt with sexually transmitted diseases) suggested that Kinsey's findings may have come as a 'surprise and shock' to the layman but: 'To anyone who has had much to do with the interviewing and treatment of venereal disease cases in British communities, the Kinsey report only serves to confirm and give statistical body to the very definite impressions gained by personal experience. Certainly, many of the case histories quoted could be paralleled in this country' (QHAR 1949–50: 22). Kinsey *et al.* found that 69 per cent of the total white male population had some experience with prostitutes although not more than 15 or 20 per cent had used their services with any frequency. While the percentage of men who were frequent users of prostitution services in the mid-1940s was the same as twenty years before, the overall frequency of contacts with prostitutes was significantly less. Kinsey *et al.* concluded 'The present-day male is making such contacts only two-thirds, or even half, as often as the older generation did … In compensation, however, there has been a definite increase in the amount of intercourse with girls who are not prostitutes, and the totals for pre-marital intercourse have not been materially changed' (1948: 595–609). This suggests that long-term changes in 'normal', non-commercial sexual relations between men and women were having a significant impact on the size of the demand for prostitution services by the late 1940s. According to Kinsey *et al.*: 'prostitution was much more important in the life of the male who lived any time between the dawn of history and World War I than we have evidence of its having been since then' (1948: 606).

While Kinsey is, thus, hypothesising a 'natural' decline in the prostitution trade, he also related this to different, class-based male sexualities. Contacts with prostitutes were more likely for 'males of the lowest social levels' while 'upper-level' males reported intercourse with prostitutes as psychically unsatisfying. This was because the 'emotionally sensitive' upper-level male needed the stimulation of erotic response in his sexual relations with women (Kinsey *et al.* 1948: 595–609).

There have been similar suggestions in the international literature that the demand for prostitution has declined since the war due to the increased sexual availability of women outside marriage. This approach clearly assumes that prostitution is primarily a substitute for, rather than an alternative to, 'normal' sexual relations and that companionate marriage is the relationship of choice for most men. This assumption may, however, be inaccurate. With the increased emphasis in post-war sexual culture on companionate relations, the demand for prostitution may now include a (masculine) desire to set aside mutuality in sexual interactions. There may have been, then, a shift between prostitution as a substitute for marital sex to prostitution as an adjunct to marital sex. This issue will be explored further in later chapters.

Prostitution: The Quiet Years

In general, prostitution generated little public debate or new legislation in the years following the war. This was in direct contrast to the situation which prevailed both during the war and for much of the preceding half-century. In South Australia, New South Wales and Victoria there were only a few minor legislative initiatives directed at the prostitution trade. In 1946 the South Australian government amended the *Police Act* to increase the maximum fines which could be applied to 'reputed thieves, prostitutes and idle and disorderly persons' (SAPD 1946: 866–70). A *Venereal Diseases Act* was also passed in 1947 although this simply brought South Australia into line with the other states.[4] In New South Wales the government amended the *Crimes Act* in 1951 in order to clarify a minor point of law in relation to the offence of having knowingly employed a girl under the age of eighteen years in a 'house of ill-fame' (NSWPD 196: 3225). In Victoria in 1952 a bill was proposed which aimed to close several legal loopholes identified by the police in relation to the prosecution of habitual drunkards and common prostitutes who behaved in a riotous or indecent manner. It sought to tighten the law in relation to keepers of disorderly houses, male persons who lived on the earnings of prostitution, the use of premises for immoral purposes (brothels), and the right of police to remove 'convicted and undesirable persons (including prostitutes) from racecourses, sportsgrounds, or showgrounds' (VPD 239: 1221–4). However, this bill lapsed largely because of opposition from the Labor Party. As in the pre-war period (see Chapter 1) the Labor Party opposed extensions of police power. In this case it was argued that the proposed new anti-prostitution measures would render young working-class men more vulnerable to arrest, even if they came from 'decent homes' (VPD 239: 2426).

This relative lack of public debate and official interest in prostitution has been explained in two ways. First, in the late 1940s the prostitution trade was said to be in the midst of a natural decline as a result of the war's end. Now that large numbers of Australian and Allied servicemen were no longer roaming city streets in search of female companionship and sexual contacts, the demand for prostitution was thought to have significantly decreased. In 1946, for example, the New South Wales police reported that 'vice' arrests had declined since the end of the war and that there were 'fewer young girls than formerly' coming to the attention of the Vice Squad: 'Many young girls who had been tempted to live immoral lives when there were many Servicemen in Sydney with substantial spending money, had now returned to legitimate work' (*SMH*, 6 February 1945). This underlines the clear distinction that was usually drawn by state authorities between professional prostitutes and 'promiscuous amateurs'; however, even professional prostitutes were not regarded as engaged in a legitimate occupation.

The end of the war clearly did have a significant impact on the prostitution industry. Professional prostitutes (as well as other women who had been sustained by the demand for sexual services during wartime) were faced with a declining market and, according to reports in the *Sydney Morning Herald*, increasingly needed to solicit on the streets in order to attract clients (6 February 1945). Some women were probably forced into overt prostitution for the first time by the departure from Australia of the large numbers of overseas servicemen that had been stationed here during the war. Many other women (who were perhaps casual prostitutes or 'kept women' during the war) were forced into low-paid jobs or into economic dependence – that is, marriage – at war's end. On her retirement in 1949, Sergeant Lillian Armfield, one of Sydney's first policewomen, said that the prostitution trade was quiet because many of Sydney's 'professional women' had married American servicemen and left the country (*SMH*, 13 November 1949).

The introduction of penicillin in the 1940s also relieved health departments and legislators of the need to be so directly concerned with the sexual practices of prostitutes and their clients. The treatment of both gonorrhea and syphilis – often with a single dose of penicillin –

was now both simple and effective. In mid-1946 the incidence of venereal disease in Queensland was said to have 'returned to a pre-war
basis' (QHAR 1945–46: 883). In fact, by 1947–48 the incidence of venereal disease was lower than it had been at any time since the early
1900s and was to decline to a record low by the early 1950s (QHAR
1955–56: 780). A similar reduction in the incidence of venereal disease
occurred in the other Australian jurisdictions at this time. This is not to
suggest that the incidence of sex outside of marriage, or of sexual
contacts with prostitutes, actually declined in this period; it is simply to
make the point that public authorities did not need to confront a
perceived nexus between prostitution and the social effects of sexually
transmitted disease.

A further reason for the relative lack of official interest in the prostitution trade has been advanced by Allen (1990: 284). She shows that
charges for prostitution-related offences such as vagrancy or being an
idle and disorderly person declined both absolutely and relatively (to
population) in New South Wales during the period. Indeed, until 1951
there were no charges for soliciting or living on earnings, and only a
few charges per year for owning a brothel. Allen suggests, however, that
these statistical patterns may simply indicate a fairly stable regulation of
the prostitution industry by police and organised crime in this period.

In Queensland and Western Australia there is clear evidence to
support this argument. The prostitution trade in both of these states
was controlled by informal arrangements between the police, state
health authorities and elements within the prostitution industry itself.
In evidence to the Fitzgerald Inquiry in 1987, several long-serving officers in the Queensland Police described their experience of policing
the prostitution trade during the war and immediately after. All of
them gave evidence of a policing practice in relation to prostitution
known as 'containment and control' which, in many cases, was tantamount to a police administration of prostitution. The Police Commissioner, Terry Lewis, said that this policy was not a secret, that ministers
were all aware of it, and that it had been policy for '50 or 60 or 70
years' (Fitzgerald Transcript: 469).

While there was some dispute at the inquiry as to whether ministers
knew of this policy, there is little doubt that a long-standing tradition
existed whereby police controlled key aspects of the prostitution industry.
Superintendent Dorries, for example, said that when he joined the police
force in 1952, there were three main brothels in Brisbane. These
brothels, he said, were there during and before the war. The police aim at
that time was to keep prostitutes off the streets and out of hotels. Thus,
the policy of containment was said to refer to the fact that sex workers
were 'confined in known premises' (Fitzgerald Transcript: 282).

Retired Assistant Commissioner N. S. Gulbransen told the Fitzgerald Inquiry that he had never heard of the policy of containment and control. Nevertheless he reported that when he served in the Criminal Investigation Branch during the late 1940s part of his job was to oversee certain aspects of the prostitution trade (Fitzgerald Transcript: 572). Gulbransen documented for examining counsel the procedure whereby prostitutes were subject to official surveillance and control via the *Health Act*. Prostitutes were not allowed to work in Brisbane's 'illegal but recognised brothels' without a weekly health check. This was performed at a special clinic for prostitutes operated by the Queensland Health Department. First attendance at the Prostitutes Clinic was said to be 'voluntary because the women knew that they would be out of a job if they didn't attend'. Gulbransen's job was to ensure that all those who were on the list attended for their examination. Those who were found to be suffering from a venereal disease were escorted to the lock hospital in the grounds of Boggo Road gaol. Those who failed to attend for their examinations were visited by members of the Consorting Squad and served with an order to attend. Workers who still refused to attend the clinic (it is hard to imagine there were many!) were taken directly to the lock hospital without an examination (Fitzgerald Transcript: 576–8).

Sulphathiazole was available for the treatment of venereal disease from 1943 onwards and penicillin from 1944 (and the number of United States troops stationed in Queensland was reduced from 1944 onwards), but women continued to undergo incarceration in the Brisbane lock hospital until mid-1946 (QHAR 1945–46: 17–18). The Health Department's Division of Enthetic Diseases noted a dramatic decline in the need for a lock hospital: 'Owing to the rapid cures with penicillin and the fact that most patients were rapidly rendered non-infectious by ordinary out-patient schedules of treatment, the daily bed rate fell away so rapidly that the need for such an institution no longer existed' (QHAR 1945–46: 12). However, an examination of the statistics for detention orders issued against women during and just after the end of the war shows that the lock hospital remained an important means for achieving control of the prostitution trade for several years after the cessation of hostilities. The Queensland Health Department reported in 1946 that the lock hospital was 'Formerly a hospital solely for the treatment of professional prostitutes, [but] the patients now mostly consist of careless or incorrigible vagrants as in-patients and certain inmates of the nearby Brisbane Prison as out-patients' (QHAR 1945–6: 16).[5] However, during May and June 1945 and again in June 1946, the number of women who had detention orders issued against them exceeded the total number of female notifications of venereal

disease.[6] So, for example, in July 1945 there were thirty-five female notifications in Brisbane for venereal disease, while forty-three detention
orders were issued against Brisbane women. While this might simply be
a statistical anomaly (reflecting detention orders relating to the
previous or next calendar month), no similar statistical anomalies
occurred in 1942, 1943 or 1944 (QHAR 1945–46: 18). It can be
suggested, therefore, that specific legal and/or institutional pressures
were being applied to sex workers at the end of the war (and that in
most cases these were additional to the measures deemed necessary to
prevent the dissemination of venereal disease). Moreover, this process
was probably related to the renegotiation of relations between the
Queensland police, state health authorities and the prostitution
industry at war's end.

In Western Australia, as in Queensland, the prostitution trade had
long been organised by informal arrangements between the police,
health authorities and entrepreneurs within the trade itself. Gail
Reekie (1985) has demonstrated that Perth women's organisations
were active on a number of sexual fronts during World War II and –
chiefly in order to protect (working-class) women from sexual exploitation by men – supported official wartime attempts to control public
drinking, prostitution and venereal disease. While conservative and
radical women's organisations disagreed about the social and
economic contexts of prostitution, they all agreed its existence represented the sexual exploitation of women and were opposed to the
system of organised brothel prostitution in Roe Street. After the war,
however, women's organisations went into decline right around
Australia. As Reekie (1985: 591) comments, 'Wartime co-operation
yielded to more enduring political factionalism in the late 1940s, and a
united women's movement slumbered until the revival of feminism
several decades later.'

In the Western Australian parliament a lone voice continued what
could be called a feminist fight against the 'state regulation of vice'. In
1955 Dame Florence Cardell-Oliver,[7] the first female parliamentarian
to speak in an Australian parliament on the issue of prostitution,
decried the fact that 'houses of ill-fame' were allowed to flourish in
Roe Street adjacent to the Perth railway station, and accused the police
as well as the government of failing to uphold the law and of
condoning graft and corruption. Cardell-Oliver said that the Commissioner of Police had told her that the government preferred the situation in Roe Street to remain as it was so that the police could 'keep an
eye on' the prostitution trade (WAPD 142: 300–3). As in Queensland,
then, the lack of official and public scrutiny of prostitution at this
time in Western Australia was most likely a reflection of a fairly

stable regulation of the industry by police, health authorities and elements within the prostitution industry itself.

The Debate about Prostitution in Parliament

Although prostitution was not a focus of new legislation, it occasionally appeared as a topic in parliamentary debate. When the matter did come up, parliamentarians continued to talk about prostitution in much the same way as they had before the war (see Chapter 1). The prostitute was still the main focus of political attention and still an object of contradictory discourses. She was represented by parliamentarians as an idle, disorderly and undesirable person (SAPD 1946: 866–70; VPD 238: 1221–4) but also occasionally as a victim who had been 'preyed' upon by men. This latter view was presented by only one parliamentarian, Florence Cardell-Oliver (WAPD 142: 300, 303). In the main, prostitutes were not regarded as victims or as workers; they were regarded as lazy and deviant women who sought an easy life. As one member of parliament argued, women who became prostitutes did so out of choice: 'No girl today is forced into prostitution by economic need. The demand for woman-power is so acute that every woman who wants a job can find it. The woman who becomes a prostitute does so not for the bread of life, but in the hope of gaining some of the jam' (SAPD 1946: 859). Thus, the post-war demand for labour was assumed to be capable of providing the 'bread of life' for women and men equally although, as Ryan and Conlon (1975: 94) have argued, women were largely displaced from the paid workforce in the immediate post-war years.

In general, clients remained relatively invisible in parliamentary considerations of the prostitution trade. The only significant exception occurred in 1955 when Cardell-Oliver raised the issue of Perth's officially tolerated brothels and described the queues of men who waited outside them on payday (WAPD 142: 300). As in the pre-war period, client invisibility tended to be threatened by official considerations of the problem of venereal disease. However, this threat was usually readily averted. Clients and their families continued to be represented as the innocent victims of diseases that were spread by prostitute women. For example, while presenting his arguments in support of the 1947 Venereal Diseases Bill, the Premier of South Australia cited several cases of women who had effectively evaded treatment despite being positively identified as the sexual contacts of men who were known to have a venereal disease. He reported the case of a young woman who had been fined in early 1947 'for committing an act of gross indecency with a man in a public place during daylight'. Another man later in the year positively identified this woman as the source of the syphilitic infection that he was suffering from. Moreover: 'Inquiries revealed that he had passed it on to his wife, who was about four months pregnant. This means that [the promiscuous woman] is known to have been responsible for infecting two persons and probably the child, making two innocent victims' (SAPD 1947: 578). The woman who was 'promiscuous' was regarded as a prostitute and as the main source of the syphilitic infection; there was no suggestion that the adulterous husband was also responsible for the state of the 'two innocent victims'. As in the pre-war period, the government – under the guise of 'public health' – was still seeking to ensure that 'infected' women did not endanger men who engaged in extra-marital sexual encounters. Women who were 'uncontrolled', that is, those who were 'freelancers' or 'amateurs', were represented as a particular threat to public health (or, often quite specifically, men's health) (SAPD 1947: 859). Although speakers did not actually say that it was natural for men to resort to prostitution (see Chapter 1), they clearly assumed that this was the case.

In another continuity with the pre-war period, men who directly or indirectly lived on the earnings of prostitution were regarded as an anathema. Cardell-Oliver argued that the businessmen and landlords who owned and operated brothels in Perth's Roe Street area made a living 'by trading the bodies of females to be made use of by males' which was an 'inhuman trade' (WAPD 142: 178). Similarly, in the Victorian parliament, the Chief Secretary argued in 1952 that proposed amendments to the *Police Offences Act* were designed to allow police to deal more effectively with bludgers and 'male sex perverts' (VPD 239: 1221–4) – a conjunction which clearly shows how men who lived on earnings were regarded. While the actual number of arrests and the penalties applied to men who lived on earning is not available, at least one case was reported in the *Sydney Morning Herald* in this period (21 January 1954). A 50-year-old man was convicted on a charge of having knowingly lived on the earnings of prostitution; he received a suspended six-month sentence.

For most parliamentarians in this period, the prostitution transaction itself was not a political issue. Cardell-Oliver was an exception to this rule. She argued that the 'legal' brothels in Roe Street, Perth, posed a direct threat to the moral health of children and families and threatened Australia's post-war immigration plans: 'if I went to England today and told the people what sort of places were waiting here for their children, we would not get many families to come here. We are definitely not encouraging migration by having in our midst places such as Roe St.' Linking the dual concerns of women's lesser economic power and the pressures on migrants, Cardell-Oliver also suggested that the prostitution trade could undermine the growth of sound citizenship practices among newly arrived migrant women: 'Many young girls who are new to this country are engaged in decent employment during the day, but are encouraged to make a few extra pounds in the evening by going to [the brothels in Roe Street] ... Does that lead these girls to good citizenship?' In a pointed and distinctly feminist critique of the practice of 'containing' prostitution, Cardell-Oliver accused her parliamentary colleagues of failing to protect women and of defending the sexual interests of men: 'I venture to say that if the houses of ill-fame in Roe St had male victims inside instead of women as we have now, and women paraded the street as men do now, all the 49 male members of this House would rise and close those houses without hesitation and ban their existence' (WAPD 1142: 299–300, 301, 303).

Cardwell-Oliver's arguments were not debated by the Western Australian parliament. But in all Australian parliaments at this time it was regarded as appropriate that there should be strong laws penalising prostitution. In most states (notably Queensland and Western Australia), such approaches did not conform with the actual means by which police and health authorities dealt with prostitution, but there was little indication of this within the parliamentary arena.

Rising Concerns

I have suggested that there was a relative lack of public and legislative concern in Australia with the prostitution industry in 1945–55. By the end of the period, however, official concerns about the prostitution trade were again becoming manifest. This first became evident in the early 1950s as new discourses about the rising incidence of sexual deviance, particularly male homosexuality, were deployed. A leading London doctor blamed the prolonged segregation of the sexes during the war for what was perceived as a growing problem of homosexuality (*SMH*, 2 April 1954). In 1952 police in Britain argued that the number of 'unnatural male offences' was more than four times the pre-war figure. They also suggested that housewives were resorting in large numbers to work in new call-girl services (*Sun-Herald*, 3 January 1954).

Similar anxieties were appearing in Australia. In 1952, the New South Wales Police Commissioner announced a drive against all sorts of vice including prostitution, but argued that homosexual offences required urgent attention: 'Offenders of this type are a cancer in the community ... It is damaging to the moral welfare of the community and must be checked at all costs' (*SMH*, 19 November 1952).

In Queensland the number of charges for 'unnatural offences' brought by the police increased fourfold in 1947–48 and then doubled in 1953–54. Arrests for female vagrancy (most of which would have been for prostitution-related offences) also doubled in the year 1954–55 before increasing again by 50 per cent in 1955–56 (QPAR 1945–57).

A review of the *Sydney Morning Herald* suggests that from 1950 onwards there was increasing official interest in the prosecution of sexual 'deviance', particularly, but not exclusively, male homosexuality. For example, between 1950 and 1955 (but not in 1945–49) the *Sydney Morning Herald* contained numerous reports of men prosecuted for offensive behaviour. This involved offences like nude sunbathing, 'staring' at girls in the surf at Bondi, and being a 'peeping tom' (15 March 1950; 20 February, 9 May 1951). There were also reports of men charged with 'misconduct with a lubra' and for offences in relation to indecent films and photographs (14 July 1951; 4, 7 December 1954). Homosexual men were arrested and charged with offensive behaviour or soliciting for 'immoral purposes' (6 January, 2, 16 March 1950; 25 April 1951; 13 September 1952; 19 February 1953, 11 February 1954).

In 1953, however, the New South Wales Supreme Court found that the *Vagrancy Act* could not be used to prosecute male persons who solicited other males for the purposes of perpetrating homosexual acts.[8] Men who were accused of homosexual soliciting were, therefore, liable only to a charge of offensive behaviour for which the maximum fine was £5 (although stiffer penalties for 'unnatural offences' were still available under the New South Wales *Crimes Act*). Consequently, in 1954, Premier Cahill argued that homosexuality was causing 'grave anxiety' in the community and that some government action was required (*SMH*, 9 June 1954). An amendment to the *Crimes Act* was passed which specifically prohibited male homosexual soliciting (whether this was for the purposes of prostitution or not).[9] The government argued that it had acted on homosexual soliciting 'because it considers that the homosexual wave that unfortunately has struck this country – though not to the extent of the continental countries – must be eradicated' (NSWPD 12: 3230). As distinct from the situation which prevailed in the early days of the Australian colony, then, prostitution was no longer regarded as an effective deterrent to the emergence of 'unnatural' sexual relations between men. Moreover, both prostitution and male homosexuality were increasingly regarded as undesirable in the new post-war sexual regime. Weeks (1981: 240) contends that this was because there was a 'heightened stress on the importance of monogamous, heterosexual love' which threw into greater relief than ever before the 'deviant' nature of both homosexuality and prostitution. Certainly, in both Britain and Australia, prostitutes and male homosexuals became subject to a range of new legal sanctions as the 1950s progressed (see Chapter 3).

Pornography: Soft-core Enters the Mainstream

Laws addressed to obscene and indecent films and to film censorship remained uncontroversial in Australia during 1945–55. Film censorship regulations were clearly aimed at mainstream films, although there is evidence to suggest that they were also applied to an embryonic trade in pornographic films. In 1953 the Chief Film Censor reported that several privately owned films of less than standard size had been prohibited. He said that it was impossible to consider requests for revision of the regulations pertaining to these films because of 'the number of attempted imports of most objectionable types of films by private individuals'. In most cases, 'according to the degree of indecency or obscenity', the films were confiscated by Customs authorities (*SMH*, 20 March 1953).

Federal customs laws were also used to launch some prosecutions of film pornography in this period. In 1954, for example, the *Sydney Morning Herald* reported the case of a man who was prosecuted for possession of a prohibited import – 'films of a very disgusting nature and obscene' said Customs officer Nathaniel P. Craig; the accused was fined £100 and given a six-month suspended sentence. He said that the films found at his flat were left there by an American seaman who asked him to mind them. He showed these films to a friend called Jack – a 'new Australian' or migrant – who had organised mixed parties to see the films. Jack had charged about 5 shillings per head (*SMH*, 7 December 1954). State obscenity laws were also occasionally used in this period against 'obscene' films produced within Australia. In 1946 the *Sydney Morning Herald* reported the prosecution of a 'sex film' producer in Melbourne. Charges against the actors in the film were dismissed (12, 14 February).

None of these particular cases provoked official comment or any obvious public debate. However, from the early 1950s onwards, there was a great deal of public debate and new legislation in the area of so-called obscene, indecent and objectionable literature. Parliaments around Australia were evaluating post-war trends in literature and establishing new regulatory mechanisms for material that was deemed to be dangerous or problematic. This included publications with themes of crime, violence or horror, as well as material that was deemed to be salacious or pornographic because of its emphasis on sex.

Almost immediately after the cessation of hostilities in 1945, there were calls to begin the dismantling of 'civil censorship'. On 2 August 1945, for example, an editorial in the *Sydney Morning Herald* – a newspaper that was to take a consistently libertarian line in relation to censorship over the next thirty years – was critical of the federal government's decision to ban the American novel *Forever Amber*, although this was done on the advice of the Commonwealth Literature Censorship Board. The editor argued that it was not necessary for a book to have literary merit to escape prohibition: 'The only issue is whether a Minister ... or anyone else, should be entitled in a democracy to impose on the public purely personal canons of taste.' This issue was to be the focus of an increasingly important political debate in the post-war period.

In 1945 nearly 500 separate texts were listed by Commonwealth Customs as prohibited imports under Section 52C of the *Customs Act*. This was literature which was considered blasphemous, indecent or obscene, which unduly emphasised matters of sex or crime, or which was calculated to encourage depravity. However, a major problem for booksellers (and others) at the time was the system of 'secret censorship', under which the list of prohibited books was not publicly available. The Minister for Customs said this was necessary because otherwise 'some people would be looking for them [banned books] all over the place' and he did not want to give publicity to books that had been banned. Booksellers were forced to rely on newspaper reports or individual inquiries to the Customs Department in order to find out if a book was on the prohibited list, and yet they were liable to prosecution if they sold a banned book (*SMH*, 15, 17 April 1946).

An important public and political debate about art, literature and state obscenity laws took place in relation to two Australian novels, Lawson Glassop's *We Are the Rats* (1946) and Robert Close's *Love Me, Sailor* (1948), and in relation to the art of Rosaleen Norton. For the sake of brevity, I deal here only with the literary cases, although the debate over Norton's art is worthy of fuller treatment.[10]

In 1946, in an action launched by the New South Wales Vice Squad, *We Are the Rats* was found to be an obscene publication. The publishers, Angus and Robertson, were fined £10 plus 8 shillings costs; the appeal against this sentence failed (*SMH*, 14, 15 June 1946). *We Are the Rats* was a story about Australian soldiers in Tobruk during World War II. The author said that he 'tried to show how men at war, repressed through lack of association with women, would react to sex'. Among the passages identified as obscene by the court was an extract from an American publication which the main character reads out to his army mates. It included the following: 'Impulsively, uncontrollably, his left hand swiftly dropped inside her low neckline, slipped beneath a silk brassiere ... She pulled her dress off. ... And, finally, he saw her glorious young body lying irresistibly nude across his lap' (Glassop 1945: 177–9). In his defence of the book, a barrister for Angus and Robertson argued that: 'There is nothing in this book which seeks to glorify pornography ... It describes only the natural reactions of gallant men of the AIF. No decent person holds any brief for pornographic literature but every thinking person must realise that literary men are bound to treat the affairs of life as real' (*SMH*, 25 April 1946). The legal action over *We Are the Rats* tended to focus public attention on this novel and on the whole issue of literary obscenity. Because it was a patriotic war text and claimed to be a true representation of men at war, the prosecution of the publishers also provoked some new public opposition to the normal procedures for dealing with 'problematic' literature.

In Victoria there was a similar public outcry about the prosecution of an author and publisher. In 1949 Robert Shaw Close was sentenced to three months' imprisonment and fined £100 for publishing an obscene libel, the novel *Love Me, Sailor*. The parts of this book regarded as pornographic described a visit to a brothel by two sailors and included the following: 'He collapsed on her fumbling with wild urgency. Strange seas drew him into a cavern of pulsing warmth. All life, all existence became a throbbing urge. A turbulent torrent swept him – the stream of life gripped in a spurting of brief ecstasy' (Close 1948: 72–9). The publishing house was also fined £500. On appeal, the sentence of imprisonment was set aside although the fine was increased (*SMH*, 16, 21, 22 April 1949). In various public statements this trial was condemned by the Fellowship of Australian Writers, the Australian Journalists Association, various state Councils for Civil Liberties, the Rationalist Society of Australia, Sydney University Union, International PEN (Melbourne Division), and the Council for the Encouragement of Music and the Arts (Mann n.d.).

It appears, then, that literary trials in the second half of the 1940s provoked both the emergence of a new opposition to censorship and the formation of new political alliances around an anti-censorship stance. But anti-censorship discourse in this period was primarily concerned with 'literature' and not with other publications which were deemed to be popular or blatantly obscene. In Victoria there were calls for reform of the *Police Offences Act* in order that a defence to the charge of having written or published an obscene book was 'that the work was written, printed, published and sold in good faith and has literary merit' (Mann n.d.). Similarly, in Western Australia, the Attorney-General agreed to consider proposals for reform of the

Indecent and Obscene Publications Act submitted by the Fellowship of Australian Writers. These proposals were particularly designed to ensure that items of literary merit were not subject to prosecution (*SMH*, 18 July 1947). This suggests that, by the late 1940s, there was rising public support in Australia for material which had literary and artistic merit to be removed from the ambit of state obscenity laws. There was, however, little opposition to the introduction of tough new controls on popular publications in the 1950s. There was also no publicly expressed support for those who breached obscenity laws with material that was blatantly commercial and/or pornographic.

Examples of the latter were frequently reported in the press. In 1951, a Brisbane firm of men's clothiers was fined £20, with £5 2s costs, for having displayed in its shop window ties with a design of semi-nude women (*SMH*, 29 March 1951). In 1954 a Sydney tobacconist was charged with publishing and exhibiting an obscene matchbox cover; he was fined £5 (*SMH*, 15 April 1954). Also in 1954, a 41-year-old shop assistant was fined a total of £65 in a Sydney magistrate's court. He was found guilty of offensive behaviour towards a boy in the State Theatrette (£5), of having twelve obscene photographs in his possession (£10) and of having brought prohibited imports into Australia (£50). The accused denied that he had intended to sell the photographs, saying that he was going to give them to people who might like them. The photos were said to represent 'nude females posed in grossly indecent postures'. The magistrate commented that 'a man with photos like this has got a diseased mind. They are disgusting' (*SMH*, January 1954). None of these cases provoked public or political comment about the need for more 'freedom'.

Popular Publications in the 1950s

In the 1950s popular magazines and comics with themes of sex, crime or horror became a specific target for new legislation throughout Australia. Calls were made in parliament for governments to do something about the 'flood' of 'salacious' literature that was said to be polluting the minds of Australian children and adolescents (see for example WAPD 1: 616; NSWPD 194: 4471; VPD 240: 1660). One member of parliament reported that by the mid-1950s Australian children were the consumers of an estimated five to six million comics annually (VPD 240: 2583). Thus, a new political problem was seen to have emerged – literature that was not legally obscene or indecent but was clearly objectionable, dangerous for children and without literary merit.

The development of uniform state laws to control the distribution of books and plays was first mooted, but rejected, at a Premiers'

Conference in 1949. No action was taken at this time, partly because of opposition from New South Wales and partly because the Commonwealth made no specific proposal to the conference (*SMH*, 18 August 1949). The NSW Minister for Housing, Clive Evatt, cited the Robert Close case (about *Love Me, Sailor*) as an example of why his state was not interested in the introduction of new censorship provisions:

> New South Wales has no enthusiasm for the proposal that there should be a Commonwealth scheme of book and play censorship ... In New South Wales there is no censorship of books. There is an Act which penalises obscene publications, the question whether a publication is obscene being determined by the Court. That Act, however, does not relate to objects of art or to literary work. On the broad question of censorship, the tendency should be towards elimination rather than towards extension of such controls (*SMH*, 18 August 1949).

This demonstrates the influence of the two key post-war obscenity trials in Australia (*We Are the Rats* and *Love Me, Sailor*) and the emergence – particularly among those on the left – of a clear anti-censorship position.

The new problems posed by comics and sex magazines were again raised at a Premiers' Conference in 1952 (*SMH*, 9 July 1952) and at a conference of state officers responsible for censorship later the same year. The states agreed that, in order to achieve Australia-wide control of undesirable comics and magazines, they would adopt a uniform and extended definition of obscene publications based on the existing Victorian Act. Provision was to be made for the exemption of works of literary merit and bona fide medical, pharmaceutical or political texts (VPD 243: 23). The proposed legislation was a direct response to intense public lobbying by groups such as Sydney Legacy, the Council of Churches, Catholic Youth Organisations, the Country Women's Association, Apex clubs, Parents and Citizens Associations, the Red Cross society, the Returned Servicemen's League, the Women's Auxiliary of the Wheat Growers Union, and the Australian Labor Party (NSWPD 11: 2711).

In 1954–55 South Australia, Victoria, New South Wales and Queensland (but not Western Australia) all passed new legislation aimed at comics and salacious magazines.[11] However, this legislation was not, in any sense, uniform. In Queensland the *Objectionable Literature Act* established a new censorship body, the Literature Board of Review. This board was given the task of examining all literature being distributed in Queensland and had the power to prohibit distribution of any material it deemed to be objectionable. The determination of 'objectionable' literature was to be made with regard to the nature of the literature under review, the persons and age groups among whom the literature was likely to be addressed, and the tendency of that literature to deprave and corrupt. Objectionable literature, then, was material which unduly emphasised matters of sex, horror, cruelty or violence; or was blasphemous, indecent, obscene, or likely to be injurious to morality; or encouraged depravity, public disorder or any indictable offence; or 'was otherwise calculated to injure the citizens of this state' (QPD 208: 1760). Provision was made under the *Objectionable Literature Act* for appeal to the Supreme Court against the board's decisions.

In Victoria, South Australia and New South Wales the establishment of new censorship authorities was considered to be undesirable. State obscenity laws were seen to be the only appropriate means for regulating the distribution of obscene, indecent and objectionable literature, with a court adjudicating on alleged breaches of the law. These three states adopted similar, although not identical, new laws to deal with indecent and obscene publications. In Western Australia no amendments to state obscenity laws were passed in the period 1953–55 although the reasons for this are not completely clear. A member of the Western Australian parliament reported in 1954 that many publications were circulating in Perth which were prohibited in Queensland. The Premier indicated at this time that a departmental committee was investigating the problem and would make some recommendations in relation to the legislative control of undesirable literature (WAPD 139: 1254). However, Western Australia was not to amend its laws against obscene and indecent publications until 1974.

The Debate in Parliament about Comics and Salacious Magazines

An examination of parliamentary debates in 1953–55 shows that a new political problem was being identified in Australia during this period. This was the set of publications – mostly comics and magazines said to be 'devoted to promiscuous sexuality and animal ferocity' (VPD 243: 83) – which had appeared on the Australian market since the early 1950s. Governments argued that existing obscenity laws were inadequate to cope with this new problem because they were 'passed in a generation that did not know the crime comic, the horror magazine and the cheap sex publications' (NSWPD 11: 2716). There was also widespread agreement among parliamentarians that obscenity laws needed to be strengthened. The overall aim of government intervention was 'to build up a better population ... one with an inherent desire to read a better class of literature' (QPD 1208: 1775). Parliamentarians said they did not want to restrict genuine literature or 'lighter reading' (that is, material designed to entertain the masses), nor did they wish to interfere 'in the legitimate occupation of reputable publishers and distributors' who catered for this latter market. The role of the legislature, therefore, was to encourage the development of a 'worthwhile and healthy appetite' in literature, one which would defend Christian values and combat the influence of Communism (NSWPD 11: 2747, 2711, 2772).

Several distinct categories of publications were regarded as problematic. There was 'sadistic literature' (QPD 208: 1773) – war, horror and crime publications[12] – as well as sex magazines (such as *Squire, Male Man,* and *Peep*), romance magazines (for example *Teenage Love* and *Love Problems*) and nudist publications (such as *Sunbather* and *Health and Vitality*). Clearly, then, while sex magazines were an important object of political concern, several other sorts of publications were also regarded as problematic. As one speaker in the Queensland parliament argued, while he was concerned to outlaw sex literature he also wanted to address material which 'exalts the horrors of war ... exalts horror and emphasises crime without showing the futility of crime'. This type of literature, he contended, was just as dangerous to the morality of the nation as literature designed 'to debase sex' (QPD 208: 1772).

The appearance of this new genre of 'objectionable publications' was frequently said by parliamentarians to be a symptom of modern life and, in particular, 'the decline of home life, the counter-attraction of the radio and cinema and all the other modern diversions and entertainments that largely tend to remove children, during their formative years, from the guidance, control and advice of their parents or others in authority over them' (NSWPD 12: 2763). The war was said to have produced 'a cheapening of life' and to have 'upset the conception of appreciation of beauty, art, thought, the relationship of man to man and man to woman'. Several parliamentarians argued that the problem of violent and salacious literature was caused by the declining standards of American culture and its influence on Australia through film and literature. American literature in general was said to demonstrate 'a complete disregard for moral and ethical standards, the sanctity of marriage and the fundamental principles of family life'. As the bearers of some of the worst aspects of American culture, then, American comics and magazines were regarded as a threat to Australian and British cultural traditions (NSWPD 12: 2624, 2770, 2763).

The main political concern, however, was that children and teenagers would be corrupted by exposure to such publications, particularly as 'temptation' was 'blatantly placed in front of them'. Adults, on the other hand, were represented as fairly invulnerable and as naturally tending to reject trashy literature and return to what was 'decent'. This capacity was clearly connected with maturity and education. For children and teenagers, a variety range of potentially adverse effects were seen to emerge from the consumption of 'objectionable' comics and magazines. These ranged from myopia (caused apparently by the small printing and poor quality paper on which pulp novels were produced) and juvenile delinquency[13] to rape and murder. One speaker in the New South Wales parliament argued that young men who commit capital offences are 'almost invariably ... avid readers of horror magazines. There can be no question of the effect of this material on their minds' (NSWPD 11: 2745). Other possible adverse effects included an increased danger of drug abuse – because of the way that American pulp novels and magazines represented the 'wonderful effects of morphia' – and sexual problems. One member of the New South Wales parliament indicated that reading pulp novels led to masturbation: 'Let us consider the case of a young man who is lying in bed reading a cheap novel.' Although the implication was that this was an undesirable sexual practice, the speaker did not indicate what he thought the specific dangers were. (Clearly, there were limits on how sexual issues and practices could be discussed in parliament.) Other speakers argued that salacious literature made 'girls' more susceptible to seduction and could, therefore, cause a rise in the number of unmarried mothers (NSWPD 12: 2718–78; QPD 208: 1772).

There was also a clear concern among parliamentarians that normal sexual relations would be distorted by young people's consumption of objectionable literature, particularly as they filled 'the minds of young people with unhealthy ideas about sex' (NSWPD 11: 2666). In New South Wales, for example, Gertrude Melville[14] argued that the consumption of romance magazines by 'young girls' could lead to unreal expectations of marriage and a higher divorce rate (NSWPD 12: 3115). Another member of the New South Wales parliament argued that young people learned inappropriate sexual roles from objectionable literature. This was because, when passing a bookstall, the first thing 'young people' noticed was the naked women displayed on the front covers. Inside this sort of literature every woman was 'fair game' and 'conquests' were described 'in a way that nobody could misunderstand. ... The details are so minute that any youth who picked up one of these books and read it may well say "Well, I will give it a go"' (NSWPD 11: 2736). Thus: 'Youths and girls who read love stories in which the man is the hunter and some member of the fair sex continually succumbs to his wiles, are inevitably conditioned to that approach to life' (NSWPD 11: 2745). The implication was that this sort of approach to sexual relations was undesirable, particularly, we might assume, in the context of the new post-war sexual culture which emphasised the importance of mutuality and, increasingly, sexual egalitarianism.

Other speakers in parliament argued that adult sexual abnormalities could emerge from the consumption of salacious literature by those who were immature: 'Every form of perversion, masochism, sadism and homosexuality is portrayed, and the child is given full opportunity to develop psychopathic tendencies. The effect of these publications is not to attract perverts but to make them' (NSWPD 12: 2779). Children exposed to the influences of objectionable literature could, then, develop disordered personalities. This would lead them, as adults, to manifest sexual (and other) excesses that would make them 'an object of pity and a subject of law' (VPD 240: 2583; 243: 99). Such individuals would also be an anathema in the new companionate sexual culture. In this context, it was suggested that 'proper' sex education material should be available for adults. As one member of the New South Wales parliament said in 1955, texts on the sexual aspects of married life should be available 'to people of maturity or young couples genuinely requiring guidance for their future married life'. But such material was not really 'fit and proper to be displayed everywhere with invitations to all and sundry to procure and study it' (NSWPD 11: 2717).

The overall concern of parliamentarians, then, was that 'objectionable' literature would produce a generation of children with 'shattered concepts of right and wrong, with distorted ideas of sex, sadistic lusts, violent colour prejudices and firm convictions that crime is a paying proposition' (NSWPD 11: 2714). The argument was made that if governments did not act then 'we could reach a position where the morality of the young child would be debased to such an extent that the moral life of the nation could be undermined' (QPD 208: 1771). Children needed to 'grow up into the decent type of citizen' and, thus, provide a 'sound foundation for the nation'. From this conservative perspective, comics and salacious literature were an evil that threatened 'the good order of society' (NSWPD 11: 2711–35).

Some parliamentarians also raised a more general concern about the representation of women in comics and pulp novels. As one member of the New South Wales parliament argued: 'when girls fall [in these novels] they always do so showing prominent bosoms. Skirts invariably billow upwards to reveal black-net panties; and the superwomen unfailingly display their "super" bosoms in a most exciting way' (NSWPD 12: 2778). Such soft-core pornographic representations were said to be blatantly disrespectful to women (NSWPD 12: 2789). One speaker in the Victorian parliament was critical of the fact that, in his opinion, women themselves were not sufficiently active in defending their own interests:

> I am astounded that women, who are noted for their volubility, have been silent on this vital issue. I expected that, when their sex was dragged into the mire, they would raise their voices in no uncertain manner, but this task has been left to the mere males who have had to exert the necessary pressure on this and preceding Governments ... From time immemorial women have been dragged in the mire, so to speak, and this practice could be stopped immediately if women were to combine and express their views (VPD 243: 97).

This approach raises several issues. In the first place there was a dearth of women in Australian parliaments at this time. So it perhaps is not surprising that women were not vigorously campaigning within parliament. Outside parliament, women's organisations *were* at the forefront in the campaign for stronger legislative controls on comics and salacious literature. The fact that their efforts were invisible to some parliamentarians is indicative of a general devaluation of women's political activities (outside parliamentary institutions) in Australian political history. There is, however, a further issue which relates to women's view of their political interests. In her speech to the New South Wales Legislative Council, Gertrude Melville argued that she was representing 'the opinion of thousands of mothers and of many organizations that have for some time been urging the government to take action on this matter' (NSWPD 12: 3113). Thus, while she and several other parliamentarians made visible the extra-parliamentary political activities of women on this issue, her main focus was on women as mothers (that is, as guardians of the next generation) rather than on the separate issue of how women were represented in salacious literature.

Opposition within parliament to the new laws against objectionable literature was typically low-key. This indicates that a significant degree of consensus existed in all Australian parliaments at this time about the need for stricter controls on popular literature. In the New South Wales parliament there were a few members who voiced their dissatisfaction with the proposed legislation. The member for Neutral Bay, for example, argued that the new laws represented 'a further proscription of our freedom', while others suggested that the legislation would 'set back the clock' and that 'the real test of a democracy' was 'the right of everyone to express himself [*sic*] fearlessly'. Thus, for a small minority, the new laws against comics and salacious magazines were an infringement of fundamental liberties and 'a nail in freedom's coffin' (NSWPD 12: 2786, 2853, 2866).

This was a position supported outside the parliament by the Australian Council of Civil Liberties (VPD 243: 97). As in the pre-war period, the editor of the *Sydney Morning Herald* argued against the principle of censorship. However, he did not defend the consumption of popular literature:

> Most people would agree that there is now a fairly large class of publications which the community would be better without. They include the lower type of American crime comics and those salacious little magazines in which sex and cruelty are mixed according to a well-tried recipe. Whether these publications actually do much harm to young people is more doubtful ... Still it will be readily conceded that, even if these publications do no harm, they certainly do no good (*SMH*, 20 October 1954).

It is clear, then, that opposition to the new laws against comics and salacious literature was premised upon an overall defence of 'literature'. It was said that the production of literature (particularly 'future classics') and the status of Australian writers would be adversely affected by the imposition of additional legislative controls (NSWPD 12: 2866–7). As one parliamentarian argued, the aim of legislation must be to control 'sex vulgarity and depravity, crime horror and violence', but 'not with the idea of killing truth or of smothering the pictures of reality that are part and parcel of modern life' (NSWPD 12: 2867). The suggestion that the fate of popular literature (such as comics and salacious magazines) was intimately connected to that of 'real' literature was strongly repudiated in the New South Wales parliament:

> to suggest that [comics and salacious magazines are literature] is a defilement itself ... publications of this sort are not literature, which is an interpretation of life at a high, gentle or comic standard, expressed in prose, verse, highly conceived poetry or some other form ... It must have ideas revealing, in either a beautiful or nasty manner, the truth of circumstances ... [this rubbish] is a warped exaggeration of truth (NSWPD 11: 2624).

Clearly, competing definitions of literature as well as disparate accounts of truth and reality could be brought into play. One member who argued against the new laws suggested that much of the literature which was deemed objectionable was simply realistic. Thus, to prohibit certain sorts of publications, such as war books, was 'to run away from truth and reality' (NSWPD 11: 2623). In contemporary terms, however, there was a very low level of political dispute in the 1950s about the institution of new laws and censorship controls over popular literature.

Conclusion

In the immediate post-war years the prostitution industry was not a major concern of government in Australia and there was little new legislation addressed to this issue. The prostitution industry appeared to be quiet in this period although, as I have shown, this could have been due to a number of different factors such as an actual decline in the demand for prostitution services, the effectiveness of new antibiotic treatments in the curtailment of venereal disease, and/or a relatively stable regulation of the industry through extra-legal arrangements. In at least two states – Queensland and Western Australia – such extra-legal arrangements were the main means of organising the prostitution industry both before and after the end of World War II. Moreover, within political discourse generally, there were clear continuities between the way that prostitution was conceptualised before and after the war. My examination of parliamentary debates shows that, as in the pre-war period, prostitutes and men who lived on the earnings of prostitution continued to be the main focus of political concern. Moreover, male clients and the prostitution transaction itself remained relatively invisible and unproblematic.

By the mid-1950s, however, new political concerns about prostitution and homosexuality were becoming evident in Australia. Prostitution was no longer regarded as an effective deterrent to the appearance of homosexuality, and the emergence of a new post-war sexual culture meant that both prostitution and homosexuality were increasingly regarded as undesirable sexual practices. In terms of political discourses about prostitution, the main impact of changes within the sexual culture was not visible until the late 1950s; this will be examined further in Chapter 3. It is not the case, however, that political discourses about prostitution remained completely unchanged. I have suggested above that the new public roles which women assumed as a result of the war led to the election of slightly more women to state and federal parliaments during 1939–55. Overall, the number of female parliamentarians remained extremely small during this period, but their individual contributions to political debate could be significant. In Western Australia, for example, Dame Florence Cardell-Oliver pointed out that existing politico-legal practices for the control of prostitution were premised upon a defence of male sexual interests. Such feminist arguments were not to appear again in any parliament until the 1970s; however, their appearance in the first post-war decade is both noteworthy and indicative of the impact that the participation of women was to have on a future political discourse about prostitution (see Chapters 6 and 7).

By contrast to the relative absence of a political concern with prostitution, there was a significant level of political debate about literary obscenity in the decade after 1945. At first this was addressed almost wholly to 'high' literature. There were some celebrated prosecutions of novels under state obscenity laws, although these cases did not provoke the passage of tougher anti-obscenity laws despite an explicit use of sexual themes and imagery in the novels at issue. Indeed, the trials of *We Are the Rats* and *Love Me, Sailor* tended to incite anti-censorship sentiment and to encourage the formation of new anti-censorship organisations.

By the mid-1950s a range of popular literature that was deemed objectionable or pornographic had become subject to increasing political surveillance and legal intervention in Australia. New laws were enacted to deal with romance and sex magazines as well as comics with themes of war, crime and horror. Both within and outside parliament there was little opposition to these new laws. This suggests that the emerging anti-censorship movement was largely addressed to a defence of 'proper' literature and shared a mainstream political concern about the nature of popular publications. The main issue appeared to be that children who consumed 'undesirable' literature were regarded as likely to develop criminal tendencies and sexual abnormalities in their adult lives. This was clearly incompatible with the acquisition of appropriate patterns of behaviour including, most notably, sexual behaviour. In the context of an emerging post-war sexual culture which emphasised the desirability of mutuality in sexual relations, the appearance of large quantities of undesirable literature in the 1950s was regarded as a distinct threat.

PART TWO

The Sexual Revolution

CHAPTER 3

The Sexual Revolution and Pornography, 1955–69

The years 1955–69 encompass most of the 'long boom' – an era of relative affluence and low unemployment in Australia. The economy expanded rapidly and Australia became a modern consumer society driven by the suburban imperative – the desire to buy a house in the suburbs, to fill the house with a range of appliances, and to acquire a car. At the level of institutional politics, the period was one of conservative ascendancy. A Liberal–Country Party government was elected federally in 1949 and remained in office continuously until the early 1970s. In all states except Tasmania and (to a lesser extent) New South Wales, Liberal or Liberal–Country Party governments held office for all or most of the years between 1955 and 1970. It seems, then, that economic prosperity and a conservative political culture were the dominant features of the society during the late 1950s and 1960s.

As I have suggested in Chapter 2, however, radical change was occurring in the intimate and sexual relations of Australians. In the first part of this chapter I examine several important features of the sexual culture in the period 1955–69. I argue that normal relations between the sexes were revolutionised under the influence of discourses about sexual pleasure, sexual companionship, sex outside marriage, and the role of women in society. This new sexual culture played a constitutive role in the lives of ordinary Australians; it created new pleasures and possibilities, but also instituted new norms of private and public life. From the mid-1950s onwards, this new sexual culture also had a direct impact on law and public policy addressed to the sex industry.

In the second part of this chapter (as well as in Chapter 4) I look at how Australian parliaments dealt with prostitution and pornography. I suggest that the sexual revolution had qualitatively different effects on sections of the sex industries and on legal regimes addressed to prostitution and pornography. While there was a trend towards liberalisation in relation to pornography, prostitution was increasingly represented as a pathological sexual practice. In Chapter 4 I will show that prostitution became the object of a range of new laws in the late 1950s and 1960s as prostitutes and their clients were increasingly constituted as deviant individuals. I suggest that this was largely due to the sexual revolution and to a perceived non-compliance with new norms of sexual behaviour. Prostitution was not regarded as a sexual practice which was compatible with modern relations between the sexes, with prevailing notions of sexual health, or with ideals of sexual equality and mutuality.

In the second part of this chapter I look at how the sexual revolution impacted upon the public political assessment of pornography. I show that there was a great deal of public and parliamentary debate about censorship and sexually explicit publications. Traditional conservative approaches, which stressed the individual and social dangers associated with pornography, were increasingly called into question. By the late 1960s a popular movement against censorship had also appeared and significant sections of the electorate as well as some parliamentarians were claiming that citizens had the right to read and view whatever they wished, even if that was pornography. As in the broader culture, arguments about sexual pleasure and sexual freedom were increasingly being attached to ideas about political modernity, social progress and health.

The Sexual Culture

In the late 1950s and 1960s the private lives of Australians changed profoundly as the power of organised religion declined and as new norms of sexual conduct, marriage and family life were instituted. This is evident in a range of different textual sources. For example, demographic and statistical data describe significant changes in patterns of marriage, divorce and childbearing in this period. While the marriage boom slowed considerably after 1955, marriage remained more popular than in any previous period of history.[1] Divorce and remarriage were also becoming more common. After reaching an all-time high of 147 divorces per 1000 marriages in 1947, the divorce rate fell away to 88 per 1000 by 1961 but had climbed back to 110 per 1000 in 1971 (Gilding 1991: 120).

The post-war baby boom peaked in Australia during 1961. Hugo (1986: 44–5) argues that, after this, there was a significant decline in Australia's net reproduction rate. In 1947 this rate was 1.42; it increased to 1.50 in 1954 and reached a high of 1.67 in 1961. By 1971 it had fallen to 1.36 and it continued to decline throughout the 1970s.

However, changes in the patterns of childbearing in this period were as significant as changes in the total number of children being born. Mathews (1984: 35) suggests that by the 1960s childbearing had become a highly concentrated activity for Australian families with 'most children (over three-quarters) ... born within a ten-year period – the first decade of marriage when the mother was between 20 and 30 years old – rather than being extended across the mother's fertile life'. It is likely that this trend both reflected and created qualitative changes in the relationships between husbands and wives.

The trend towards smaller and more discrete families was facilitated by the increasing acceptance of the desirability of contraception and family planning. The diaphragm was the contraceptive method of choice in the 1950s, but it was rapidly displaced when the oral contra-ceptive pill became available in Australia in 1961. Interestingly, Siedlecky and Wyndham (1990: 43–4) report a higher rate of oral contraceptive use in Australia during the 1960s than in either Europe or the United States. In fact, the rate of oral contraceptive use in Australia was almost twice that in the United States; between 1960–63 and 1970–71 the proportion of married women in Australia using some form of birth control (the contraceptive pill was by far the most popular method) rose from 67 to 87 per cent.

While the advent of the Pill did not fundamentally change fertility patterns (these were already well established before 1961), it did increase the likelihood of preventing unwanted pregnancies and of planning the timing and spacing of pregnancies. Thus, changing tech-nology gave added impetus to discourses about the desirability of family planning. This supported the development of new public and private roles for women. The demand for labour and consumer goods meant that an increasing proportion of women participated in the paid workforce. This trend was particularly evident in relation to married women; while the proportion of women in the workforce increased overall from 22 per cent in 1947 to 32 per cent in 1971, the proportion of married women in the female workforce rose steeply from less than one-fifth to more than one-half over the same period (Gilding 1991: 117–18; O'Donnell and Hall 1988: 7).

Although women's average weekly earnings remained well below those of men, their emerging economic independence increasingly challenged the traditional economic underpinnings of marriage and of men within families (Gilding 1991: 116–18). Of course, for the majority of women in the 1960s, particularly women with children, marriage continued to be the basis of economic well-being. However, economic independence also became more possible for women in this period and it is likely that this had a direct impact on the style of normal marital (and non-marital) relations between the sexes. Gilding (1991: 118–20) says that companionship, sexual fulfilment and personal development came to be regarded as the main basis for marriage in this period. The failure to achieve or maintain satisfactory levels of companionship, sexual fulfilment and personal development was increasingly cited as the reason for marriage breakdown and divorce.

The advent of reliable contraception also substantially undermined arguments about the need for female virginity at marriage. Indeed, it was now often argued that sexual experience before marriage – for both men and women – was conducive to the establishment of a good marriage bond (Weeks 1981: 260). This discursive shift was evident in various items published by the *Sydney Morning Herald* in the 1960s. For example, the Marriage Guidance Council of New South Wales called for a more 'reasoned' attitude towards pre-marital sex (*SMH*, 18 November 1966). The Young Women's Christian Association argued that some features of the sexual revolution, visibly under way by the 1960s, were 'good', particularly as they produced a 'liberation from the frightened attitude towards sex we inherited' (*SMH*, 13 September 1966). There were also increasing public calls for adequate sex education in schools and, by the late 1960s, this was even supported by the churches (*SMH*, 3 June, 27 July 1967).

In sexological discourse during the 1960s there was increasing emphasis upon the role of sex and orgasm in the construction of good relationships. This was partly due to the work of psychoanalyst Wilhelm Reich, who argued that orgasm had a mystical, redemptive power to heal and inspire. However, as Ehrenreich *et al.* (1986: 43–4) argue, his influence was limited to an intellectual avant-garde, and 'most Americans learned to think of sex in terms of orgasm from Kinsey'. From the mid-1960s onwards, the work of William Masters and Virginia Johnson also achieved widespread recognition. Their 1966 text, *Human Sexual Response*, is regarded as a central text of the sexual revolution. Masters and Johnson aimed to examine the physiological basis of male and female sexuality (as opposed to what they termed the 'sociological' studies of Kinsey) and, thus, to look at the physical reactions which develop as the human male and female 'respond to effective sexual stimulation'. This knowledge was said to be necessary 'if human sexual inadequacy ever is to be treated successfully'. Sexual inadequacy was defined as the inability to achieve orgasm in the context of a loving relationship.

Masters and Johnson emphasised the similarities in the sexual responses of men and women, but pointed out that women have a greater orgasmic capacity (longer and multiple orgasms) than men.[2]

From this perspective they argued for a revaluation of female sexuality because 'eroticism has become so synonymous with maleness that it has progressed beyond acceptability' (1966: 121, 301). It is not surprising, then, that Masters and Johnson were taken up by the emergent Women's Liberation movement in the late 1960s.

Human Sexual Response was the basis of a treatment program for orgasmic 'dysfunction' and impotence, the details of which appeared in Masters and Johnson's later text, *Human Sexual Inadequacy* (1970). One interesting aspect of this therapeutic approach was its debt to the knowledge of prostitutes. Masters and Johnson initially developed their investigative techniques with a group of male and female prostitutes (although their main study was conducted on married couples and a few single people who were non-prostitute volunteers). The prostitute group was said to have provided invaluable advice about:

> techniques for support and control of the human male and female in situations of direct sexual response. [The prostitutes] described many methods for elevating or controlling sexual tensions and demonstrated innumerable variations in stimulative technique. Ultimately many of these techniques have been found to have direct application in therapy of male and female sexual inadequacy [Masters and Johnson 1966: 10].

So the special knowledge obtained by prostitutes in the course of their working lives was reformulated as general, scientific advice to the heterosexual population.[3]

Discourses about the importance of sexual pleasure and sexual freedom were also central to the emerging counter-culture of the 1960s which blended New Left politics (and, in particular, the Freudian Marxism of Marcuse) with a characteristic youth culture. In the 1960s and 1970s New Left and counter-cultural politics began to have a direct impact on mainstream Australian politics. This was particularly evident in the appearance of new political demands in this period for abortion law reform, homosexual law reform and de-censorship.

From the early 1960s onwards, it is clear that major changes in sexual attitudes and behaviour were occurring throughout the Western world, including Australia. There is, however, little agreement among contemporary scholars as to what these changes meant. Authors such as Ehrenreich, *et al.* (1986) argue that the sexual revolution liberated people from 'the straitjacket of Victorian sexuality'. However, they argue that it was women's sexual behaviour (rather than men's) that was 'revolutionised' between the late 1950s and 1980s:

Put briefly, men changed their sexual behaviour very little in the decades
from the fifties to the eighties. They 'fooled around', got married, and often
fooled around some more, much as their fathers and perhaps their grandfathers had before them. Women, however, have gone from a pattern of
virginity before marriage and monogamy thereafter to a pattern that much
more resembles men's. ... It is not only that women came to have more sex,
and with a greater variety of partners, but they were having it on their own
terms, and enjoying it as enthusiastically as men are said to [1986: 2].

The main evidence cited by these authors to support the claim that
women had been sexually liberated was the decline in 'female sexual
dysfunction', with an increasing proportion of American women
reporting orgasms in their sexual relations (1986: 2). Their approach,
then, is premised upon the analysis of human sexual response developed by Masters and Johnson and assumes that more sexual pleasure
necessarily means a better, freer life.

Jeffreys argues that the sexual revolution of the 1960s needs to be
understood quite differently. In her text *Anticlimax* (1990), Jeffreys
contends that the sexual liberation offered by the sexual revolution was,
in fact, only 'the freedom for women to take pleasure from their own
eroticised subordination'. In her view, heterosexuality has an explicit
political function which is to maintain the oppression of women. Sexual
pleasure is used to overcome women's resistance to their oppressed
status. From this perspective, more sex and more sexual pleasure for
women do not translate into greater freedom. Jeffreys (1990: 2)
concludes: 'The 1960s was a period when greater opportunities were
open to women and the "sexual revolution", rather than being liber-
ating, helped to defuse the potential threat to male power.'

A third approach to understanding the sexual revolution – one that
has some distinct commonalties with Jeffreys's approach – has been
advanced by various followers of Foucault. Weeks, for example, argues
that the proliferation of new sexual discourses and the greater freedom
in talking about sex which characterised the 1960s signalled not a liberation but the development of new modes of social regulation in which
sexual discourses and the institution of new norms of sexual conduct
played a key role in 'disciplining' individuals (both male and female)
and whole populations (1981: 112). As I have already suggested, in
their focus on equality, mutuality and companionate heterosexuality
these new sexual norms tended to designate some sexual pleasures as
more 'appropriate' than others. In this context the legal and cultural
sanctions against apparently non-reciprocal sexual practices, such as
prostitution, were likely to be intensified. As I show in Chapter 4, this is
what happened in relation to prostitution. In relation to pornography,
however, the situation was somewhat more complicated, perhaps

because the consumption of pornography could be represented in this period as a marital aid.

Pornography and Censorship

In this section I show that sexually explicit literature became consti-tuted as a new social and political problem in Australia during 1955–69. I begin with a discussion of an important literary trend in Britain and the United States during the same period when the legal sanctions against sexually explicit publications were significantly reduced. This trend had a major impact both on the publications avail-able in Australia and on the politico-legal culture. I examine changes in the political regulation of literature in three Australian states – New South Wales, Victoria and Queensland – to demonstrate the range of legislative and institutional responses to the problems posed by sexu-ally explicit publications in the 1960s. I conclude with an analysis of the representation of the main issues and concerns associated with the censorship of literature in Australian parliamentary debates, demon-strating a trend away from conservative approaches and towards more liberal approaches.

International Trends

As discussed in Chapter 2, a new generation of sexually explicit publi-cations – novels and magazines – was produced in Britain and the United States after World War II. In the late 1950s there were legal changes in both these countries which effectively opened up the literary field to an expansion of sexually explicit publications.

In 1957 a United States Supreme Court decision marked an impor-tant legal shift away from the traditional (Hicklin) definitions of obscenity and towards the more relative concept of community stan-dards in the determination of legal obscenity (Kendrick 1987; Williams 1989; Talese 1980). *United States v. Roth* resulted in a conviction for mailing a magazine (*American Aphrodite*) which contained nude pictures and erotic stories. Justice Brennan ruled that hard-core pornography did not fall under the ambit of constitutionally protected speech or press. However, not all sexual representation fell into this category, only material which was 'utterly without redeeming social importance' and which deals with sex 'in a manner appealing to prurient interest'. As Williams comments: 'the ironic effect of Brennan's clarification was that subsequent to this ruling all sorts of surprising works were discovered to be not without some "nugget" of social, historical or aesthetic worth.' This decision led, then, to 'a gradual legal acceptance of publications which depicted sex' (Williams 1989: 89). As Talese (1980: 131) comments, it also led to an 'opening of the pornography floodgates' in the decade after 1957.

A similar process was under way in Britain by the late 1950s. The *Obscene and Indecent Publications Act* of 1959 established, for the first time, a statutory basis for obscenity law. While the Act followed Hicklin in its definition of obscenity – that is, it formally required proof of a tendency to deprave and corrupt those who were the likely consumers of a publication – it also provided that a publication could not be found obscene if it was justified as being for the public good on the ground that it was in the interests of science, literature, art or learning. In the decade that followed, academics, literary critics and other so-called experts were frequently called upon to testify as to the 'public good' of sexually explicit novels such as *Lady Chatterley's Lover*. Thus, a legal process – one which John Sutherland has called the 'road to freedom from censorship' – began in the late 1950s and led to the release in Britain of a significant number of formerly prohibited novels. Sutherland (1982: 1–2) reports that during the 1960s the 'tide of liberalisation' was 'irresistible'. After 1967 there were no further prosecutions of literary novels on the grounds of obscenity.

While arguments about the irresistible tide of liberalisation in the 1960s are now commonplace, Hunter *et al.* (1987) offer an alternative and convincing explanation. They argue that the use of expert witnesses in the literature trials of the 1960s 'allowed the alignment of the novel with sexuality to be recognised as a public good, and hence strongly defended'. But this could occur only because of changes in the field of literature and because of the role which literature itself was coming to play in the regulation of sexuality more generally. In the twentieth century literature adopted 'the terms and images of sexually explicit writing (previously associated with pornography), while aestheticizing and valorizing them in a novel way as paths to the deepest truths of the individual' (Hunter *et al.* 1987: 7–10). From this perspective, literature was assuming an increasingly important role in the 'disciplining' of individuals and, more generally, literate populations. But in this process the law was left to guard 'a boundary between serious writing and the obscene that is no longer maintained within literary fields themselves, since the serious novel, in particular, has become both literary and pornographic' (Hunter *et al.* 1987: 7).

In the 1960s, then, there was an increasing deployment of sex in all types of literature and, at the same time, its politico-legal surveillance became more problematic.

Australian Trends

Because of the important role that British and American culture played in the constitution of Australian culture, these overseas trends in relation to 'obscene and indecent' literature had a significant impact. Both the 1959 *Obscene and Indecent Publications Act* and the *Roth* decision were often cited by Australian parliamentarians during the 1960s and after.

In general, the period between 1955 and 1969 in Australia was one of intense public and governmental concern with the issue of literary censorship. However, different types of literature were deemed to be problematic at different points during this period. In the late 1950s there were ongoing concerns in many states about the effects of comics on children. While some argued that these publications were harmless, groups as diverse as the English Teachers Association, the Catholic Church and the Communist Party of Australia adopted vehement anti-comic rhetoric (Coleman 1974: 122). In the late 1950s state governments like the one in Victoria, as well as statutory authorities such as the Queensland Literature Board of Review, were concerned with the policing of anti-comic legislation which had been passed in the mid-1950s (see Chapter 2).

From the late 1950s onwards, however, the political focus of the censorship debate shifted from comics to novels designed for an adult audience. In 1957 a new approach to the censorship of novels began in Australia. This was a direct result of a public outcry over the prohibition of *Catcher in the Rye*. After 1957 it became Customs Department policy to refer all publications which claimed literary and/or artistic status to the Commonwealth Literature Censorship Board. At this time the minister also asked the board to review the list of banned books, and several hundred titles were released. The list of banned books was also made public so that importers would be aware of what titles were prohibited, thus ending the system of secret censorship.

Coleman (1974: 22) suggests that, as a result of these reforms, very few novels were classified as prohibited imports after 1957 and many formerly prohibited novels were released. For example, James Baldwin's *Another Country* was released in 1966. However, both *Lolita* and *Lady Chatterley's Lover* were prohibited anew in the 1960s. Norman Mailer's *An American Dream* was prohibited in 1967 and Phillip Roth's *Portnoy's Complaint* in 1969. In many respects, then, increasing liberalisation only focused public attention on the novels that were still prohibited.

The 1957 reforms also tended to shift the primary site of political battles about literary censorship from federal to state arenas. After this time, state laws against obscene, indecent and objectionable literature were increasingly called upon to deal with novels which had been passed by federal Customs; this trend was particularly noticeable in Queensland and Victoria. Federal Customs officers did, however, continue to take direct action in relation to publications that were 'obviously pornographic'. This included material which today would be regarded as soft-core pornography. For example, the July 1963 edition of *Playboy* magazine was banned for publishing photographs of a naked Jayne Mansfield, 'enjoying the luxuries of a bubble bath and a double bed' (*SMH*, 7 March 1966). *Playboy* was then scrutinised by the Customs Department on an issue-by-issue basis. However, by the end of 1967, fifty-one issues out of fifty-one had been prohibited. The ban on *Playboy* was eventually lifted in 1967.

It was a perceived need to defend novels with literary merit which provided the initial impetus for the growth of a popular opposition to censorship laws and practices in Australia. By the mid-1960s there was significant public support for publishers who attempted to 'beat the Customs Department ban' by printing prohibited publications within Australia (see *SMH*, 7 March 1966). Consequently, most state governments were forced either to permit the circulation of publications which were not prohibited imports or to launch unpopular prosecutions which were unlikely to succeed; Queensland was an exception here because of its Literature Board of Review. As the 1960s progressed, the states adopted quite disparate approaches to the issue of obscene and pornographic publications. Consequently, there were also renewed calls for more uniformity in censorship decisions.

In 1967 the Commonwealth and state governments (excluding Queensland) agreed to establish a joint advisory board to consider publications for which literary, artistic or scientific merit was claimed, but which might otherwise be considered indecent or obscene. The overall aim was to achieve some uniformity throughout Australia in regard to the censorship of literature. A National Literature Board of Review was established to replace the existing Commonwealth Censorship and Appeal Board. This new board was to have six members nominated by the Commonwealth government and three selected from a panel of nominees submitted by the states. Its main role was to advise Commonwealth and state ministers on matters of literary censorship, although the states retained the right to decide whether a prosecution was to be instituted in any particular case. There was, however, an informal agreement among the states that any publication passed by the National Literature Board of Review would not be the subject of a state prosecution. For material that was not passed by the board, it was agreed that individual states should take whatever action they thought appropriate.

Not surprisingly, this agreement did not resolve the political problem surrounding literary censorship. In part this was a result of differences in the legal, institutional and political culture of the states in the late 1960s; these regional differences undermined the possibility of a national consensus on literary censorship. The failure of the 1967 agreement was also, however, an effect of rapid changes in the literary field and in popular opinion. By the late 1960s it was becoming increasingly impossible to distinguish literature from pornography in any authoritative way. There were now novels on the market which were extremely sexually explicit but whose authors claimed both literary merit and the support of literary experts for their work. There were also increasing calls within the Australian electorate – especially in states like New South Wales – for an end to censorship. By the late 1960s the anti-censorship position was attracting widespread public support. And, for the first time, this support was beginning to be addressed to *all* publications produced for adults, whether these were literature or commercially produced pornography.

This shift in popular opinion is reflected in the new censorship policy adopted by the Australian Labor Party in 1969. The party's federal conference decided that, as a general principle, adults should be entitled to 'read, hear or view what they wish in private or public' but also that individuals, and children in their care, should not be exposed to unsolicited material offensive to them. The Leader of the Opposition in South Australia, Don Dunstan, was an important advocate for the new censorship policy. He argued that what an adult person could read or view should be a matter for their own judgement, 'not [some politician's], not some tribunal's, not some academic's and not some Customs officer's' (*SMH*, 31 July 1969). Arguments such as these were explicitly linked to the claim that censorship suppressed political freedom – for example, by preventing the dissemination of information about the Vietnam War. Lionel Murphy, leader of the Labor Opposition in the Senate and a strong supporter of de-censorship, argued that it was 'a great myth' that Australians lived in a free country (*SMH*, 29 September 1969). Arguments like these were to be important in debates about censorship policy in the late 1960s and 1970s.

In the next part of this chapter I examine some important regional differences in political debates about pornography and censorship.

Queensland

The establishment of the Literature Board of Review in Queensland in 1954 (see Chapter 3) subjected the distribution of all objectionable publications to an administrative body with independent and quasi-judicial powers. This made Queensland unique among Australian states by effectively shifting responsibility for obscene or pornographic publications away from the courts and parliament. Between 1955 and 1969 there were no significant new legislative initiatives in Queensland directed at obscene and indecent literature.

In its annual reports to parliament, the Literature Board of Review indicated that it saw its functions quite broadly in terms of 'the field of the mass media', although this was said to be 'limited ... to the group of publications put out mainly for children, adolescents and young people' (QLBR 1958–59: 2; 1954–55: 1). The board interpreted this mission quite widely to include a range of war, crime, western, humour and romance comics as well as 'sexy category' magazines, paper-covered novels, glossies and nudist magazines (QLBR 1954–55: 2–3). At least some of these publications were clearly intended for an adult audience. For example, magazines prohibited in the sexy category included *Peep*, *Stag* and *Bikini Beauties*. They were said to 'frankly make sex their business' and 'emphasise sex to the exclusion of all else'. The main reason that these magazines were subject to prohibition orders was that they were 'cheap, well within the price range of youths and girls whose taste and conduct cannot fail to be debased by a substantial diet of such rubbish' (QLBR 1954–55: 3).

Comics prohibited in the war category had titles like *War Battles* and *The United States Marines*. These publications were said to be excessively brutal although, in general, war was 'not an objectionable theme'. The board argued that publishers needed to realise that there was 'abundant scope and interest for boys in aspects of war which emphasise courage, chivalry, daring, comradeship and self-sacrifice' (QLBR 1954–55). Comics prohibited in the crime category had titles like *Dragnet*, and were said to contain 'blueprints for how to plan and carry out robbery, violence and murder' (QLBR 1954–55: 2). Those in the romance category included *Teenage Love* and *First Love*. While other categories of comics were regarded as harmful to boys, the romance comics were seen to be a particular danger to girls.

Between 1955 and 1970, the Literature Board of Review issued 123 prohibition orders, although forty-seven of these were in its first year of operation. The board did not confine its activities to review and prohibition. It also negotiated with publishers (indicating what were acceptable standards for literature that was to be distributed in Queensland), issued warnings to publishers and distributors, and commented on publications (for example, newspapers) that did not fall directly within the legal ambit of the board's functions (QLBR

1954–55). This multi-faceted approach had a significant impact on the number and type of publications distributed in Queensland and, indirectly, on the publications produced for the rest of the Australian market (Coleman 1974: 56).

By the late 1950s the Literature Board of Review was claiming a major achievement in relation to the standard of publications being distributed in Queensland. In spite of a successful High Court appeal in 1956 against the prohibition of romance comics,[4] the board claimed that the comic problem was now under control in Queensland (QLBR 1957–58: 3). Such reassurances continued well into the 1960s.

Between 1957 and 1961 the board also adopted a new high profile in relation to paperbacked novels. Prohibition orders were issued against two novels by Marc Brody (*Headlines for a Hussy* and *Deadline for a Dame*), six by Carter Brown (for example, *The Temptress*), and one each by John Thompson and William Woolfolk; these were, of course, novels which had been passed by the Commonwealth censor. The board found that novels like these had 'gaudy covers and sensational titles'; they were also said to combine sex and violence in ways that were unacceptable for the community at large (QLBR 1960–61: 2). In its seventh annual report (1960–61) the board discussed this problem in terms of the 'pornography of violence'; the proper relationship between sex and love was being replaced with the idea of sex as 'associated with, and ... symbolic of, the hatreds and hostilities, the angers and cruelties, that lie deep in men and women'. This was clearly a process which was gendered in highly significant ways; the 'image of evil' on the cover of prohibited novels was not a man but a 'semi-nude woman with a smoking gun in her hand'.

The board argued that the emergence of a problem with paperback novels in Queensland in the late 1950s was a direct result of 'the abolition of [federal] import restrictions' (QLBR 1959–60: 2). While the board said that it did not wish to constitute itself as a second line of censorship or provide supervision additional to that already in place at Commonwealth level, such action was 'increasingly being forced upon it' in order to protect the Queensland community (QLBR 1959–60). Although paperback novels were clearly 'adult literature', the board contested the right of adults to consume such publications:

a very large proportion of this [adult fiction] would be definitely harmful to adolescents. Must the adult population expect to go on indefinitely reading and asking for sordid stories in the name of freedom? What must an adolescent generation think of its adults if it is so anxious to preserve its rights to read sex-soaked literature? [QLBR 1959–60: 2]

Thus, the question was 'whether serious literature can escape the charge of pornography', particularly as a deterioration in the standards of literature could be expected to have a direct impact upon the standards which could be expected in popular publications (QLBR 1959–60: 2, 3). In 1963, however, the board noted a marked improvement in the paperback novels being distributed in Queensland. This had been achieved by a direct 'co-operative liaison' with the Customs Department rather than through prohibition orders (QLBR 1962–63: 1). In 1961 Carter Brown's *The Blonde* became the last paperback novel to be prohibited by the Queensland Literature Board of Review. (Novels which created major controversies in other states during the 1960s – for example Mary McCarthy's *The Group* – were not released for distribution in Queensland.)

From the late 1950s onwards, 'sexy category' magazines were an increasingly important object of concern for the Literature Board of Review. In 1957, for example, the board argued that literature which displayed 'sex provocation' was partly responsible for the problem of juvenile delinquency in Queensland (a problem that was seen to be particularly associated with the cult of bodgies and widgies in Brisbane) (QLBR 1956–57: 3). However, in 1955 and again in 1958 the Queensland Supreme Court upheld appeals by publishers against the prohibition of the magazines *Peep* and *Gals and Gags*. In his judgement on the *Gals and Gags* case, Judge Townley said:

> As the name indicates, the publications all deal with girls and jokes. The 'girls' portion, with which somewhat over 50 per cent of each issue is concerned, consists of photographic reproductions of girls either in scanty bathing costumes or other scanty attire. In each reproduction emphasis seems to be given to the notorious fact that girls, adult or adolescent, have breasts. I may be artless but I must confess that it does not appear to me that any other than the mammary portions of the female anatomy are emphasised in the pictures except the legs. The fact that women have legs has also, in the last fifty years or so, come to be publicly recognized. It seems to me that the tendency to become pre-occupied with the contemplation of the female torso which might result from the photographic portions of the publication would probably be disturbed by the 'gags', some of which are humorous and some of which are not, but all of which seem to me fairly innocuous ... [cited in QLBR 1958–59].

The judge argued that, while the pictures in this magazine could induce 'thoughts of sex' in the minds of young men, this could also happen 'without any extraneous stimulation whatsoever' and was not necessarily indicative of depravity or corruption. Thus, *Gals and Gags* was not found to be objectionable under the terms of the Queensland Act.

The Literature Board of Review implied that its ability to constrain the circulation of publications in the 'sexy category' had been significantly undermined by this legal decision (QLBR 1958–59: 2). But the Board did press the Commonwealth Customs authorities on this issue, and it continued to warn Australian publishers of sexy magazines about any objectionable content (QLBR 1961–62: 1). Moreover, in general, the board continued to obtain significant judicial support for its campaign against sexy magazines. By a unanimous decision of the Queensland Supreme Court in 1964, the publishers of *Playboy* failed in their appeal against the prohibition order placed on their magazine. *Playboy* was found to be an objectionable publication under the Act because it unduly emphasised matters of sex and was likely to deprave and corrupt its reading audience, 'notwithstanding that those persons are likely to be of a higher order of education than the average'. According to the board, the main problem with *Playboy* was that it adopted a cynical and amoral attitude towards sexual relations with 'promiscuous sexual intercourse between young people ... presented not merely as a matter of course, but as something actively to be encouraged' (QLBR 1963–64: 1–2).

From 1963 until its abolition in 1990, the main target of the Literature Board of Review for new prohibition orders was sexy literature. This does not mean that other sorts of literature were ignored; during the 1960s the board issued prohibition orders against a wide range of literature. This included Sydney-based publications, such as the *Kings Cross Whisper* and *Censor*, which combined sex and political satire. Prohibition orders were also made against several nudist magazines, a Maoist publication called *The Little Red Schoolbook*, sex magazines such as *Topless* and *Ribald*, and a calendar called *The Girls from Man Calendar 1969*.

By the late 1960s public criticism of the censorship functions which the Literature Board of Review performed was becoming more widespread in Queensland. The board itself saw this as a direct effect of the sexual revolution and of the permissive society (QLBR 1964–65; 1968–69). In the Queensland parliament, though, there was remarkably little criticism of the board's censorship activities during the late 1950s and 1960s. In other states by the late 1960s many Labor parliamentarians had adopted a strong anti-censorship rhetoric. In Queensland the only questions raised in parliament about the Literature Board of Review concerned how much it cost to run or whether it was being strict enough in its censorship functions.[5]

Victoria

Throughout the period 1955–69, the problems of undesirable literature, obscene publications and policing and censorship practices were consistently raised in the Victorian parliament. Indeed, of all the state parliaments, the Victorian parliament was the most vigorous in its review of these issues. This was primarily a result of the pro-active role undertaken by the Victorian government (particularly when Arthur Rylah was Chief Secretary) and the Victorian police in relation to undesirable publications. During the late 1950s and early 1960s a large range of undesirable publications – comics, popular magazines and hard-core pornographic publications as well as novels which claimed artistic merit – were prosecuted under Victoria's *Police Offences Act.*

This provoked significant public debate and political activity around the issue of literary censorship in Victoria during the 1960s. As a Labor member of the Legislative Council argued: 'Because of the Government's illiberal attitude, various organizations such as the Freedom to Read Association have been formed to protect what are, in effect, the rights and liberties of the individual citizen' (VPD 1282: 3855). Thus, it was the government's illiberal pursuit of objectionable literature in this period that was seen to be responsible for the emergence of a popular opposition to censorship laws and practices.

As in Queensland, a major focus of political concern in Victoria in the late 1950s was crime and horror comics. The argument that crime comics 'may conduce towards wrong doing and even, in rare instances, to horrifying crimes' was widely accepted by the Victorian public, particularly after a criminal case in which it was claimed that a youth murdered his sister after reading crime comics (VPD 252: 1803–4). In 1957 Chief Secretary Rylah appointed the sergeant in charge of women police to investigate complaints that objectionable comics and obscene literature were circulating in Victoria. The government's aim, therefore, was to monitor the effectiveness of the 1954 *Police Offences (Obscene Publications) Act.* One year later Rylah reported that there had been six prosecutions under the Act, and six convictions had been achieved with monetary penalties ranging from £20 to £30; one order had been made for the destruction of obscene books and magazines. At this stage, one Policewoman Mackay was submitting fortnightly reports to the government about the problem of obscene and indecent literature (VPD 254: 3909).

In the late 1950s popular magazines also became a focus of political concern in Victoria as the publishers and distributors of *People* and *Reveille* were successfully prosecuted by the police. The first of these magazines had published excerpts from a book called *Love in the South*

Seas by a Danish anthropologist who argued that Polynesian ideas about sex were better than Western ones. The second magazine published two articles – 'I Went to a Sex Key Orgy' and 'Unmarried Mother by Choice'. Both of these magazines were found to be obscene, under the terms of the Victorian Act, because they unduly emphasised sex and offended against community standards.

In 1959 a novel, *God's Little Acre* by Erskine Caldwell, was seized by the Victorian police apparently following complaints from members of the public. *God's Little Acre* had already had a chequered career; it had been banned by the Customs Department in 1933 but released in 1958 on the advice of the Literature Censorship Board. In 1959 this novel was found to be an obscene publication under the Victorian *Police Offences Act*; an appeal to the Supreme Court failed. In 1960 the novel *Carlotta McBride* suffered a similar fate (VPD 274: 3323). As both of these novels had recently been released by the (Commonwealth) Literature Censorship Board, there was a significant amount of criticism in the Victorian parliament about the system of 'double censorship'. The fact that novels such as these were 'withheld' from citizens was said by some parliamentarians to be 'intolerable in a twentieth century pluralist society' (VPD 261: 1067, 135–6). At the time, Chief Secretary Rylah defended the application of state obscenity laws to comics, popular magazines and novels. He argued that a publication should not be given free rein in Victoria 'just because it comes into Australia through the Customs'. The member for Fitzroy, Mr Lovegrove, said that it was this sort of approach which was 'fast making Victoria the laughing stock of Australia' (VPD 262: 1325–6).

In 1964 Mary McCarthy's novel *The Group* became the centre of a new storm of criticism for the Victorian government and for Chief Secretary Rylah. This novel was allowed into Australia by Customs but, following public complaints and on the recommendation of the Vice Squad, was withdrawn from sale in Victoria by its distributors. (*The Group* contained relatively explicit descriptions of sexual intercourse between young unmarried adults and of contraceptive practices.) The procedure whereby book distributors in Victoria were 'warned off' problematic publications was said to be a voluntary arrangement designed to prevent prosecutions against innocent booksellers (VPD 273: 3252). However, the Labor Party was completely opposed to such procedures and argued that they amounted to a system of pre-censorship, one which was 'inappropriate', 'undemocratic' and detrimental to civil liberties in Victoria. The danger was that 'it could give rise to a situation whereby unqualified persons make decisions in secret on matters which are properly the concern of the public'

(VPD 274: 3401–7). For the Labor party the courts were the only valid means of assessing the legality of publications.

It is relevant to note, though, that the prosecution of material which was obviously commercial and pornographic was not regarded as a political issue in this period. In 1961, for example, a man was found guilty of two charges of selling obscene articles and three charges of keeping obscene articles for gain. He was fined a total of £220, in default fourteen days' imprisonment. The court ordered destruction of all of the books seized, which included titles such as *House of Lust, Video Virgin, Women on the Loose, Taken, Sex Cruise, Playground of Violence, Vagabond Lover, Brute Madness, Song of the Red Ruby* and *Oriental Orgy* (VPD 274: 3323). No voices were raised in support of defendants like these.

Despite the public furore over the government's handling of *The Group*, the prosecution of a wide range of literature under the *Police Offences Act* continued in Victoria. In response to a question in parliament during 1965, the Chief Secretary indicated that charges had been laid against a number of indecent books and magazines. The titles listed included sex literature, nudist publications, photographic publications, novels such as *God's Little Acre* and a number of scientific texts such as Kinsey's *Sexual Behaviour in the Human Male*[6] (VPD 278: 4411–13).

There were two separate legislative attempts during the mid-1960s to resolve the issue of literary censorship in Victoria. In 1965 and again in 1966 a private member's bill – the Indecent Publications Bill – was debated in the Victorian Legislative Council. This bill attempted to introduce a new definition of indecency (modelled on the *Roth* decision in the United States) and to establish an Indecent Publications Tribunal (modelled on the recently established tribunal in New Zealand) (VPD 279: 708–15). For different reasons, the bill was opposed by both the government and the Labor Opposition and was never debated in the Legislative Assembly.[7]

In 1967, however, the Victorian government did amend the *Police Offences (Obscene Publications) Act*. This was in order to implement the Commonwealth–State agreement on the censorship of books of literary, artistic or scientific merit which might otherwise be regarded as obscene or indecent (see above). This measure was supported by the Labor Opposition because 'there is a need for censorship against the commercialization of smut' and for 'a step towards some uniformity in the approach to literary censorship' (VPD 289: 3330). Moreover, the Labor Party succeeded in amending the original bill so that obscenity prosecutions could no longer proceed without the prior authority of the Chief Secretary. Together with the political demise of Rylah, this

eventually brought to an end the large number of police-initiated prosecutions in Victoria in the area of obscene and indecent publications.

New South Wales

Unlike the situation in Victoria, the censorship of literature was not a
major concern of the New South Wales parliament in the late 1950s
and early 1960s. The 'comic problem' appears to have been successfully addressed by the 1955 *Obscene and Indecent Publications (Amendment) Act* and there were few questions raised about this issue in the
parliament. Unlike the concerns raised in other institutions at this
time (particularly the Victorian parliament and the Queensland Literature Board of Review), there was also very little debate in the New
South Wales parliament about the censorship of novels which claimed
literary merit. Despite this apparent liberalism, the possession of material which was blatantly obscene continued to be dealt with harshly by
the courts. Several convictions for possession of obscene publications
were reported by the *Sydney Morning Herald* in the late 1950s. In April
1956, for example, a 66-year-old Wollongong dentist was sentenced to
six months' gaol for being in possession of twelve books containing
obscene photographs, 572 obscene photographs and 1030 negatives.
A hypodermic syringe and a number of phials of a 'sex drug' were also
seized at the time of the arrest. The *Herald* reported that legal action
had been instituted against a woman in some of the photographs (she
was said to be a well-known Sydney prostitute), while, in others, the
defendant had superimposed the heads of 'a number of decent girls
residing in this district' upon the original (obscene) photograph. In
his defence the dentist said that many of the photographs had been in
his possession for seventeen years and that photography was his only
relaxation (although in 'late years it has developed into something
twisted') (*SMH*, 28 April 1956). A further two cases of convictions
for the possession of imported books and obscene photographs
were reported by the *Sydney Morning Herald* in the late 1950s
(23 September, 23 December 1958). Cases like these did not occasion
significant public comment or a mobilisation of anti-censorship
forces.

However, from 1964 onwards, questions began to appear in both
houses of the New South Wales parliament about 'the undue emphasis
being placed on sex by many of our newspapers and the display of unfit
and indecent photographs in newspapers and magazines'. There was
said to be a 'growing concern of people at the commercialising of sex
in publications that are readily available, particularly the daily newspapers' (NSWPD 152: 702; 54: 1566–7).

Public debate was also influenced by the appearance in the mid-1960s of a strain of radical politics which used sexually explicit publications to challenge the status quo. According to Wendy Bacon, a prominent activist of the period, this group was composed of libertarians, anarchists and 'non-authoritarian socialists'; they were clearly influenced by the work of Freudian Marxists such as Marcuse. Bacon (1972: 46), for example, argued that: 'there are connections between various forms of repression, economic, political and social. ... [We] believe that sexual repression, maintained through the authoritarian family and monogamous marriage in a capitalist society, has a central place in the development of the servile, conformist personality found in any repressive system.' The idea, then, was to 'de-repress' sexuality. In relation to censorship this meant that the main focus of concern was 'freedom not literary merit' (Bacon 1972: 48). According to one vociferous critic of this approach (Coleman 1974: 62–3), this meant that pornography or blatant obscenity was used as 'a technique of liberation and subversion'; it was said to fulfil the same role as petrol bombs or counterfeit currency for other revolutionaries.

Libertarian politics was a particularly important feature of life at Sydney's three universities in this period. In 1964, prosecutions were launched under the state *Obscene and Indecent Publications Act* against two publications, *Oz* and the student newspaper of the University of New South Wales, *Tharunka*. The defendants were convicted by a magistrate on charges of printing and publishing an obscene publication. However, appeals against these convictions were subsequently upheld.[8] As Judge Levine[9] commented on the *Tharunka* case in the Court of Criminal Appeal:

> We are living in times when great freedom of expression on matters of sex is accepted by the community. Indeed even a casual glance at current newspaper topics and advertisements, the nature and types of magazines available to be purchased and the films shown in the theatres and on television clearly indicate that the community accepts today an open discussion of matters of sex which would never have been tolerated in the days of our Victorian forebears [*R v. Sharp* (1964) 82 WN 132].

For the New South Wales parliament, the decision in the *Oz* and *Tharunka* cases 'clearly established' that for a prosecution to be successful, the court had to be fully satisfied that any publication that was the subject of a prosecution had a tendency to corrupt or deprave (NSWPD 61: 4912). As proof of this was difficult to establish, the effect was substantially to liberalise the application of the law against obscene and indecent publications.

A range of new newspapers and magazines then began to be produced in Sydney. These included the satirical newspaper *Kings Cross Whisper*, which published photographs of topless and partially clad women (later full nudes in outline or beneath see-through clothing) alongside articles which satirised prominent political figures, the Sydney City Council, the Vietnam War, and Sydney's flourishing prostitution industry.[10] After complaints in parliament, the *Kings Cross Whisper* was examined by the government, which decided against a prosecution on the grounds that the courts would be unlikely to find the publication obscene (NSWPD 62: 4912). (Other states – for example, Western Australia – also decided that prosecution of the *Kings Cross Whisper* would be unlikely to succeed because of the many 'double meanings' in this publication.)

An important amendment to the *Obscene and Indecent Publications Act* was debated and passed during 1967. This Act had three main purposes. First, it aimed to give effect to the Commonwealth–State agreement on the uniform censorship of material with artistic or literary merit which might otherwise be regarded as obscene or indecent (see above). Second, it instituted trial by jury in obscenity cases and established a State Advisory Committee on Publications. This committee was to make recommendations as to which publications should be referred to the National Literature Board of Review, which should be prohibited from public sale, and which could be published, sold or distributed without prosecution. While publishers were not required to submit their publications to the committee, they were liable to prosecution under the Act if they did not. Publications which were passed by the State Advisory Committee were to be immune from prosecution under the *Obscene and Indecent Publications Act* (NSWPD 69: 1690–1).

The third purpose of the 1967 Act was to create a new category of restricted publications. These were publications that, in the opinion of the minister and on the advice of the State Advisory Committee, gave undue emphasis to sex, drug addiction, crimes of violence, gross cruelty or horror, or otherwise had a tendency to deprave, corrupt or injure the morals of any persons, class of persons or age groups, or were undesirable reading for children under the age of sixteen. Restricted publications were to be sold only within a shop and could not be exhibited to public view (NSWPD 69: 1777).

One of the main aims of the Act, then, was to achieve some legislative control over 'magazines of a cheap, salacious type which ... are being sold on the streets and finding their way into the hands of children and adolescents' (NSWPD 62: 1946). This was clearly addressed to publications such as the *Kings Cross Whisper* and *Censor*. The urgency of this measure was underlined by the Chief Secretary, who said that he had received a petition from the League of Welfare and Decency signed by 70,000 persons as well as a great number of letters, almost all from parents, complaining about 'smutty publications containing jokes with double meanings and references to sex, and nudes in suggestive or vulgar poses' (NSWPD 62: 1775–6).

The Labor Opposition basically supported the measure, although it was concerned about the lack of appeal mechanisms and about the fact that the legislation did not prohibit the sale of restricted publications to young persons under the age of sixteen (the government said that it was unwilling to legally prohibit the sale of restricted publications to children and that such a measure would be both difficult to police and unfair to newsagents). The government argued that the new legislation was a measure which protected the rights of minorities – both the minorities that did not want 'this trash' pushed under their children's noses in the street *and* the minority of parents who did not mind if their children could buy these publications at the local bookshop (NSWPD 62: 1934, 1938, 2065).

The uncertainty which surrounded the issue of obscene and indecent literature in New South Wales was intensified by a series of conflicting legal decisions in the late 1960s. The case of *Crowe v. Graham*[11] related to the prosecution of four men for having published indecent or obscene material, in particular the magazines *Censor No. 2* and *Obscenity No. 2*. The defendants included a newsagent, a printer, a street seller and a publisher (who was a member of the New South Wales Council for Civil Liberties). In the Sydney Magistrate's Court both publications were found to be indecent but not obscene. However, on appeal to the Supreme Court, the convictions were quashed on the grounds that the magazines concerned were not exposed to public view and because 'the partially uncovered female bosom on the cover of *Censor* magazine was not indecent ... in view of the widespread and tolerant depiction of the uncovered female breast in other contexts in the community' (cited in Perry 1968: 2). In 1968 this Supreme Court decision was reversed by the High Court and the original conviction of the four men allowed to stand. It is evident, then, that by the end of the 1960s, the legal system was increasingly unable to adjudicate – in any consistent manner – on obscene and indecent publications.

Parliamentary Debates about Censorship

As I have already suggested, Australian parliaments became increasingly concerned with (and unable to resolve) censorship issues during the late 1950s and 1960s. In this section I want to look at how the problems associated with obscenity, pornography and censorship were being defined by authoritative public actors and how this changed as a result of the sexual revolution. My examination of parliamentary debates indicates that the main divisions were not so much Labor versus Liberal and National/Country Party supporters as conservatives versus (small-'l') liberals. Conservatives and liberals deployed fundamentally different approaches to sexuality and gender relations.

Conservatives argue that a society is partly constituted by its traditional code of morality. This code, they suggest, should be reflected in the laws which govern society because laws constitute a public acknowledgement of virtue and vice, right and wrong ways for human beings to live. For conservatives, then, it is the proper role of government to protect this moral code by punishing those who engage in immoral acts (such as homosexuality, prostitution and the consumption of obscene publications). In the conservative view, if governments do not act in this way then the health and well-being of society will be damaged, perhaps irretrievably. It can be seen that conservatives emphasise the connections between the public and private lives of individuals; the virtuous private lives of individuals are integral to the maintenance of a strong and healthy public sphere (see Devlin 1965; Coleman in Turner 1975).

Liberals, however, tend to disconnect public and private and to stress the rights of individuals to pursue their own goals and ends in all areas of life. They argue that society does not have a right to make laws which restrict the private sexual behaviour of adults, even where there is a common view that a certain sexual practice is immoral or aberrant. Following an approach initially advocated by John Stuart Mill, liberals argue that privately conducted sexual acts which do not harm other people, even those which are considered disgusting or degrading by most members of society, should not be punishable by law. In this view it is not the law's business to make people better or more moral; adult citizens should be free to do as they wish in their private lives so long as doing so does not harm others. Consequently, liberals call for the repeal of laws which prohibit homosexuality, the use of pornography, prostitution and abortion (see Hart 1963; Bacon in Turner 1975). As might be expected, this call is vehemently rejected by conservatives.

In the period 1955–69, conservative approaches were adopted by members of all political parties and tended to dominate parliamentary debate. Conservative parliamentarians argued that no clear dividing line could or should be established between different types of publications like literature and pornography. In 1964, for example, the Victorian Chief Secretary, Sir Arthur Rylah, was concerned to refute the suggestion that there was a category of publications – those which claimed literary merit – that were beyond the scope of laws against obscene and indecent literature: 'there is a pretty thin line between what is plain pornography – good, clean dirt, as one of my friends refers to it – and this pornography which is supposed to be submerged by some literary merit but which to my mind is usually fairly hard to find' (VPD 273: 3250). In support of this statement Rylah quoted passages from a novel, *The Group*, and from another publication called *The House of Lust*. He argued, quite convincingly, that the representation of sexual activity in these publications was similar and that it was common overseas to see 'pornography masquerading under the name of literature'. The main issue appeared to be that harm would accrue to individuals as well as to the common good from 'the flooding of the country with seamy pornographic literature'. Young people, in particular, would be 'depraved and corrupted by this filth' (VPD 273: 3253). This position was supported by many other parliamentarians. One member of the Victorian parliament argued that young people were now in an

> extraordinarily difficult position in regard to matters of sex, because convention and social and economic conditions have so arranged things that they are unable to satisfy their natural desires in the normal way by choosing a mate at maturity. For several years between puberty and independence, they are necessarily in a stage of disquiet, turbulence and vulnerability from the point of view of having suggested to them disturbing and provoking thoughts which will spring up quite easily enough without the assistance of ... literature which will make their struggle more difficult [VPD 1274: 3414].

In this view, youth could be corrupted – or at least rendered more vulnerable to corruption – by the increased availability of 'unseemly' publications. It was the government's role, then, to protect children and young adults from their own natural sexual impulses.

As in the years before and after the war (see Chapters 1 and 2), it was mainly children and adolescents who were represented as vulnerable to the effects of sex literature. However, some adults were also seen to be in danger and the combined effect was represented as able to compromise the common good of society. As one member of the Victorian Legislative Council argued in 1966, censorship restrictions were necessary 'to enlarge the field of over-all liberty' and to protect the public against 'the exploitation of human weaknesses' (VPD 280: 1454). From this perspective, laws against gambling, prostitution, drug abuse and obscene literature were designed to prevent injuries to the individual, to the general public, to community standards and 'the good order of society'.

In a specific extension of the conservative approach – indicative of the growing influence of psychiatric and psychoanalytic discourse on public life in the post-war period – this speaker also suggested that a justification for strong censorship laws could be found in the writings of modern psychiatrists. Erotic or pornographic material was said to have the effect of

> lifting the lid ... off repressions or unconscious urges, allowing them to bubble to the surface and produce or stimulate fantasies in which a dream world is substituted for reality, and self-gratification for love and affection ... The result can be a blurring, or even a blotting out, of the dividing line ... between propriety and impropriety, between normality and perversion, between the acceptable and the socially offensive or harmful [VPD 280: 1454].

Such a breakdown in the forces 'inhibiting us from lapsing into anti-social conduct ... naturally increases the prospect of the commission of anti-social behaviour'. Thus, society was interested in controlling pornography for the benefit of the individual and for the protection of the common good (VPD 284: 1453–5). The argument that the increasing incidence of sexual violence was due to the consumption (by children and adults) of sexually explicit publications was frequently reiterated by conservative parliamentarians during this period (see for example NSWPD 52: 702).

In the 1960s, however, a liberal discourse began to assume increasing prominence in Australian parliaments and to contest conservative approaches. Initially, parliamentarians who deployed this discourse tended to argue for a modified liberalism, one in which a clear distinction was drawn between literature and pornography. In the modified liberal approach, pornography should be prohibited but literature remained a realm of legitimate freedom and its restriction was untenable. For example, in New South Wales during 1967 one parliamentarian argued that it was possible to mark out a clear legislative distinction between books that were 'adult, mature type of literature', and 'yellow, guttersnipe-type' material that is 'not literature at all'. While the censorship of adult, mature literature could not be justified, gutter material was rightfully subject to legal sanctions (VPD 289: 3330; NSWPD 62: 1697).

Similarly, in Victoria, the member for Albert Park contended that pornography was 'a hideous debasement of literature' and should be banned. But he also argued for a proper distinction to be drawn between literature and pornography, particularly as 'many decent and intelligent people oppose the State's intrusion into their private affairs, believing that the individual conscience is the first and final arbiter in such an exercise as reading and that there is no place in a pluralist society such as ours, for the State as a dictator of moral attitudes' (VPD 289: 3333). In this view the censorship of literature needed to be conceptualised in terms of 'the rights and liberties of individual citizens', rather than in terms of the need to protect individuals or preserve a common good.

The certain relationship identified in the immediate post-war years – and maintained in conservative discourse – between the consumption of sex literature and juvenile delinquency, adult sexual pathology and sex crimes was also increasingly called into question (VPD 274: 3407; NSWPD 69: 1943). Members of parliament who deployed a liberal discourse called for censorship standards that could 'reasonably be applied to intelligent, adult human beings', for the community standards of '50 or 100 years ago' were said to be out of date and inappropriate for a modern society. In this view, while pornography should be prohibited, sexually explicit novels ('socially realistic publications') with literary merit were suitable reading material for modern adults (VPD 274: 3409; 289: 3330).

With the growing influence of New Left political thought in Australia during the 1960s, a much stronger version of this liberal, anti-censorship discourse began to emerge in some state parliaments. A few parliamentarians now began to argue for a more thoroughgoing liberalism in relation to sexual matters – a position that I will term 'libertarian'. In the mid-1960s libertarian parliamentarians began to argue for de-censorship and to link this to what was regarded as a much-needed de-repression of sexuality. They argued that an 'interest in sex is natural' and that talking about sex openly was a sign of health because erotica contained 'nothing really objectionable' (VPD 282: 3861). As the member for Warren in Western Australia argued: 'Would anybody in this House, or anywhere else, be prepared to say that the human form, as the Creator made it, is indecent or obscene? It is only the use to which the human form is put which makes it indecent or obscene; there is nothing wrong with it as it exists.' He argued that other cultures did not regard the representation of nudity or sexual matters as smut and that 'after all is said and done' women do have breasts and sex organs. The problem was that Australians had been raised 'in a prudish and prurient fashion, where we come to look upon sex as something dirty' (WAPD 176: 739). The display of (women's) naked bodies was, then, associated with sexual and cultural health.

Libertarians argued that the arrival of the sexual revolution and of youth culture meant that the 'false prudery' of existing social values was increasingly being challenged by young people (NSWPD 162: 1775–6, 1941). Again the member for Warren best exemplified this position. He argued:

> In the light of modern-day thinking some liberalisation of censorship is most essential. A great writer once said we will have no liberalisation of censorship until all the middle-aged and aged people die, because they associate the pleasures which are connected with sexual activity with something evil, repulsive, and degrading. In general this is sometimes the attitude of censors. Why do they not face up to elemental facts? [WAPD 176: 38]

Such 'elemental facts' were clearly related to the 'naturalness' of (hetero)sexual activity and the display of women's bodies.

Libertarian parliamentarians increasingly challenged the distinction drawn by moderate liberals between publications with literary merit and those without. Some parliamentarians, for example, argued that the cheaper types of sex publications (such as the *Kings Cross Whisper*) had artistic merit and that whether one sees anything as obscene really 'depends on one's mind' (WAPD 176: 590–1, 738). The distinction between pornography and literature was, therefore, represented as subjective and political. Through censorship,

> members of the public are deprived of the opportunity to choose for themselves. Why should someone else choose and decide what literature or book I should read? ... A book is read in private ... in complete privacy and secrecy: and because of that it is entirely different from ... publications ... which are exhibited publicly ... where censorship may be necessary for the public eye generally, it is quite wrong to censor a book which is read in complete privacy and which is something entirely between the reader and the author's written word [WAPD 176: 739].

Thus, the private nature of reading meant that censorship was an illegitimate interference by government in the rights and liberties of individuals. This was particularly so if what was offensive and obscene could not be determined in any final, objective fashion. In the end, all censorship mechanisms were potentially oppressive for adult citizens.

In the 1970s this sort of thoroughgoing libertarian discourse was to be of major importance (see Chapter 5). In the years between 1955 and 1969, however, it was confined to the margins of mainstream political debate. But during this period the dominant discourse about pornography and literary censorship became less conservative and more liberal in all jurisdictions except Queensland. By the end of the 1960s, then, there was clear and growing support among many parliamentarians for the argument that, while pornography should be prohibited, adult literature should be relatively free of oppressive censorship controls.

Conclusion

In the period 1955–69 pornography was increasingly constituted as a new sort of problem within Australian political institutions. I have suggested that this occurred for two main reasons, both of which are related to changes in the dominant sexual culture in the wake of the sexual revolution. In the first place, there were significant changes in the literary field, with a range of new sexually explicit publications – novels, magazines and newspapers – being produced for adult audiences. Changes in the dominant sexual culture meant that 'normal' Australians were now also more interested in reading and talking about sex and in intensifying sexual pleasure via their reading and viewing practices. As I have suggested, this trend should probably be regarded as indicative of changing sexual norms (and the deployment of new forms of social regulation) rather than a straightforward extension of freedom.

In the second place, a popular opposition to censorship emerged in Australia during the 1960s. Initially anti-censorship movements were directed at literature and film which claimed some artistic merit. However, by the late 1960s, the anti-censorship movement was also embracing a demand for the freedom to use sexually explicit material for which no artistic merit was claimed.

My examination of parliamentary debates shows that at least two competing discourses about pornography – conservative and liberal – were in play during this period. Conservatives tended to emphasise the dangers associated with all sexual representation and to call for strong legal controls. In contrast, liberals were concerned to distinguish between the sexual representations in pornography and those in 'good literature'. While they thought the former should be prohibited, the latter were not regarded as an appropriate object of state regulation. During the 1960s this sort of liberal discourse became increasingly ascendant in Australian political institutions.

CHAPTER 4

Revolutionary Limits: Governing Prostitution, 1955–69

In the last chapter I showed how conservative approaches to pornography dominated political debate in the 1950s and early 1960s; by the end of the 1960s these were increasingly displaced by liberal and libertarian approaches. A similar trend is *not* apparent in relation to prostitution. In this chapter I look at the range of new anti-prostitution measures enacted by Australian parliaments during the period 1955–69. It appears that, while the sexual revolution led to a liberalisation of attitudes towards pornography, new social and political concerns about prostitution were becoming apparent.

In the first part of this chapter I discuss the role of the Wolfenden Report in this process. The Wolfenden Report on homosexuality and prostitution was published in Britain in 1957 but had a substantive (and ongoing) impact on Australian law and public policy. The main recommendations of this report were that private, consensual sexual behaviour should be removed from the jurisdiction of the criminal law. In relation to prostitution, however, the report also offered a range of new justifications for laws against street prostitution and public soliciting. In the period after 1959 the Wolfenden Report was frequently cited by Australian law-makers and used to justify the deployment of new anti-prostitution measures.

In the second part of this chapter I trace several key changes in Australian prostitution laws and assess the impact of the Wolfenden Report in this process. I then go on to look at how parliamentarians understood the law reforms that they were engaged in during this period. Of particular interest here are changes in the representation of prostitution transactions, with clients becoming both more visible and more problematic. As in the decades before and after World War II, female prostitutes and men who lived on the earnings of prostitution were regarded as deviant, pathological individuals. However, from the late 1950s onwards, male clients also began to be represented in this way; men who went to prostitutes were no longer regarded as totally normal, natural men. In the wake of the sexual revolution and the increased sexual availability of women outside marriage, it was thought that normal men had no need to visit prostitutes. Prostitution increasingly came to be regarded as the arena of abnormal sexual desire (for men) supplementing its existing constitution as an arena of abnormal labour (for women). Significantly, this shift also occurred as the assumed heterosexuality of prostitution transactions was called into question; from the early 1960s Australian prostitution law became implicated in the formation of new cultural definitions of male homosexuality.

The Wolfenden Report

The *Report of the Committee on Homosexual Offences and Prostitution* (Wolfenden Report), published in Britain during 1957, was formulated as a direct response to rising public concerns about the incidence of homosexuality and prostitution in the mid-1950s (see Chapter 3). As Weeks (1981: 239) suggests the report had its origins in the 'search for a more effective regulation of sexual deviance' although its recommendations later came to be regarded as a blueprint for liberal reform. The Wolfenden Report argued that the law was not the most appropriate or effective means of controlling sexual deviance:

> Prostitution is a social fact deplorable in the eyes of moralists, sociologists and, we believe, the great majority of ordinary people. But it has persisted in many civilizations throughout many centuries, and the failure of attempts to stamp it out by repressive legislation shows that it cannot be eradicated through the agency of the criminal law [para. 225].

In this view prostitution could be eradicated only 'through measures directed to a better understanding of the nature and obligations of sex relationships and to a raising of the social and moral outlook of society as a whole' (para. 292).

As a result, the report contended that laws against prostitution (and homosexuality) should address only issues of immediate public concern: 'It is not, in our view, the function of the law to intervene in the private lives of citizens, or to seek to enforce any particular pattern of behaviour, further than is necessary to carry out the purposes we have outlined' (paras 13–14). The 'purposes outlined' were, in fact, far-reaching. They included the need to protect the common good from that which was offensive, injurious or inimical to it; also the need to have safeguards against the exploitation and corruption of others – particularly those who are specially vulnerable because they are young, weak in body or mind, inexperienced, or in a state of special physical, official or economic dependence (para. 13).

While this gave significant scope for justifying legal intervention in the lives of ordinary citizens, it also established the principle that private sexual behaviour between consenting adults was not an appropriate concern of the law. Thus, the Wolfenden Report recommended that homosexual behaviour between consenting adults in private should not be a criminal offence (and that questions relating to 'consent' and 'in private' should be decided by the same criteria as those which already applied in the case of heterosexual acts between adults). It also recommended, however, that the laws and penalties pertaining to street prostitution (as a public and, therefore, intrinsically offensive form of sexual behaviour) be tightened up. The suggestion was that maximum penalties for street offences by prostitutes be significantly increased, that a system of progressively higher penalties for repeat offences be introduced, and that the law pertaining to street soliciting be reformulated so as to eliminate the legal requirement to establish proof of annoyance (because street soliciting was a 'self-evident' public nuisance). Taken together, these recommendations provided for much harsher criminal sanctions against street prostitutes and made prosecution more likely.

The Wolfenden Committee justified this approach to street prostitution by arguing that the aspect of prostitution which caused the greatest public concern was the 'visible and obvious presence' of prostitutes on the streets (para. 229). This was because normal, decent citizens had the right to be in public places without their 'sense of decency' being affronted by prostitutes touting for business (para. 249). There was, then, no requirement to prosecute clients:

> If it were the law's intention to punish prostitution *per se*, on the grounds that it is immoral conduct, then it would be right that it should provide for the punishment of the man (client) as well as the woman (prostitute). But that is not the function of the law. It should confine itself to those activities which offend against public order and decency or expose the ordinary citizen to what is offensive or injurious; and the simple fact is that prostitutes do parade themselves more habitually and openly than their prospective customers, and do by their continual presence affront the sense of decency of the ordinary citizen. In doing so they create a nuisance which, in our view, the law is entitled to recognise and deal with [para. 257].

This contained an implicit judgement that the behaviour of prostitutes was always more offensive than that of clients. Even where clients were explicitly involved in forms of soliciting that caused public nuisance (for example, by kerb-crawling, driving around soliciting prostitutes) it was still argued that the law could not be adequately designed to address client behaviour. There was said to be too high a risk that innocent men would face soliciting charges (para. 267). The public nuisance afforded by some men was not, then, regarded as seriously as the public nuisance afforded by prostitutes soliciting for business. Thus, it can be argued that the conceptualisation of 'public offence' in the Wolfenden Report contained an implicit assumption that it was prostitutes (women) who were offensive. The ways in which clients might be publicly offensive could not easily be addressed within existing legal discourse because of cultural norms which regarded this sort of public behaviour by men as indistinguishable from normal male behaviour.

The representation of female prostitutes in the Wolfenden Report indicates that they were seen as dangerous people who, simply by being visible, had the power to corrupt both men and 'good' women:

> the very presence of the prostitutes on the streets provides an example which some young women, to whom a life of prostitution had not yet become a fully formed intention, might be tempted to follow. Again, while we recognise ... that the prostitute could not exist in the absence of a demand for her services, demand and supply are not unrelated, and the mere presence of prostitutes on the street creates a demand for their services. Many men, especially younger ones, who now avail themselves of the services of prostitutes would be less inclined to do so if these services were less readily and obviously available [para. 289].

Underlying the Wolfenden Report recommendations, then, was a specific attitude towards the prostitute, the client and the prostitution transaction. Women who became prostitutes were clearly regarded as sexual deviants for, 'whatever may have been the case in the past, in these days, in this country at any rate', economic pressures were not a determining cause of women adopting a life of prostitution. Although it was accepted that there could be 'precipitating factors' ('a bad upbringing, seduction at an early age, or a broken marriage') there was always 'some additional psychological element in the personality of the individual woman who becomes a prostitute': 'Our impression is that the great majority of prostitutes are women whose psychological make-up is such that they choose this life because they find in it a style of living which is to them easier, freer and more profitable than would be provided by any other occupation' (para. 223). Clients were not psychologised in this way. They were simply men who were vulnerable to diversion by prostitutes (para. 306).

The relationship between prostitutes and men who lived on the earnings of prostitution were also represented as both entirely voluntary and based on mutual advantage. A prostitute was said to be less susceptible to 'coercion or exploitation against her will' than in the past because of the relative absence of economic pressures (para. 304). Thus, it was an 'over-simplification' to think that men who lived on earnings were exploiting the prostitute. What they were really exploiting was the whole complex of the relationship between prostitute and customer; 'they are in effect exploiting the human weaknesses which cause the customer to seek the prostitute and the prostitute to meet the demand' (para. 306). For this reason the Wolfenden Committee argued against increasing the legal sanctions against those who lived on the earnings of prostitution. It also argued against stronger penalties in relation to the use of premises for the purposes of prostitution for, 'as long as society tolerates the prostitute, it must permit her to carry on her business somewhere'. The only tolerable situation was said to be prostitution which occurred in individual premises where public visibility (and thus, public offence) was minimal (para. 320). As a result the committee was opposed to the establishment of licensed brothels because this would encourage 'indulgence in promiscuous intercourse by men who might be less inclined to avail themselves of the services of prostitutes if these services were less readily and obviously available' (para. 293).

The Wolfenden Committee openly acknowledged that its recommendations in relation to street prostitution would, if adopted, produce a reorganisation of the industry into less public forms of prostitution (such as call-girl services where greater opportunities existed for the exploitation of prostitutes).[1] The committee argued, however, that the law was already adequate to combat such exploitation and that the proliferation of off-street prostitution 'would be less injurious than the presence of prostitutes in the streets' (para. 330). It is clear, then, that the potential injury posed to the common good by prostitution derived more from its visibility than its existence and had little to do with the exploitation of women. Women who resorted to a life of prostitution were clearly represented as consenting or as prepared to accept money in place of their explicit consent to sexual activities with clients. From this perspective, private prostitution could be represented as a legitimate contract between individuals.

The significance of the Wolfenden Report is that it sought and largely established a new separation of law and morality. From the late 1950s onwards the idea that the law should protect and defend a public morality was increasingly displaced by the idea that individual consent should be a central consideration in determining the nature of laws which governed sexual behaviour. If two individuals freely consented to a particular sexual practice – and if that practice was conducted in private – then, increasingly, it was not deemed appropriate for the criminal law to intervene. As Weeks (1981: 252) argues, this signalled a crucial shift in the balance of decision-making from the public to the private sphere, from society to the individual. This shift established new boundaries between the public and private aspects of citizens' lives, with sexuality marked out as an innately private sphere of human activity.

This change was to have important consequences. The Wolfenden Report established the basis for much of the permissive legislation passed in Britain (and Australia) during the 1960s and 1970s. New laws decriminalised homosexuality, abortion and the consumption of pornographic literature. It is clear, however, that Wolfenden-type reforms could both sustain and strengthen social control. The principle that private consensual sexual behaviour should not be subject to legal penalties was used to liberalise the laws against male homosexuality and to strengthen the legal sanctions which could be applied to street prostitutes. As Weeks (1981: 252) argues:

> What needs to be understood in this period of legislative reform is the balance of liberalisation and control and the rationale for the changes. For what was taking place in the 1960s was not a simple reform of outdated laws, but a major legislative restructuring, marking an historic shift in the mode of regulation of civil society.

This historic shift was to have important consequences for the direction of prostitution law in Australia.

New Australian Laws

The Wolfenden Report significantly influenced the direction of prostitution law in Australia during (as well as after) the late 1950s and 1960s. This does not mean that Australian legislatures took up all or even most of the specific recommendations of Wolfenden. Rather, it was the general approach which this report adopted in relation to the (de)criminalisation of private sexual behaviour between consenting adults which was so influential. Moreover, when the Wolfenden Report became available in Australia, there were already important differences between the states in institutional arrangements and official attitudes to the prostitution industry (see Chapter 2). In the period 1955–69

these regional differences continued – and to some extent even intensified – although in all jurisdictions prostitution became subject to a
range of new cultural and legal sanctions from the late 1950s onwards.
The main dimensions of the political debate about prostitution during
this period will be demonstrated by reference to four states – Victoria,
New South Wales, Queensland and Western Australia. I examine
changes in the legal domain around prostitution in these states before
proceeding with an analysis of what parliamentarians saw as the
problem and the solution.

Victoria

In 1957 the Victorian parliament amended its *Police Offences Act* to
outlaw loitering for the purposes of prostitution. Women who were (or
who were reputed to be) common prostitutes could now be arrested
simply for being in the street, regardless of whether they were soliciting
or not. Thus, the new law greatly facilitated the prosecution of sex
workers. Loitering for the purposes of prostitution was, however,
already an offence under the by-laws of the cities of Melbourne, South
Melbourne, Fitzroy and St Kilda. The Chief Secretary, Arthur Rylah,
said that the new measure was necessary because, according to the
Victoria Police, street prostitution was now 'spreading beyond what was
once a well-defined area'. Police, therefore, needed increased powers
to control 'the evil of prostitution' (VPD 253: 2074).

Street prostitution was the particular concern of Victorian parliamentarians at this time. The visible presence of prostitutes on a street
was said to be 'an embarrassment' for 'decent men going about their
lawful business'. Moreover, as the motor car had become part of 'the
modern locale' for prostitution, with clients gutter-crawling and soliciting women on the street, a significant new traffic hazard had been
created in some Melbourne suburbs:

> Public order in the roads and streets ... has been disturbed by offenders
> who make the night hideous with shouting, the screeching of motor tyres,
> brazen solicitings and importunings, insults hurled at residents pursuing
> their lawful occasions, and all the rest of the modern aspects of the world's
> oldest industry or profession, which was never before so lucrative as it is now
> [VPD 253: 2425].

While this meant that both sex workers and their clients were creating
a public nuisance, the 1957 provisions were addressed to sex workers
only. It was not until 1967 that these loitering provisions were extended
to cover clients and gutter-crawlers.

The 1957 amendments also extended the legislative provisions which related to living on the earnings of prostitution. Previously the law addressed only male persons who lived with or were habitually in the company of a prostitute, an offence which was said to be 'not common these days'. A more usual offence was said to be the case of people (male and female) who promoted prostitution. They could be men who had women working for them on the street or who took women 'from house to house for the purposes of prostitution'; they included women who set up or managed brothels and got off scot-free when prostitutes working for them were arrested. The new provisions, then, covered any person who exercised control, direction or influence over the movements of a prostitute in such a manner as to show that the person was aiding, abetting, procuring or compelling her prostitution (VPD 253: 2075). Five years earlier, the Labor Party had argued that stronger anti-prostitution measures were unnecessary (see Chapter 2), but in 1957 it did not oppose the passage of this legislation in the Victorian parliament.

In 1961 a Prostitution Bill also amended the Victorian *Crimes Act* in relation to the procuration and sexual use of young women and girls. This was prompted by charges that some migrant men, particularly southern Europeans, were seducing and procuring Australian girls into a life of prostitution. These charges emerged from a television interview in which a young prostitute claimed that she had been brutally attacked by an Italian procurer and then hawked around espresso bars in Melbourne. While the woman later retracted these claims, police evidence presented in parliament suggested that some migrant men were involved in procuring and that many of Melbourne's espresso bars were implicated in networks of prostitution. The Vice Squad had reported that about forty espresso bars in the Melbourne metropolitan area were 'pick-up joints'. The usual practice was for the proprietors to allow soliciting on their premises although the sexual acts were carried out in a van or truck, 'a mobile brothel'. The chief of the Melbourne Vice Squad was reported as saying that 'in the past 4 years, 46 men had been charged with [procuring] ... 90 per cent of whom were migrants, mostly southern European migrants' (VPD 263: 2412, 2414, 1930, 1940–1, 2200, 2761).

In parliament, a sex imbalance in Australia's immigration program was said to be the fundamental cause of this problem. The total migrant intake between 1955 and 1960 was close to 750,000 but, in Melbourne, there was 'a majority of the best part of 30,000 males'. Migrant men – 'sex-starved bachelors' – were, therefore, easy targets for the 'agents and touts' who hawked young girls around Melbourne's espresso bars. The general thrust of this argument was contested by the

Commonwealth Department of Immigration, which argued that prostitution was not necessarily related to the rate of male migration. The department contended that more than 50 per cent of those charged in Victoria with procuring for the purposes of prostitution were in fact Australian-born and not migrants. They also reminded parliamentarians that prostitution flourished even in countries where there was an excess of females (VPD 263: 2411, 2422, 2197, 2200).

The changes to the *Crimes Act* in 1961 prohibited *all* procuring of women under the age of twenty-one (previously prostitutes and women 'of known immoral character' had been exempt from these provisions) and more than doubled the maximum penalties for this offence. The new law also prohibited the act 'of knowingly inducing or persuading any male person to have unlawful carnal connection with any girl under the age of 18 years' (VPD 263: 2199) and extended the liability of householders who permitted the 'defilement of young girls' on their premises (previously, this had been an offence only when the girl was under sixteen years of age). The penalties for abducting and detaining women and girls with intent to have carnal knowledge of them were also significantly increased. In line with the recommendations of the Wolfenden Report , the 1961 amendment also extended the legal sanctions against soliciting so that they applied to both men and women.

Despite these new laws, large numbers of prostitutes and male clients continued to congregate on the streets of St Kilda (Winter 1976). In the mid-1960s there was a public outcry about blatant street soliciting, and police took drastic action. Reports in parliament show that in the first six months of 1966 'police arrested some 400 prostitutes in the St Kilda district'. In a controversial move, female police were also deployed on the streets in an effort to catch clients. One parliamentarian praised the Victoria Police for achieving the first conviction of a male client, although it had hardly been a difficult catch. The client had responded to the request of a 'working girl' that he take her to the police station, where she wanted to bail out a friend. At the police station, he was asked if he had been soliciting for prostitution. He said that he had, was convicted and fined £5 or five days in gaol (VPD 280: 2318–19). Winter (1976: 42) suggests that, because of a spectacular rise in the incidence of sex crimes following police activity against clients, police decided to abandon their pursuit of male clients at this time.

In 1967, however, a Summary Offences Bill was passed by the Victorian parliament. It specifically extended the 1957 loitering provisions to include male clients and gutter-crawlers. It became an offence 'for a male person to loiter in a public place for the purpose of inviting a female to prostitute herself for pecuniary reward with himself or with another person' (VPD 288: 1339). The main target of this legislation was said to be young men, particularly those who were causing worry and distress to 'innocent women' by their public behaviour.

Queensland

In Queensland there were only two minor legislative initiatives directed at the prostitution industry in the period 1955–69. The first of these was an amendment in 1955 to the *Vagrants, Gaming and Other Offences Act* which significantly increased penalties for behaving in a riotous, violent, disorderly, indecent, offensive or threatening manner; penalties were increased from £5 or one month's imprisonment to £50 or six months' imprisonment. In parliament it was said that this measure was prompted by community concern over the behaviour of teenagers during the visit of rock-and-roll singer Johnny Ray to Brisbane. However, in other states, 'disorderly conduct' was a charge frequently laid against prostitutes and, as one member of the Queensland parliament argued, the bill was also designed to deal with 'sexual perverts' (QPD 211: 1758).

A further amendment to the Act in 1967 repealed Section 55(v), which related to rules of evidence in the case of brothels:

> Proof that any house or part of a house wherein any female of Asiatic or Polynesian race dwells, or is lodged, or is found, is frequented by or is the resort of any male person not of Asiatic or Polynesian race at any time between the hours of 9 o'clock in the evening and 6 o'clock in the morning, shall be prima facie evidence that such house or part of house is a brothel [QPD 245: 2380]

This amendment was introduced by the Minister for Education, Jack Pizzey, who suggested that removal of the offending section was urgent because of the numbers of Asian and Polynesian student-visitors now attending the University of Queensland. He said that the section first appeared in bills that were not proceeded with in 1909 and 1911. It then appeared in the new *Vagrants, Gaming and Other Offences Act* in 1931 'and no-one ever asked that it be removed or questioned it being there' (QPD 245: 2380).

While these two minor changes were the only legal initiatives directed at the prostitution trade in Queensland, there were significant alterations in the organisation of the industry and in its relationship to various state institutions. In 1959, Brisbane's tolerated houses of prostitution (see Chapter 2) were closed by the Police Commissioner, Frank Bischof, and the Health Department discontinued its weekly examination of prostitutes. This dramatic shift (without any legislative changes or debate in parliament) was clearly related to the election of a conservative government in 1957. As Finnane (1988) suggests, the end of almost forty years of Labor rule disrupted the long-standing but largely informal arrangements whereby the prostitution trade was policed in Queensland.

There was clearly some public pressure on the new Nicklin government to close the tolerated brothels. Correspondence tabled years later at the Fitzgerald Inquiry in Queensland referred to a pamphlet published in 1958 under the auspices of the League of Moral Reform. This pamphlet named four inner-city brothels and accused the Nicklin government of protecting them, thus contributing to the 'defilement of womanhood'. At the time, the Solicitor-General said:

> In approaching this matter, one has to bear in mind that at least some of these houses have, as a matter of notoriety, been in existence for very many years. (One brothel ... has existed from at least the turn of the century.) The keeping of these houses is definitely unlawful but every government has refrained from enforcing the law to such an extent as not to close all these places up, there being little doubt that strict enforcement of the law would, generally speaking, be against the public interest, not only from a health point of view but also in many cases on the grounds of public safety [Fitzgerald Inquiry, Exhibit 22].

The Solicitor-General argued that a prosecution launched against the author and printer of the pamphlet was unlikely to succeed and might attract unfavourable publicity for the government over the issue of 'tolerated' brothels. The Solicitor-General's letter was endorsed 'Cabinet decided to take no action.'

Phil Dickie (1988: 7–8) suggests that the closure of Brisbane's brothels in 1959 had little if anything to do with moral reform campaigns. He found that the actions of Police Commissioner Frank Bischof in closing the tolerated houses of prostitution was a successful attempt to divert an inquiry into police graft and corruption associated with the prostitution trade. Shirley Brifman, a prostitute who worked at one of the tolerated brothels, said that the close-down occurred when Bischof went on holiday in 1959 and certain police decided to increase the protection fees for brothels. According to Brifman, one of the brothel madams lodged a formal complaint with the police and an official investigation was launched. Upon his return, Bischof was forced to close the brothels as part of the action required to save the police involved in the extortion racket (allegedly they included future Police Commisioner Terry Lewis).

According to evidence presented at the Fitzgerald Inquiry, most of Brisbane's prostitutes operated on the streets and out of hotel lounges after the closure of the brothels. In October 1963 public allegations were made that senior police officers condoned and encouraged a call-girl service which operated from the inner city National Hotel. A Royal Commission was called to inquire into these allegations. However, Mr Justice Gibbs found no evidence of police condoning or participating in breaches of the *Liquor Acts*, call-girl services, prostitution and the like at the National Hotel. He merely recommended that the *Liquor Act* be amended with respect to 'guests' and that police procedures regarding the reporting of offences against the *Liquor Acts* be revised (Borchardt 1986: 239–40). Dickie (1988: 11–25) has since documented substantial evidence that police in the 1960s were involved in the operation of a prostitution racket from the National Hotel.

Western Australia

In Western Australia tolerated brothels continued to operate in Roe Street, Perth, until 1958 when police took action to close them (Winter 1976: 49). As in Queensland, then, the shift away from a regime of tolerated houses of prostitution was accomplished by police action alone and without resort to new legislation. An article in the *Observer* (6 September 1958) suggested that the Commonwealth government was behind the closure of Perth's famous brothel area. The Commonwealth was said to have seized several properties in Roe Street – and six of the eleven brothels – because they were officially 'enemy property', having been owned by a woman who became a German citizen during World War II.

In 1968 an amendment to the *Police Act* extended to women the provisions which prohibited male persons from living on the earnings of prostitution. This occurred in response to a request from the Commonwealth that state laws meet the requirements of the United Nations *International Convention for the Suppression of the Traffic in Persons and of the Exploitation of Others*. Opposing this amendment, the member for Wembley, Dr Henn, raised some concerns about the application of these new provisions to brothel madams. Henn said that he had worked in a medical practice adjacent to the old brothel area in Roe Street and that the lives of prostitutes were 'not as sordid as one would imagine'; they 'wish to do this [prostitution] and, in the main, it is their business'. The madams were an important factor in keeping a house orderly:

I do not think it can be said that they themselves operate in the business; they are there as an overseer of sorts ... They look after the girls, and see they behave themselves properly while they are not on duty and misbehave themselves properly while they are on duty. It is a very important function. ... if they are run off the road and the girls are left to themselves, the houses will not be conducted quite so well.

However, Henn was also critical of the continuing toleration of brothels on the goldfields for, 'it is cant and humbug for any Government ... to say it [prostitution] cannot be eradicated'. He said the law should be enforced or other alternatives explored (WAPD 180: 1244–5). In general, this was not a view adopted by the Western Australian parliament in this period. Tolerated brothels continue to operate in Kalgoorlie.

New South Wales

While no new anti-prostitution laws were enacted in New South Wales during the late 1950s and early 1960s, prostitution became an increasingly important political issue in this period. Winter (1976: 32–9) reports that a 'bordello district' located in the inner Sydney suburb of Darlinghurst was closed by the Heffron Labor government in 1962; however, many of the brothels in this area reopened the following year. The election of a Liberal–Country Party coalition government in 1965 led to renewed police action against the brothels although, by the late 1960s, brothels again occupied large frontages in Darlinghurst and East Sydney. On the day before the state election in 1968 police carried out a huge raid on this red-light district; 168 customers and sightseers and seventeen prostitutes were arrested. This suggests that prostitution was increasingly being connected to other political agendas (such as law and order) and that governments were increasingly prepared to use the policing of prostitution as a means of establishing and conserving political power.

A new configuration of pressure-group politics was also emerging around prostitution in Sydney during the 1960s. One of the most influential of these was the Civic Reform Group, an alliance of businessmen and inner-city residents which supported several aldermen on the Sydney City Council. In 1967 the Civic Reform Group complained publicly about 'blatant' prostitution in the Kings Cross area and the display of undesirable photographs 'outside certain places of entertainment' (SMH, 3 April 1967). It also applied consistent pressure to both the state government and the Sydney City Council in order to extend the legal controls on prostitution.[2]

At the same time, however, some individuals and pressure groups began to lobby publicly in favour of a decriminalisation of prostitution. In an address to the Australian Convention of Councils for Civil Liberties in 1968, Ken Buckley, a lecturer in economic history at the University of Sydney, called for the establishment of an official red-light district and an end to the legal harassment of prostitutes (*SMH*, 8, 11 October 1968). He described prostitution as 'a private matter in so far as it is engaged in between consenting adults in a private place', and argued that the existing laws against vagrancy and prostitution reflected class-bound assumptions about public behaviour which positively disadvantaged working-class men and women.

Such arguments did not impact upon official attitudes to prostitution in the 1960s. In 1968 the New South Wales government introduced an extensive range of new legal sanctions against prostitution with an amendment to the *Vagrancy, Disorderly Houses and Other Acts*. This measure was said to be necessary for several reasons. First, the government claimed that its ability to control prostitution had been significantly undermined by a legal decision in 1966, *Ex parte Fergusson*.[3] In this case Justice Brereton found that the use of a house by one prostitute (working alone) did not constitute it as a disorderly house under the terms of the New South Wales Act. In 1967 this decision was upheld by the Supreme Court.[4] Subsequently, police said that they were unable to act against the large number of small brothels in the East Sydney red-light area. The Chief Secretary argued that prostitutes 'and, more particularly, racketeers and bludgers who live on the proceeds of their illicit trade' were now able to 'thumb their noses' at the law.

The second reason which the government put forward to justify the 1968 amendment related to a perceived expansion of prostitution activities as a result of the influx of United States servicemen on rest and recreation leave from Vietnam. The appearance of three and a half thousand new GIs every fortnight was said to have had a 'skyrocketing' effect in Sydney on the price of food, accommodation and 'girls' (NSWPD 75: 1641–3). There was also said to be a visible increase in the number of crooks and standover men in the prostitution business. Questions were raised in parliament about the alleged murder, arson and police corruption associated with prostitution. Newspaper articles drew public attention to the extensive red-light district in East Sydney and to the long history of ineffective police crackdowns and government inaction on prostitution (*SMH*, 30 May). On 11 November 1968 the murder of 'prostitution czar' Joe Borg was reported in the *Sydney Morning Herald* amidst calls for 'proper controls' to be applied to the prostitution industry, including heavy penalties for those who organised and lived on the earnings of prostitution.

The 1968 legislation introduced significant new penalties for prostitution-related offences, but only marginally addressed the issue of clients, bludgers and owners. It created, for example, a new offence of loitering in, or in view of, any public place for the purpose of prostitution or of soliciting for prostitution. Similar laws in Victoria were applied to common prostitutes, that is, to women who had previously been convicted for a prostitution-related offence. In New South Wales, however, there was no requirement to prove that the accused was a common prostitute. The Chief Secretary said that this clause was designed to facilitate the prosecution of women who solicited from just inside the doorway of their houses, 'especially from premises with doors right on the footpath' as in many parts of the Darlinghurst and East Sydney red-light area (NSWPD 75: 1384). Previously, prostitutes who worked in this way were exempt from prosecution because they were not considered to be soliciting in the public domain.

The 1968 legislation also provided new penalties for a known prostitute who was simply found in premises habitually used for the purposes of prostitution, and for soliciting for prostitution. A lesser penalty applied to known prostitutes who were found on premises which were only 'reasonably suspected' of being habitually used for the purposes of prostitution or soliciting. Other new penalties applied to prostitutes who, for the purposes of prostitution or soliciting, used premises which purported to be available for massage, sauna, steam baths, etc. (NSWPD 75: 1385).

In relation to living on the earnings of prostitution, the law was extended to cover women as well as men, as had occurred in Victoria in 1957. The Chief Secretary argued that this was necessary in order to allow for the prosecution of 'madams who are now operating quite openly'. All penalties for living on earnings were significantly increased and women, like men, became liable to a period of imprisonment if they were convicted more than once of this offence (NSWPD 75: 1384).

The penalties applied to owners and operators of premises were also increased, and a second offence in this category now attracted both a fine *and* imprisonment. For a third or subsequent offence, the owner, manager or occupier was liable to a gaol term not exceeding twelve months. Owners retained their existing right to evict tenants who were practising prostitution. Penalties were also increased for 'being an owner or occupier of any house, room or place [and] knowingly permitting any female suffering from venereal disease to occupy such house or room for the purpose of prostitution'. Owners who harboured diseased prostitutes were clearly more liable in the eyes of the state than owners whose tenants were 'clean'.

Importantly, the 1968 legislation also amended the *Disorderly Houses*

Act. This Act already cited drunkenness, disorderly or indecent conduct, entertainment of a demoralising nature, the presence of reputed criminals, and unlawful liquor, drug-taking or sales as grounds on which premises could be declared a disorderly house and closed down (NSWPD 75: 1385). The amendment added 'habitual prostitution' to these grounds, and thus significantly extended the application of the law to brothels. This part of the bill was clearly prompted by the legal decision in *Ex parte Fergusson*, mentioned above.

Community response to the new anti-prostitution laws varied. Some correspondents to the *Sydney Morning Herald* called for the licensing of brothels in order to control both the criminal racketeering associated with prostitution and the rising incidence of rape and venereal disease (8 October 1968). The licensing of prostitutes and/or houses of prostitution was, however, specifically rejected by the government because 'licensing would only make respectable what society regards as immoral and distasteful' (NSWPD 75: 1383). Other correspondents in the *Sydney Morning Herald* argued that the new laws were aimed at 'the poor man's beer' (working-class men's sexual outlets) and would simply increase the cost of living for migrant men. However, one female writer suggested that prostitution would disappear 'if men did not over-indulge their carnal appetites' (15, 17 October 1968).

That the new legislation was primarily applied to sex workers (and not to owners and operators) was evident in a statement by the Chief Secretary, Eric Willis, during 1969. Willis reported that in the five months that the new Act had been in force it had been successful in 'suppressing blatant and offensive forms of prostitution in Sydney'. Although some massage parlours remained, twenty-four had been closed. There had also been 112 arrests consequent upon the changes to the Act:

> 55 of these were in respect of known prostitutes being found on premises habitually used for prostitution; 33 were for soliciting for prostitution in massage parlours or the like; and 24 were in respect of occupiers, managers and so on suffering prostitution on their premises. To date no applications for declaration of premises as a Disorderly House have been made but one is said to be imminent [NSWPD 79: 5120–8].

Thus, more than 80 per cent of the charges made by police in the first five months after the declaration of the Act were laid against sex workers. Allen (1990: 192–3) argues that the 1968 legislation did provide 'occasion and means to harass brothel keepers, owners and landlords, at least in the short term'. Charges for keeping or owning a brothel underwent an eightfold increase in 1969 and then doubled again in 1970. However, after 1970 a steady downward trend began in arrests for this category of offence. Also, the bulk of prosecutions continued to fall on prostitutes and these actually increased in the early 1970s. Charges for soliciting, for example, jumped from 90 in 1969 to 3631 in 1970 (Allen 1990: 192–3).

The Debate in Parliament about Prostitution

The legal changes described in several states during 1955–69 indicate that the laws against prostitution became more extensive. My aim in this section is to ask 'Why did this happen?' In a period when discourses about sexual liberation and the desirability of sexual plea-sure were widespread, why was prostitution marked out for increased legal penalties (especially as the opposite was tending to happen with pornography)? As in previous chapters, I address these questions by looking at what parliamentarians said when introducing new laws against prostitution.

As I have shown, prostitution was not a major concern of parlia-ments in Queensland and Western Australia. However, it became a visible political concern in Victoria at this time and in New South Wales during the late 1960s. An examination of parliamentary debates in these states shows that there were no significant changes in the ways that prostitutes were represented by parliamentarians. However, there were some important changes in the ways that clients were repre-sented, as well as in the perceived causes of prostitution and the nature of appropriate government controls over the industry.

As in the years before and after World War II (see Chapters 1 and 2), it was prostitutes, rather than clients, who were the main focus of parliamentary attention in the late 1950s and 1960s. Moreover, the prostitute was still predominantly a female figure, although the spectre of male prostitutes, catering for a homosexual clientele, also emerged in parliamentary debates of this period. The Victorian Prostitution Bill of 1961, for example, extended the legal sanctions against street solic-iting so that they applied to male and female prostitutes (although the inclusion of men was not widely commented on by members of the Victorian parliament at the time). This marked the beginning of an important shift in Australian legal culture. As Arnot (1986: 126–7) argues, until the early 1960s, the legal meaning of the words *prostitute* and *prostitution* was 'entirely bound up with heterosexual relationships'. From 1961 onwards prostitution law became deeply implicated in the formation of new cultural definitions of male homosexuality in Australia.

As in previous decades, prostitutes were still subject to a set of contradictory discourses. On the one hand they were labelled as lazy, deviant and the purveyors of disease. On the other hand they could also be represented as victims of their social circumstances. For example, in the New South Wales parliament during 1963, prostitutes were identified as the major source of a new venereal disease problem becoming evident in the Australian community (NSWPD 46: 4319–63).[5] Prostitution was also described as 'a most unnatural act so far as a woman is concerned', one that women resorted to not out of poverty but out of 'sheer greed' and a desire for 'fine clothes and a faster life' (VPD 253: 2422–3).

However, in New South Wales in 1968 the member for Illawarra, George Petersen, argued that his 'prime objection' to the prostitution trade was 'the damage it does to the women who engage in it'. In his view, then, prostitutes were objects of pity rather than objects of desire:

> prostitutes in the mass must be admitted to be a pathetic sight. They are not the blowsy, attractive women of *Man* magazine or the other girlie publications. … a sizable number of them are mentally subnormal and a great number, if not the majority, are emotionally deprived. So far from being evil women … they are poor devils exploited by pimps, bludgers, landlords and stand-over merchants of all kinds [NSWPD 75: 1500].

Thus, the prostitute was represented as a victim of her economic and psychological circumstances. Moreover, as prostitution was 'essentially service by social inferiors to social superiors', the situation of the prostitute was a paradigm of the inferior position of women more generally in society (NSWPD 75: 1499–500).

Overall, however, the number of speakers in the Victorian and New South Wales parliaments who adopted a sympathetic approach to the position of prostitutes was significantly less during 1955–69 than in any period before 1955. This suggests that the status of women working in the prostitution industry was actively declining. The Wolfenden Report was probably instrumental in this process, particularly as it labelled female sex workers as lazy and deviant. For example, in the Victorian parliament during 1967, the Wolfenden Report was cited in support of the argument that prostitutes choose their occupation because their 'psychological make-up' was such that they sought 'an easier, freer and more profitable' occupation (VPD 288: 1702). Similarly, the Leader of the Opposition in New South Wales cited the Wolfenden Report in order to explain why women resorted to 'this immoral way of earning a living when there is plenty of work about' (NSWPD 75: 1442–3).

While arguments like this were also deployed in Australian parliaments during the first decade after the war (see Chapter 2), they were used more widely and consistently from the late 1950s onwards. In this view women did not 'choose' prostitution because they were particularly attracted to a life of immorality or because they liked sex. For prostitutes: 'it is business and a way of earning a living. ... While sexually unexcited, [the prostitute] believes it is a good way of life, better than working in an office pounding a typewriter' (NSWPD 75: 1443). While the prostitute was now represented as a woman who freely chose her profession (for apparently rational if not moral reasons) she was not seen to be a worker in the proper sense of the word. In the New South Wales parliament, otherwise sympathetic parliamentarians talked about the need to encourage prostitutes 'back to work'; that is, into any work that was not sex work (NSWPD 75: 1449).

A major focus of concern for parliamentarians during this period was the young, innocent girl inadvertently drawn into prostitution. Given that older women were represented as freely choosing sex work, it would appear that the main issue here was whether sufficient maturity had been achieved for the prostitute's consent to be, in some sense, meaningful. But this discourse was also subject to pressure from a sexual discourse that made explicit the pathological nature of all prostitutes. For example, one of the main concerns of parliamentarians debating the 1961 Prostitution Bill in Victoria was that young, innocent girls would be coerced or encouraged into the prostitution trade by migrant men. The Chief Secretary argued that girls as young as thirteen and fourteen were being procured for immoral purposes in espresso bars and cafés. It was said that these girls were lured into espresso bars by rock-and-roll music on the juke boxes and that, once inside, they were rendered powerless by the addition of drugs to their coffee and Coca-Cola. However, girls who had been led astray in this way were also said to be the product of broken homes and homes where mothers went out to work. They were 'wayward girls who are uncontrollable, insensitive and lack all those things expected of normal girls' (VPD 263: 1933, 2767). As girls who were already 'bad' (and 'ruined' by parental neglect rather than by the men who procured or hired them) they were naturally more likely to end up as prostitutes. It was clear that they were to some extent also regarded as less worthy of state protection.[6]

As in previous periods, men who lived on the earnings of prostitution were not represented sympathetically by parliamentarians. One speaker in the New South Wales parliament in 1968 described them as 'squalid and disreputable specimens ... standover men and ... "spivs" – who live and apparently thrive on the earnings of prostitution'

(NSWPD 75: 1383). Thus, while the Labor Opposition opposed many features of the legislation introduced in 1968, it did not oppose the introduction of tougher legal penalties for bludgers and pimps. As the deputy leader of the Opposition argued, 'is there anything more abhorrent than the person who is living off prostitution – a man who will live on the earnings of a girl who makes her living by prostitution' (NSWPD 75: 1446). The only exception here was the approach adopted by Asher Joel, who argued in the Legislative Council that 'there are … some bludgers who provide the prostitute with a certain degree of warmth and comfort which is denied to her elsewhere in the world' (NSWPD 75: 1640). While, in several states during this period, the ambit of the law was extended to include both men and women who lived off the earnings of prostitution, it was still men – and not women – who were singled out during parliamentary debate as the main exploiters of prostitutes.

While the clients of prostitutes had been relatively invisible during parliamentary debates in the period before and after the war, they now became significantly more visible. Clients also became subject to a set of new contradictory discourses at this time. While the resort to prostitution was still regarded as natural and inevitable for some men, a discourse which marked clients as sexual deviants began to be deployed in Australian parliaments during the 1960s.

In both Victoria and New South Wales concerns about the sexuality of migrant men tended to focus political attention on the role of the client in prostitution transactions. Men of southern European extraction were represented as more passionate by nature and, therefore, less able to control their sexual impulses. For these men the resort to prostitution was regarded as natural and inevitable. As one member of the Victorian parliament argued in 1961:

> the very crux of the problem which has led to the procuring of young girls in the streets, in cafés and in espresso bars can be looked at in three ways. The first is the disproportion between the sexes of migrants who have come to this country in the last ten years, the second is the natural loneliness of men when deprived of female company, and the third is the biological urge [VPD 263: 2762].

Thus, a perceived imbalance in the sexes of those who were brought to Australia under assisted immigration policies combined with the fact of (men's) uncontrollable biological urges meant that there was bound to be an increased demand for prostitution, particularly as 'Australian girls have shown … a certain reserve about marriage with members of European races' (VPD 263: 2197, 2762). For men without wives, the resort to prostitution could still be regarded as natural and a useful means of containing the social dangers posed by pent-up male sexual urges. Thus, the figure of the desperate and biologically driven male migrant assumed some explanatory force in parliamentary debates: 'The reason for [the upsurge in prostitution] seems to be that there are now in Sydney thousands of healthy, virile migrants. They are lonely and woman-hungry, and their only chance of sex contact is through the prostitutes' (NSWPD 75: 1444). Of the clients in East Sydney's red-light area, 90 per cent were said to fall into this category, that is, to be men who 'had to fall back on this immoral and abhorrent form of prostitution to enjoy a woman's company'. According to one member of parliament, this did not mean that the migrant was 'more sexual or immoral than the Australian man; it is simply impossible for him to make sex contact except through prostitutes' (NSWPD 75: 1444).

This approach suggested that the only men who used prostitutes were those without a 'normal' sexual outlet. However, as in previous decades, some parliamentarians still argued that because 'the male is always polygamous by nature', prostitution was an inevitable feature of all human societies (VPD 263: 2424). As the Deputy Leader of the Opposition in New South Wales argued in 1968, prostitution was 'a social problem that has existed from the beginning of human history'; because it served an 'obvious need' – servicing 'males seeking sexual contact' – it was probably 'inherent and inevitable in organised society'. Indeed, the resort to prostitution was said to be less disruptive to society than adultery (VPD 253: 2422; NSWPD 75: 1440–1). As a means of countering 'free and indiscriminate love', prostitution was conducive to the good order of society (NSWPD 75: 1442).

By the late 1960s, however, this sort of functionalist approach was meeting overt challenge from the forces of the sexual revolution. The member for Port Kembla, George Petersen, argued that as prostitution was defined by the absence of reciprocal desire, it was 'a blot on our society' because 'the most intimate of all relationships is reduced to a cash nexus'. He proposed, therefore, that prostitution was *dysfunctional* for society because the formation of loving sexual relationships between men and women was 'the whole basis of society' (NSWPD 75: 1499).

By the late 1960s all normal Australian men, including those who were unmarried, were assumed to have access to such loving sexual relationships with women. As one speaker argued: 'Sexual contact between the sexes has become much freer, and women, with the aid of modern medical safeguards, ... more agreeable to love outside marriage' (NSWPD 75: 1444). Thus, men were said to have less need to resort to prostitution for the servicing of their sexual needs. As 'ordinary' women were now 'liberated from the shackles of Victorian sexuality', they made fine 'sexual companions' (NSWPD 75: 1501) – unlike prostitutes. In a quotation remarkably reminiscent of Kinsey on the deficiencies of prostitutes for middle-class men (see Chapter 2), Petersen cited the following: 'If you have had a sexual relationship with a woman in which both of you have obviously enjoyed yourselves you are not going to be satisfied with the sneeze in the loins that is all you can get from a prostitute' (NSWPD 75: 1501). Petersen told the parliament that he had walked around the Sydney red-light area and seen 'the class of men who visit prostitutes'. They were all said to be young migrants or middle-aged Australians, that is, 'persons who for one reason or another have no sexual attraction to women'.

It appears, then, that the use of prostitutes was becoming less culturally acceptable in the late 1950s and 1960s, at least for so-called normal men. As companionate forms of sexuality (emphasising the importance of love and mutual sexual desire) became more dominant within mainstream Australian culture, prostitution (which, it was assumed, could never involve love or mutuality) was increasingly represented as not normal.

Even among parliamentarians who favoured a more liberal approach to prostitution law, the deviancy of clients was becoming an issue. For example, in the NSW Legislative Council during 1968, Joel argued strongly for a new, more compassionate, approach to the problem of prostitution and 'a new concept of dealing with sexual relations that will ... remove the sadness of the world of those who are compelled to be deviants, of those who practise the calling of prostitution or of those who apply to them for their bodily comfort' (NSWPD 75: 1636). This is a clear statement of changes in the status of clients. While prostitutes had been regarded as deviant women for most of the preceding decades (see Chapters 1 and 2), the activities of clients were usually conceptualised in terms of the normal desires of men with no other sexual outlet. Now, however, men who made use of the services of prostitutes were those with aberrant desires:

> Many men ... patronize prostitutes, for one reason alone – because of their deviant behaviour. If their deviant behaviour were not ... worked out on these unfortunate women, there would be a far greater incidence of crime. ... many persons who seek prostitutes upon whom to wreak their passion hesitate to make the same demands of their wives, fiancées or girlfriends [NSWPD 75: 1640–1].

That girlfriends and fiancées could now be publicly represented, like wives, as catering to men's sexual needs showed a significant change in sexual mores. Moreover, the idea that prostitutes serviced deviants (and not normal men with no other sexual outlet) was a new one. While normal men sought liberated women, rather than prostitutes, for the satisfaction of their sexual desires, prostitutes could increasingly be represented as an outlet for the expression of abnormal, deviant sexual desires.

While sexual deviance and the imbalance in Australia's immigration program were the most frequently cited causes of prostitution in this period, the increasing use of soft-core pornographic images was also regarded as an important reason why the prostitution industry had not disappeared. This possibility had also been raised before the Wolfenden Committee; the British Medical Association argued that the suggestive nature of popular magazines and films stimulated sexual over-activity, 'so creating an appetite that was gratified by prostitutes' (cited in VPD 263: 2420). A link between 'sex in magazines and on the covers of paperbacks' – material which 'excited, aroused and developed immoral thoughts' – and the demand for prostitution was proposed by several members of parliament in Australia (VPD 263: 1943, 2424–5). In 1967, for example, one member argued that the sexualisation of mainstream advertising was both 'deplorable' and an exploitation of women. But he also suggested that 'prostitutes should be grateful for the trade it helps to create for them' (VPD 288: 1702). Similarly in New South Wales in 1968 Joel cited the views of Dr Eustace Chesser (an American psychoanalyst) who said that one of the major causes of prostitution was the over-emphasis placed upon sex in modern society: 'In all media, in every form of literature and in every film we emphasize sex to such a degree that we set young men upon the path to prostitution' (NSWPD 75: 1642). Thus, the suggestion was that the constant titillation induced by repeated exposure to sexual representations in popular literature produced a new demand for sexual services, one that apparently could not be satisfied by wives and girlfriends.

My analysis of parliamentary debates in the period 1955–69 shows that Australian parliaments had several different objectives when passing new laws addressed to the prostitution industry. While they were concerned to control the criminal element said to be associated with the prostitution trade (VPD 263: 2422; NSWPD 75: 1444), their main concern was the visibility of prostitution and the public offence said to be caused by street prostitution. This was obvious in Victoria during 1957 when several members argued that the mere presence of prostitutes on the streets was 'an embarrassment' for men: 'Men have

the right to go about the streets, and the presence of women [prosti-
tutes] who adopt these practices should not affront their dignity' (VPD
253: 2422). From this perspective, street prostitutes were a hazard to
male dignity, in addition to being a moral danger or a health hazard.

Similarly in New South Wales in 1968 it was the visibility of prostitution that was seen to lead to public offence. As the Deputy Leader of
the Opposition argued:

> Our concern should be only for those activities associated with prostitution
> that are against the public interest ... the too overt factors of the profession.
> ... When prostitution is put on public exhibition, it becomes a nuisance and
> is obnoxious. It is then the job of the legislature to stamp it out [NSWPD 75:
> 1445].

The aim of legislation, therefore, was to 'put prostitutes out of the
public gaze' and to end 'the blatant and vulgar way in which prostitution is being flouted before the community' (NSWPD 75: 1454, 1382).
This was consistent with the approach recommended in the Wolfenden
Report. It also meant that legislation which outlawed loitering by prostitutes could be justified as in the public interest and as a defence of
the rights of 'respectable citizens'. While this was usually posed in
terms of men's ability to walk the streets without being solicited by a
prostitute, the rights of innocent women (that is, women who were not
prostitutes) were also raised. It seems that there were two main dangers
here. In Victoria during 1957 it was argued that innocent women were
in some danger from prostitutes, for the harassment to which 'decent
men going about their lawful business' were subjected was nothing in
comparison to 'the insults which these foul harpies heap upon innocent women' (VPD 253: 2424). However, in Sydney in 1968 it was the
activities of clients that were seen to endanger women: 'Respectable
citizens who live or work in [the red-light district in East Sydney] have
complained that their wives and daughters have been offended and
molested by the men who throng to these places' [NSWPD 75: 1382].
In Victoria during 1957, when the loitering provisions were extended
to include men, several members of parliament raised concerns about
the possibility of innocent men being charged. As one argued:

> No matter how noble the objectives of the Bill may be, they should not
> infringe on the rights or civil liberties of individuals. ... The danger is the
> effect on a person [sic] who may be engaged in an innocent pursuit and
> who is standing around in areas which prostitutes might frequent; it might
> be an old man who is out for a little fresh air ... many people like to watch
> the pretty girls walking along the street [VPD 288: 1702].

The argument that anti-loitering provisions might infringe the rights of sex workers to walk in the streets was not specifically raised in Australian parliaments at this time.[7] As it was assumed that 'good' and 'bad' women could be readily discerned on the street, they could be treated accordingly. Loitering provisions were not an infringement of the rights of 'real' citizens or of 'decent women' who were merely waiting around to keep appointments (VPD 253: 2422). The New South Wales government argued in relation to its new anti-loitering provisions that there would be 'no room … for the rights of a citizen to be transgressed'. It was clear, however, that this did not refer to the rights of sex workers, for the bill was said to be 'aimed at protecting the rights of law-abiding citizens' (NSWPD 75: 1383, 1386).

Throughout 1955–69, as in the preceding decade, there was substantial agreement among members of parliament about the nature of appropriate legislative controls on the prostitution industry. As one commented in 1968, 'honourable members on both sides agree on the fundamentals of this matter [prostitution]' (NSWPD 75: 1496). But the grounds of this consensus were shifting as the Wolfenden Report established a new basis for appropriate government controls on the sex industry.

The Wolfenden Report was cited for the first time in an Australian parliament in 1961, during debate on the Prostitution Bill in Victoria. One member argued: 'Modern thinking is opposed to the crimination of private acts of immorality between consenting adults' (VPD 263: 2418). By the late 1960s this view was becoming dominant in Australian parliaments and was influencing official attitudes towards prostitution. In 1968 the Deputy Leader of the New South Wales Opposition argued that, while prostitution was definitely immoral, it was not a proper object of legislative concern. This was because: 'personal morality is a matter for the individual and his [sic] moral conduct, his right to sin in private, causing no offence to the public, is inalienable' (NSWPD 75: 1445).[8] From this perspective, it was appropriate that the legislature should take some action only when a sin became public and created a public nuisance. When committed 'in private [in a manner] which does not result in an offensive situation and does not annoy people, the government should not interfere'. Thus, while prostitution could be personally abhorrent, private prostitution (for example, call-girls) belonged more appropriately in the category of 'non-offensive' prostitution (NSWPD 75: 1446).

But this sort of approach and the application of a (Wolfenden-type) distinction between public and private behaviour, between law and morality, did not meet with unanimous support in parliament in this period. Some conservative members repudiated the notion that acts of immorality committed in private were no concern of the legislature. As one argued, if this was so then 'it would be true to say that ... a man could shoot his wife so long as he did it in private' (NSWPD 75: 1496). Edna Roper – President of the Federal Labor Women's Committee and the only female member of parliament to participate in the debate on prostitution in New South Wales during 1968 – also supported the maintenance of laws against prostitution. In her view, prostitution could exist only in societies where women were relegated to an inferior status; granting women equal pay was the best means of raising the status of women and combating the growth of prostitution (NSWPD 75: 646). Like Petersen, then, Roper saw the social position of women as intimately related to the continuance of prostitution. However, unlike Petersen, she argued strongly for political measures directed at ending prostitution and did not envisage a liberal solution such as decriminalising all private sexual acts to the prostitution problem.

While there was increasing support in Australian parliaments during the 1960s for the idea that private sexual behaviour between consenting adults was not an appropriate concern of the legislature, there was also clear resistance to the application of this principle to sexual practices like prostitution. During 1955–69, Australian parliamentarians voted strongly in favour of new laws against street soliciting. However, they also voted in favour of new laws against private (brothel) prostitution and ostensibly private matters such as living on earnings. So while the *idea* underlying Wolfenden was being widely proclaimed, there was clear resistance to the application of this principle to prostitution law reform. This resistance was due to the (changing) status of prostitution within the broader sexual culture; a sexual practice which was not visibly premised on mutual sexual desire, and which remained firmly located in traditional patterns of sexual-economic exchange, was not readily transformed into a vehicle of the sexual revolution.

Conclusion

In the late 1950s and 1960s the sex industry began to emerge as an important political concern in Australia. This is evident in the range of new legal and cultural sanctions that were brought to bear on the prostitution industry from the late 1950s onwards and in the increasing intensity of political debate about literary censorship and sexual representation in the 1960s. While the sexual revolution which occurred in this period brought about new demands for the dismantling of political controls on literary censorship, it also led to a cultural reconceptualisation of prostitution and changes in official attitudes towards the industry.

In two states – Victoria and New South Wales – tough new anti-prostitution laws were enacted, while in Queensland and Western Australia a long period of tolerated brothel prostitution drew to an end in the late 1950s. I have suggested that this shift was due to several specific changes in the sexual culture and to the impact of the Wolfenden Report. My analysis of parliamentary debates certainly indicates that changes in the sexual culture had a significant influence on political discourses about prostitution during 1955–69. The sexual revolution meant that women who were not prostitutes were more sexually available outside marriage, and that 'normal men' were no longer forced to seek out the services of prostitutes in order to find a sexual outlet. Moreover, there was an increasing emphasis within 'normal' relationships over this period on orgasm and mutual sexual pleasure as the basis of successful, companionate relationships. There was, then, an increasing disparity within Australian sexual culture between prostitution and 'normal' sexual relations. As a result, prostitution could be perceived (by parliamentarians as well as the general public) as an increasingly deviant sexual practice.

Perhaps as a result of this change, the prostitution transaction and the needs of clients came under political scrutiny for the first time. Increasingly, men who needed prostitutes were represented as sexual deviants (that is, with sexual desires which could not be accommodated within normal sexual relationships) or as social misfits (that is, unable to forge relationships with normal women, perhaps because of a lack of English). This was most obvious in the mid-1960s when the issue of migrant men's sexual needs – and the representation of migrant men as a sexual 'other' to normal male sexuality – provided the occasion for parliaments publicly to assert the deviancy of prostitution within Australian culture, for the first time. In this context it is not surprising that parliaments moved to increase the legal surveillance and criminal penalties attached to prostitution.

My analysis of parliamentary debates shows that the Wolfenden Report was frequently cited by Australian parliamentarians from the late 1950s onwards and that its general approach – particularly pertaining to the privacy of sexual behaviour, the consensual nature of prostitution, and the desirability of a separation between law and morality – was widely adopted by Australian legislators in the ensuing decade. I have suggested that this had a particularly detrimental impact upon the way that prostitute women were represented within political discourse; the balance of competing discourses about prostitutes shifted in the post-war period so that prostitutes were increasingly regarded by parliamentarians as bad and lazy women rather than as victims. This trend intensified in the period 1955–69 as a result of the negative, parasitic images of prostitutes deployed within the Wolfenden Report and as result of Wolfenden's conceptualisation of prostitution as a wholly consensual sexual transaction.

CHAPTER 5

Libertarian Moments,
1970–75

In the early 1970s the sex industry in Australia appeared to be expanding rapidly; there was a significant increase in the number of sexually explicit publications available on the Australian market as well as a proliferation of visible prostitution in the form of massage parlours in most capital cities. At the same time traditional political approaches to the control of the sex industry were increasingly being called into question. In the late 1960s a popular opposition to censorship laws and practices emerged in Australia and this made less tenable the comprehensive prohibitions on the purchase of sexually explicit material which were in place. The increasing importance of sexual discourses that emphasised the liberatory potential of sex and the illegitimacy of legal intervention in the private, sexual activities of adults also tended to reduce the effectiveness of additional controls on the prostitution industry.

This chapter is in four sections. The first examines important features of Australian sexual culture in the 1970s. I show that premarital sex had become a 'normal' feature of sexual relations by the 1970s and that in sexological discourse there was increasing emphasis upon the desirability of sexual experimentation. The pornography industry expanded considerably and sexual liberation movements – such as the Women's Liberation Movement and Gay Liberation – appeared in Australia. Libertarian discourse was, then, becoming an increasingly important feature of Australian sexual culture.

In the second section of this chapter I examine the politico-legal regulation of the pornography industry in Australia during 1970–75. In this period censorship became an important political problem in Australia and governments were increasingly forced to reassess their approach to the control of sexually explicit publications and films. This occurred as libertarian discourse became more influential in the

Commonwealth and in some state parliaments. This will be demonstrated in relation to various censorship reforms – but, in particular, the
introduction of the R classification for adult-only films – proposed and
debated by the Commonwealth parliament between 1969 and 1972.

In the third section of this chapter I show that between 1970 and
1975 the main focus of attention in the political debate about censorship shifted from literature and modern pornographic novels, such as
Portnoy's Complaint, to hard-core magazine pornography which claimed
no literary or artistic merit. In the late 1960s and early 1970s, public
concern focused on the official censorship of literary novels, but the
establishment of sex shops in many capital cities during 1972 fundamentally reoriented the political debate about censorship towards the
issue of commercial pornography. I argue that this shift (in all states
except Queensland) was due to the expansion of the pornography
industry, the establishment of an international trade in hard-core
pornography, and a growing domestic concern to ensure that adults
had the freedom to consume sexually explicit material, including
pornography, if they so desired. As a result, between 1973 and 1975, all
states except Queensland adopted new regulatory schemes for the
control of pornography. These maintained strict controls on the sale of
pornography to children and on the public display of material which
could cause public offence, but extended to adults the right to purchase and consume what they chose. I argue that the establishment of
regulatory schemes represented a significant shift away from traditional political strategies which emphasised the need to prohibit
pornography. This shift was due to the increasing unpopularity of
censorship controls on adults and to aspects of the sexual culture
which linked the right to consume pornography with a more general
sexual freedom. My analysis of parliamentary debates demonstrates the
key role played by libertarian discourse in this process.

In the fourth section of this chapter I examine the politico-legal
regulation of the prostitution industry in Australia during the early
1970s and the emergence of feminist and civil libertarian claims that
prostitution should be decriminalised. I show that while new anti-prostitution measures were adopted by the Queensland government in
this period, two Labor state governments actively resisted the elaboration of additional legal controls on prostitution. This was in spite of
fairly intense pressure associated with the growth of prostitution in
massage parlours. I argue that an emerging political resistance to the
laws against prostitution was due to the growing political importance
of discourses which emphasised the illegitimacy of state intervention in
the private, consensual sexual activities of adults. Although these
discourses had been influential for some time (see Chapters 3 and 4)

and were widely deployed within the anti-censorship movement (that is, in relation to pornography) they had not previously been applied to the issue of prostitution.

Australia in the 1970s

In the 1970s Australia's long period of post-war prosperity came to an abrupt end. The growth in gross domestic product declined rapidly from 8.6 per cent in 1968–69 to 3.8 per cent in 1972–73. There was also a marked acceleration in price and wage inflation from 1969–70 onwards and a steep increase in unemployment, particularly after 1974. However, the political culture became visibly less conservative during this period with the election of Labor governments in South Australia (1970) and Western Australia (1971) and with the election of the Whitlam government federally (1972).[1]

As a result of both the sexual revolution and long-term demographic changes, the status of normal relations between men and women was visibly transformed by the early 1970s. Australians clearly began to delay marriage and childrearing[2] while the incidence of divorce increased rapidly, particularly after the introduction of easier, no-fault divorce in the *Family Law Act* (1975).[3] One important indicator of new family patterns and of long-term changes in the status of women was the increase in married women's participation in the paid workforce; between 1966 and 1983 the proportion of married women in the workforce increased from 29 to 42.6 per cent (Hugo 1986: 266).

By the early 1970s pre-marital sexual intercourse had also become commonplace and perhaps the new norm. In his 1974 survey of 1442 Australian women, Bell found that younger women were more likely than older women to have experienced pre-marital sexual intercourse; in fact he found a progressive resort to pre-marital intercourse by successive generations of women. Thus, 92 per cent of women aged 25 years or less, 85 per cent aged 26–30, 70 per cent aged 31–40, 58 per cent aged 41–50 and 38 per cent of those over 50 years of age had had pre-marital sex (1974: 97). Among those who were married, the younger women had more communication with their husbands about sex, initiated sex more frequently, enjoyed a more diverse range of sexual practices with their husbands, and were more likely to have regular orgasms (1974: 128–32). At least if measured by Masters and Johnson's concept of sexual adequacy (see Chapter 3), it would appear that the sexual revolution had significantly improved the lives of young Australian women and married couples.

The generalisation of pre-marital sexual intercourse was supported by the wide application of contraceptive practices. By the mid-1970s, nearly one-third of Australian women aged 15–44 were taking the contraceptive pill, a trend that was facilitated by the removal of a sales tax on the Pill and its inclusion on pharmaceutical benefit lists after 1973. With the introduction of Medibank in 1975, abortion too attracted a medical rebate (Siedlecky and Wyndham 1990: 63). Laws against abortion were liberalised in South Australia in 1970 and in the Northern Territory during 1974. Similar measures were introduced through new case law in both Victoria and New South Wales.[4] Hugo (1986: 73–4) suggests that as a result of these legal changes there was a significant increase in the number of abortions performed during the 1970s and the number of sterilisation operations increased threefold over the decade.

These trends were examined by the Royal Commission on Human Relationships (chaired by Justice Elizabeth Evatt), which was appointed by the Commonwealth in 1974 to investigate 'the family, social, educational and legal and sexual aspects of male–female relationships with particular emphasis on the concept of responsible parenthood'. In its *Final Report* (3: 1) tabled in 1977 the commission noted that the modern 'capacity to avoid pregnancy affects social controls on sexual behaviour'. Now that sexual behaviour could be perceived independently from its consequences, the traditional link between human sexuality and fertility (and the social customs and values that proceeded from this link) were said to be disintegrating. In the wake of this trend, new sexual roles – emphasising sexual intimacy, pleasure and experimentation – also became available for men and women.

This changing emphasis within normal sexual relations is evident in the sex advice literature of the 1970s. Popular sex manuals – such as Alex Comfort's *The Joy of Sex* – became runaway best-sellers. *The Joy of Sex* was first published in 1972 and had sold more than 7 million copies by the early 1980s (Brunt 1982: 161). As D'Emilio and Freedman (1988: 330) argue, texts like these openly endorsed sexual experimentation and did so 'in language that twenty years earlier had been the province of pornography'. They aimed at the 'childfree' heterosexual couple and promoted 'high-grade sex' as a full-time leisure activity for adults (Brunt 1982: 161–3).

The early 1970s was also a period of significant and world-wide expansion in the pornography industry. In the United States triple-X-rated films – such as *Deep Throat* and *The Devil in Miss Jones* – attracted mass audiences and, for the first time, a large number of ordinary married couples (D'Emilio and Freedman 1988: 328; Williams 1989: 99–100). In the field of publications, adult bookstores which sold hard-core sex magazines and paperbacks opened in many American cities. Moreover, 'A substantial portion of newsstand sales came from publications that the police would have seized a decade earlier' (D'Emilio and Freedman 1988: 328).

In Australia a significant increase in the number and range of pornographic publications was visible by the early 1970s. This was due to several interrelated factors. First, changes in printing technology – in particular the development of multilith printing and photocopying machines – significantly reduced the cost of producing printed material: the result was an upsurge in the total number of all publications (including pornographic ones) on the Australian market (NSWPD 103: 3909). Second, the growth of the pornography industry in the United States imposed new cultural and economic pressures on nations such as Australia. Third, as will be shown later in this chapter, changes in the political mode of regulating the distribution of obscene and indecent literature within Australia significantly expanded the range of what adults were legally permitted to read and view from 1973 onwards. The combination of a reduction in legal controls and an increase in both supply and demand meant that the pornography industry expanded rapidly in Australia during the early 1970s.

Various sexual liberation movements – Women's Liberation and Gay Liberation (Altman 1971) – also appeared in this period. The Women's Liberation Movement in particular was to have some influence on political debate in Australia during the 1970s. Members of the Women's Liberation Movement joined mainstream political parties (particularly the Labor Party) and formed pressure groups such as the Women's Electoral Lobby. As a result, an increasing feminist influence on law and public policy is evident in Australia after the election of the Whitlam Labor government in 1972.

Censorship Debates in the Early 1970s

By 1970 censorship had become an important political issue in Australia. Dutton and Harris (1970: 6) argue that there was an 'urgent public feeling' which suggested that current censorship practices were outdated and undemocratic. Politicians, police officers, magistrates and judges were no longer regarded as competent to decide 'what expressions are aesthetically accepted in the community standards of modern Australians'. For a growing number of Australians, then, the call to end censorship was a call for a thoroughgoing cultural freedom.

Initially, this was a call that pertained to high culture – art films and literature – and not to popular culture and pornography. However, by the early 1970s, this distinction was becoming less viable. On the one hand, many modern novels, such as *Portnoy's Complaint*, adopted pornographic codes of representation. On the other hand, adult citizens were increasingly demanding the right to consume pornography as a sign of their cultural and sexual freedom. Thus, what began in the post-war period as a political movement against the censorship of novels with literary merit became, in the late 1960s and early 1970s, a movement against all censorship.

An important turning point in the political history of Australian censorship occurred during 1970–71 when the Commonwealth parliament debated the issue of censorship for the first time in more than thirty years. The Minister for Customs and Excise, Don Chipp, argued that, because censorship had become a significant political issue (and 'an organised movement against censorship' had recently appeared within the Australian community), a complete overhaul of censorship policy and practice was necessary. As 'the pace of social change had quickened', the existing censorship regulations were inadequate to cope with the demands of a modern society (HofR 68: 3372). Thus, there was a new 'problem' for government to deal with.

Chipp did not, however, make a case for the abandonment of all censorship. While he saw censorship as a direct infringement of individual liberties, he argued that it was a necessary evil, one that was required for the protection of society, and children in particular. Citing J. S. Mill's famous 'harm principle', Chipp said that the only purpose for which mankind was warranted, individually or collectively, in interfering with the liberty of action of others was self-protection. Mill, however, argued that the harm principle should not usually be applied to actions that were merely objectionable, or to ideas, speech and publications (Mill 1859). Chipp, on the other hand, argued that the community had a right, through its democratically elected government, to inhibit the circulation of material which it as a community found objectionable (HofR 68: 3372–3).

Signalling a major change of direction in Commonwealth censorship policy, Chipp told the parliament that, while censorship decisions had previously been made by reference to the concept of obscenity (that is, the tendency to deprave and corrupt), future decisions would be made by reference to the more flexible entity of community standards. Although citizens were entitled to 'as little censorship as possible within the limits set by community standards', and were ultimately responsible as individuals for their own censorship decisions, citizens were also members of a state established for their common good. Thus, there were limits on both individual liberties and the degree of government intervention with respect to censorship. This approach sought a new balance between individual rights and the demands of the common good (HofR 68: 3373–6) and, as such, resembled the modified liberal approaches deployed during the 1960s (see Chapter 3).

While this balanced approach won widespread support among state and federal parliamentarians, it did not meet with universal approval. Some conservatives argued that the preservation of standards of 'normal, decent conduct' and the repudiation of 'extreme permissiveness' were more important than the extension of individual freedoms because 'permissiveness ... eventually sows ... the seeds of [social] destruction' (HofR 71: 449–51, 464, 491; SAPD 1971–2, 2: 2076, 2141). As in the 1960s, therefore, there was no support among conservatives for the suggestion that adults should be free to view whatever they wanted. On the other hand, there were those who emphasised the priority of individual freedoms over the common good and adopted a thoroughgoing libertarianism along the lines suggested by J. S. Mill. As one member of the Commonwealth parliament argued, 'some significant social harm must be shown to be caused before free speech should be interfered with'. In this approach, any determination of the common good was regarded as both arbitrary and repressive: 'The creative spirit and genius of man [sic] cannot and should not be inhibited, restrained or controlled by a monolithic state big brother' (HofR 71: 453, 448). This process was exacerbated by what was said to be the irrationality and subjectivism of Australia's censorship laws and practices. As Bill Hayden argued:

> I find censorship today in Australia a mass of confusing and conflicting laws, and of censorship bodies. I have doubts about the qualifications of many people who are censors. I find that there is much inconsistency in the way in which censorship practices are applied. I find that there is an inability in the law to define obscenity as, indeed, there must be because after all it is a subjective term [HofR 68: 3382].

The libertarian discourse had some of its most voluble advocates among Labor members of the Commonwealth parliament. At least three members – Moss Cass, Dick Klugman and Gordon Bryant – advocated the complete abolition of censorship (HofR 71: 442–3, 451–3, 466–7). Others – such as Bill Hayden and Clyde Cameron – argued for a complete de-censorship of sexual material in relation to adults, but suggested that there was a need to maintain censorship controls over the representation of violence (HofR 68: 3376–82; 71: 457). This latter view was based on social science data which suggested 'the possibility' of a connection between anti-social behaviour and the viewing of violent films, particularly among children. Evidence of a similar relationship between the viewing of pornography and the perpetration of sex crimes was said to be lacking (HofR 68: 3377, 3380).

The use and counter-use of social science data, which first became evident in the 1970–71 censorship debate in the Commonwealth parliament, was to remain an important feature of all subsequent debates in parliament about censorship and pornography. In 1971 several parliamentarians cited a study by the Kinsey Institute as well as the report of the US Commission on Obscenity and Pornography (Lockhart 1970) which suggested that a lack of exposure to 'erotica' in adolescence could be linked to the appearance of anti-social behaviour in adults. In this view, the inability to achieve 'fantasy release' with pornography was a distinguishing feature of rapists and child molesters (HofR 68: 3380; 71: 451–3). For the first time, then, some parliamentarians were arguing that the consumption of pornography was an *aid* to sexual health.

The libertarian approach to censorship was premised on several distinct assumptions, some of which were to have important long-term consequences for future censorship laws and practices. In the first place libertarians assumed that representations were not real in the way that actions were. This meant that, even though a representation was offensive or objectionable, it could not legitimately be prohibited because the basis of all personal liberty was freedom of thought. Representations were 'only ideas' and as such were not an appropriate object of government action; anyway, as Bill Hayden argued, 'we have nothing to fear from them' (HofR 68: 3378). The designation of representations as ideas – and the clear distinction between ideas and actions – was (and remains) an important feature of libertarian approaches to pornography and censorship.

In the second place, the libertarian approach to censorship was premised upon the assumption that photography and film 'mirrors life' (NSWPD 91: 737) and was a medium that could tell the truth about sex and about violence. Chipp was reported to have said to a public meeting in Brisbane that 'the greatest obscenity we can inflict upon our young people is the obscenity of denying them the truth' (cited in QPD 258: 2034). Not to allow the truth to be told permitted distorted, possibly untruthful accounts of life and human behaviour to circulate uncontested in the public domain. As Moss Cass argued, 'because of censorship we render violence almost acceptable because we remove the repugnant aspect' (HofR 71: 443). Thus, allowing young people to view films which depicted the full horror of war (rather than only the heroic fantasies of John Wayne) made it more likely that they would grow up with an aversion to interpersonal violence and war (QPD 258: 2034). In the context of widespread opposition to Australia's involvement in the Vietnam War in 1971, this argument had a great deal of cogency. The suggestion that pornography could tell the truth about women or sexual relations remained uncontested in this period.

In the third place, the libertarian argument for a complete de-censorship of sexual material was premised upon a belief in the essential goodness of sex and on the notion that free sexual expression was both healthy and desirable if personal and social liberation was to be achieved. People were said to have a fundamental right to happiness, 'particularly through sexual experience' (NSWPD 91: 748), while those who opposed the liberalisation of censorship policies were said to have 'a problem of repressed sexuality' and 'something sick in their own sex lives, their own attitude to life and normality' (HofR 68: 3380; HofR 71: 442). Moreover, the consumption of pornography was seen to have some distinct therapeutic effects for the sexually disadvantaged. As Clyde Cameron argued, 'pictures of nudity provide an outlet for the person [sic] who is unmarried or has a sex problem' (HofR 71: 459). Others also suggested that the use of pornography might be necessary for those 'people [sic] who can't get a beaut bird into bed' (Henry Mayer, cited in NSWPD 91: 748).

It appears, then, that the libertarian argument against censorship was also premised on the assumption that good sex was both heterosexual and a social activity that men controlled. Debate clearly took place on terms that were both heterosexist and masculinist. One member of parliament argued that there was 'a strong case for allowing those who want to see films containing sex scenes ... to do so'. However, this speaker said he was 'talking about normal, natural sex scenes' and not 'perversions' such as homosexuality (HofR 71: 457–8). In his comments on the scientific study which showed a relationship between a lack of exposure to pornography and the appearance of sexual deviations (see above), Dick Klugman concluded that 'a reasonable exposure to erotica, particularly during adolescence, reflects a high degree of sexual interest and curiosity that correlates with adult patterns of acceptable heterosexual interest and practice' (HofR 71: 452).

Thus the free availability of erotic material was seen as capable of preventing the appearance of 'perversions' such as homosexuality; pornography could have a beneficial effect by educating young people into normal adult patterns of sexuality. But the scientific evidence cited by Klugman dealt only with *male* sexual offenders and did not address the absence of women from this category of criminals. Moreover, in most Western cultures, a high degree of heterosexual interest and curiosity is considered unproblematic only in *male* adolescents. So, while the scientific evidence presented in parliament during 1970–71 indicated that the consumption of pornography assisted in the construction of so-called normal male sexuality, there was no acknowledgement of the often problematic nature of this normal male sexuality (for women and/or non-heterosexuals).

In his closing comments during the 1971 censorship debate, the Minister for Customs and Excise said that the changes in censorship policy did not mean that hard-core pornography would be allowed into Australia and suggested that material 'with no literary, sociological or artistic merit' would continue to be banned. However, he raised an explicitly masculinist standard for this process by nominating *Playboy* magazine as the 'benchmark beyond which we will not go in permissiveness as far as sex is concerned' (HofR 71: 500–1). While *Playboy* was described as 'a high quality magazine' with 'excellent articles on political and sociological subjects' it was not generally noticed that *Playboy* pictorials displayed naked women only and that the magazine was marketed for a male viewing public.

The new approach to censorship mooted in the Commonwealth parliament during 1970–71 was applied in the first instance to film censorship. In October 1970 Chipp announced the introduction of a new R (Restricted) classification for films which were deemed suitable for adults only (HofR 70: 2928–9). This meant that, for the first time in Australia, children between the ages of six and eighteen were to be legally excluded from the exhibition of films which were found to be unsuitable for them.[5] The introduction of the R classification signalled an important shift in censorship policy and significantly extended the range of what adults were legally permitted to view in Australian cinemas.

Enabling legislation for the R film classification was passed in all Australian states during 1971.[6] While there was a marked level of consensus in state parliaments about the need for an adults-only category of films, there were also some important regional variations. In the New South Wales parliament, for example, members deployed a set of arguments similar to those in the federal parliament. A balanced approach to the issue of film censorship was proposed by the government and this attracted wide cross-party support. However, the proposal was opposed by conservatives as well as by several radical libertarians (NSWPD 91: 742–8). Moreover, for the first time in an Australian parliament, explicitly feminist arguments about pornography were deployed (although not by a female member of parliament). The member for Port Kembla, George Petersen, said that he supported the arguments made by the Women's Liberation Movement that pornography 'treats women as sex objects for male gratification'. At this point, the Acting Speaker (Douglas Darby) ruled that Petersen's comments were out of order on the grounds that 'problems of sex and the equality, so called, of the sexes' were not directly relevant to the bill under debate (NSWPD 91: 748–9). This sort of comment would be extremely unlikely in the present political context!

By contrast to the situation in New South Wales, conservative discourse was widely deployed during debate on the R classification in the Queensland parliament. However, the government assured members that the new legislation did not mean an end to film censorship, even for adults, and that pornographic films would definitely not be permitted (QPD 258: 2026). While the Labor Opposition supported the R classification, members did not offer any libertarian or feminist arguments. Instead, they emphasised the urgent need for more family films and for a local film industry which reflected Australian cultural values.

Pornography in the Political Arena

In spite of the pro-pornography stance adopted by some parliamentarians during the censorship debates of 1970–71, it was the soft-core magazine *Playboy* that marked the limit of what was legally available in this period by way of pornography. Moreover, the main focus of political concern was still the censorship of high literature and film and the need to ensure that films and publications with literary merit were not subjected to oppressive censorship requirements. As in the 1960s, then, debate in parliament tended to focus on the distinctions between literature and pornography. While pornography was still seen to be a legitimate object of censorship concerns, literature was not.

In the early 1970s this situation was subjected to a set of intense challenges. Australian publishers began to confront state obscenity laws and Commonwealth censorship regulations by printing, within Australia, texts that had already been classified by the Commonwealth as prohibited imports. Jerry Rubin's *Do It*, C. H. Rolph's *The Trial of Lady Chatterley*, Barry Humphries's *The Wonderful World of Barry MacKenzie*, Stephen Vizinczey's *In Praise of Older Women* and Leonard Cohen's *Beautiful Losers* were all produced in this way.

But the most controversial banned book in the early 1970s was Philip Roth's *Portnoy's Complaint* which, in June 1969, was classified as a prohibited import on the advice of the National Literature Board of Review. This prohibition was not lifted until June 1971, although *Portnoy's Complaint* was published within Australia during 1970. This left a response squarely in the hands of state governments as to whether they would launch prosecutions under state obscenity laws.

In New South Wales, the Australian publishers of *Portnoy's Complaint* were taken to trial twice although, on both occasions, the jury could not agree on a verdict. The case was eventually dropped by the Attorney-General. Coleman (1974: 47) comments that after this debacle, the New South Wales government decided against the prosecution of novels which claimed any literary merit. This included novels such as Leonard Cohen's *Beautiful Losers* which was published in New South Wales during 1972 despite a Customs ban instituted in 1969.

In South Australia the (Labor) Attorney-General refused to allow a prosecution to proceed against *Portnoy's Complaint*. Premier Don Dunstan argued:

> with regard to adult persons, the view of the Government is that they should read and see what they choose to read and see, however unfortunate we think their choice to be. It is not for the Government or anyone else to tell people what they may read or what they may not read: it is for the people themselves to say [SAPD 1970–71: 1140].

Conditions for the adults-only sale of *Portnoy's Complaint* were set down in South Australia.

In Western Australia, the same book was found to be an obscene publication. However, as the court also established its literary merit, all charges were dismissed (HofR 71: 17). In Victoria the Australian publishers of *Portnoy's Complaint* were fined $100 despite the fact that two well-known authors testified as to the literary merit of the book. In Tasmania an indictment was secured, but not enforced, against a book-seller who distributed *Portnoy's Complaint*. In a similar case in Queensland a bookseller was fined $20 (Coleman 1974: 47).

In the end, then, *Portnoy's Complaint* was sold legally in South Australia, New South Wales and Western Australia but not in Tasmania, Victoria or Queensland. This inconsistency provoked a large number of questions in Australian parliaments during 1970–71. It also led to claims that point-of-entry (Customs) regulations and the 1967 agreement between the Commonwealth and state governments on texts of literary and/or artistic merit (see Chapter 3) were unable to deal with the problems posed by a new generation of literature. In the first place, this was said to be because Customs regulations were easily circumvented by publishers printing Australian editions; once publishers adopted this strategy, state governments could not win. They could take no action (a move which would be unpopular among the more conservative sections of the electorate) or they could choose to launch unpopular prosecutions under state obscenity laws. In the second place, existing laws and regulations were seen to be inadequate because literature itself was changing; novels which claimed literary merit were increasingly assuming many of the same codes as pornography. Consequently, clear distinctions could not always be drawn, by censors and policy-makers, between literature and pornography.

But probably the most important reason why existing laws were seen to be inadequate was that influential sections of the electorate were now demanding the right to consume pornography. Thus, even if a distinction could be drawn between literature and pornography, there was no longer general agreement that this was a distinction between legitimate and illegitimate publications (that is, between publications which should or should not be censored).

Sex Shops

The public debate in Australia about *Portnoy's Complaint* was one of the last occasions that the issue of censorship focused on novels which claimed literary merit.[7] After 1972 the censorship debate focused almost entirely on commercial sex establishments or sex shops which sold imported pornographic magazines and sex aids. Sex shops opened in several Australian capital cities in 1972 and provoked a variety of official responses. In Victoria, the government moved to prohibit the public display of goods offered for sale within sex shops by amending the *Police Offences Act*. Introducing this legislation, the Chief Secretary, Rupert Hamer, said: 'In the view of the government, it is contrary to the public interest that [a sex shop] ... should be at complete liberty to display itself and its goods and make open invitation to the public at large' (VPD 306: 4886). The new laws increased the penalties for being in possession of obscene articles for commercial gain and for the exhibition of indecent or obscene pictures and printed matter; higher penalties were imposed where the offender was a company. The Labor Opposition in the Victorian parliament raised no substantial objections to this amendment (VPD 307: 5639–41).

In Perth the opening of a sex shop called Ecstasy in 1972 also produced a public furore and calls for government action (see, for example, WAPD 193: 1008; 194: 1700, 1830, 1565). Although Premier Tonkin indicated his commitment to closing this shop down, the Labor Party caucus and the Trades Hall argued that this was contrary to Labor – and therefore, government – policy; that is, adults were to be free to read and view whatever they wished as long as children were protected and there was no public exposure of offensive material (WAPD 193: 508, 650).

After a meeting of Commonwealth and state ministers in August 1972, the Commonwealth agreed to restrict the importation of sex aids in an attempt to restrict the stock available to sex shops (WAPD 196: 4435). In 1973, Premier Tonkin indicated that several prosecutions of sex shop proprietors were proceeding under the *Indecent Publications*

Act although 'many articles for sale in the [sex] shop are not covered by this Act' (WAPD 198: 554).

Two sex shops opened in Adelaide during 1972. As a result there were repeated calls by Opposition members in parliament for the government to take some action; there were also a large number of public petitions on this matter. However, the Dunstan government emphasised Labor policy and the importance of preserving individual freedoms, as it had done in the case of *Portnoy's Complaint*. Thus, even if people made the 'unfortunate move of patronising sex shops' and consuming pornography, it was not the government's role to intervene (as long as children were protected and there was no public offence caused by the display of unseemly material). Between 1970 and 1973 the Dunstan government faced repeated questions and criticism in parliament about what the Opposition called its non-policy on the censorship of pornography and on sex shops.

By the end of 1972, then, the attention of state governments around Australia was beginning to focus on an emergent pornography industry rather than on the issue of how or whether literary novels should be censored. In 1975 one member of the New South Wales parliament argued that a 'dramatic deterioration in the standard of material available to the public' was occurring and that no 'enlightened person' was now bothered about the censorship of hardback novels such as *Portnoy's Complaint* and *Fanny Hill*. Hard-core commercial pornography was now the main problem.

The Shift from Prohibition to Classification

In 1972 a reforming Labor government came to power at Commonwealth level. Its attempts to reform the existing censorship system raised the pitch of political debates about pornography and censorship in the early 1970s. In 1973, for example, the new Minister for Customs, Senator Lionel Murphy, announced that there would be no further prosecutions under Section 4A of the *Customs and Excise Act* which pertained to the importation of obscene and indecent publications. This amounted to a virtual abandonment of point-of-entry controls over pornography, a move which forced the states to look to their own laws.

In 1973 and again in 1974 state ministers responsible for censorship met with the Commonwealth minister in order to forge an agreement about national uniformity in relation to obscene and indecent literature for which no literary or artistic merit was claimed. The idea was that the new laws and regulations would not constrain the rights which adults were now deemed to have to read and view whatever they wished, even if that was hard-core pornography. The new laws and regulations were also to apply at the point of sale (that is, retail outlets) rather than at the point of entry into Australia.

All states, except Queensland, agreed that pornographic publications which would normally be prosecuted under state obscenity laws would, in future, be subject to classification. Classified publications that were distributed according to the established guidelines (designed to protect children and prevent public offence) would be exempt from laws relating to obscene and indecent publications. The Commonwealth was to be responsible for the initial classification of both imported and locally produced publications, but the states were to be free to establish their own classification processes if they deemed this necessary.

Between 1973 and 1975 South Australia, Victoria, Western Australia and New South Wales all passed legislation designed to implement this scheme. Significant regional variations are evident in the legislation enacted; these variations were often indicative of particular historical and political configurations around the issue of pornography. In South Australia, for example, the Dunstan Labor government clearly sought to extend the freedom of adults in relation to the consumption of pornography while also protecting the interests of minors. *The Classification of Publications Act* (1974) established a Classification of Publications Board which had the power both to review and to classify all publications distributed in that state. Publications that dealt with matters of sex, drug addiction, crime, cruelty, violence or other 'revolting or abhorrent phenomena', in a manner that was likely to cause offence to reasonable adult persons, or that was unsuitable for minors, could be classified as restricted publications. It was up to the board to determine the conditions under which the sale, exhibition or dissemination of a restricted publication was to be allowed. The board could also classify a publication as an unrestricted publication or refuse to classify it altogether (such a publication was not illegal but it was vulnerable to prosecution under state obscenity laws).

As with Labor policy generally, two principles guided the actions of the board in South Australia. First, adults were regarded as entitled to read and view what they wished in private or in public; second, members of the community were entitled to protection (extending both to themselves and those in their care) from exposure to unsolicited material that they found offensive. Where the application of these principles led to conflicting conclusions, the board was required to exercise its powers in a manner that would achieve a reasonable balance. This issue of balance created some dissent in the parliament. The Legislative Council returned the original bill to the House of

Assembly with a series of amendments, the most important of which aimed to change the balance of decision-making in favour of the protection of minors. The government refused this amendment (SAPD 1973–74: 2795).

In Victoria the *Police Offences (Publications) Act* had two principal purposes – to establish an advisory board on publications and to substantially increase penalties for breaches of the Act in relation to obscene and indecent material. The government argued that these latter measures were necessary because 'the volume of erotic and obscene material circulating in the community has increased dramatically'; the Vice Squad was said to have 19 tons of pornography currently awaiting destruction (VPD 312: 5409).

The Victorian board was empowered to advise the minister on the sale, distribution and exhibition of all publications in public places. Publications which the board deemed restricted could not be displayed in public – that is, in the window of a shop or on open shelves within a shop. The sale of restricted publications was prohibited to persons under the age of eighteen years. The board could also decline to classify a publication (leaving it vulnerable to prosecution under state obscenity laws). While final authority lay with the minister, he or she could not restrict a publication except on the advice of the board (but could decide not to restrict a publication that the board had recommended should be restricted).

In 1973 an Obscene and Indecent Publications Bill was debated in the New South Wales parliament. This bill had a much wider ambit than either the South Australian or Victorian legislation, and eventually lapsed due to lack of support. It prohibited advertising by sex shops and the display of sex aids, 'in a manner visible from a public place or to a person who has not consented to or requested them to be shown to him [*sic*]' (NSWPD 102: 3849–50). It also aimed to re-enact the provisions relating to restricted publications which had been introduced in 1967 (see Chapter 3) and to extend these so that the sale or hire of a restricted publication to a person under eighteen years of age was prohibited. Restricted publications were not to be exempt from the operation of the indecency laws (NSWPD 102: 3850–1). The bill also sought to tighten the law in obscenity cases; the terms *obscenity* and *indecency* were to be assimilated, in order to avoid 'the confusion which at present exists by material being variously labelled obscene or indecent' (NSWPD 102: 3847). It was intended that the new law could find a whole publication obscene even if part of that publication was not. These measures were clearly designed to address some of the difficulties that had been raised by *Crowe v. Graham* (see Chapter 3) as well as the intense legal and political activism which surrounded the issue of obscenity in New South Wales during the early 1970s (Bacon 1972).

The 1973 New South Wales bill also sought to revoke provisions (introduced in 1967) for trial by jury in all obscenity cases. The government argued that this was necessary because of the huge backlog of cases waiting to be heard at jury trials; it was said that these would be more efficiently dealt with by a magistrate and that 'the time and expense involved in jury trial' was unwarranted because publications presently being prosecuted were only 'cheap, salacious [publications] with no possible claim to literary merit' (NSWPD 102: 3847–8).

The bill attracted a great deal of criticism both inside and outside parliament. Some Labor members, for example, opposed the removal of trial by jury and those aspects of the bill which aimed to extend police powers in relation to obtaining search warrants and entering premises. The Leader of the Opposition, Neville Wran, argued that the proposal to abolish trial by jury in obscenity cases had caused widespread public concern. He cited a range of organisations and newspapers that supported the Labor position on this, including the Bar Council of New South Wales, the Council for Civil Liberties, the Literature Board of the Australia Council for the Arts, the Women's Conference of the Labor Party, the State Council of the Liberal Party, the Australian Journalists Association, the *National Times*, the *Sydney Morning Herald*, the *Australian* and the *Sunday Telegraph* (NSWPD 102: 3858–9).

While the 1973 bill eventually lapsed, a new bill – one that focused more on the classification of pornography – was presented, and passed two years later. The 1975 Indecent Articles and Classified Publications Bill provided for the establishment of a Publications Classification Board to replace the existing State Advisory Committee on Publications. The board's role was to advise the minister on the classification of all publications referred to it; referrals were to be by individual publishers or the minister. Classified publications that were distributed according to their classification guidelines were to be exempt from prosecution under existing obscenity laws (NSWPD 116: 4553).

Whereas the 1967 Act (see Chapter 3) provided for the classification of publications as either restricted or unrestricted (and did not prevent the sale of restricted publications to minors), the 1975 bill provided for three classification categories: restricted, unrestricted and direct sale. The sale or hire (and the offer to sell or hire) of a restricted or direct-sale publication to a person under the age of eighteen years became an offence under the new Act. As in the 1967 Act, the public sale and display of restricted publications was prohibited; sale and display was to be permitted only within the confines of a shop. However, direct-sale publications could not even be displayed within a shop; they could be sold only as a result of an unsolicited personal request or by mail order (NSWPD 116: 4554).

The 1975 legislation also addressed sex shops in response to the 'many complaints' which had been received by the government. Most of these were apparently about 'flagrant advertising' and the public display (for example in sex shop windows) of articles for sale. The new Act prohibited sex shops from advertising the nature of their business and from exhibiting or displaying any sex aids in or within view of any public place. Thus, it was the 'objectionable advertising and public display that will be prohibited by the legislation, not the sale of the so-called sex aids themselves' (NSWPD 116: 4552).

By 1975, then, all states except Queensland had shifted from an approach which emphasised the need to prohibit pornography to one which regulated its consumption and display. In the next section of this chapter I look at changes in discursive formations within parliamentary debates which made this legal shift both likely and possible. I then go on to examine the situation in Queensland in order to ascertain why this state took a different path at this time.

The Debate in Parliament about the Classification of Pornography

In the early 1970s parliamentarians began to use the term *pornography* to denote a new field of mass-produced pictorial representations of explicit sexual activity. The concern with literary material (that is, novels) disappeared and parliamentarians focused on both identifying and managing problems seen to be associated with hard-core pornography. In 1975 one member of the New South Wales parliament commented on this change. He said that there had been a 'dramatic deterioration in the standard of material available to the public' over the previous two years. No enlightened person was now said to be bothered about the censorship of hardback novels such as *Portnoy's Complaint* or *Fanny Hill* because, all over Australia, 'cheap filthy tabloid publications' such as *Screw* and *Ribald* were available. These contained explicit pictorial depictions of sex and there was said to be a 'vast difference' between sex being depicted pictorially and by the written word (NSWPD 116: 4565–7).

As in the 1960s, a range of competing discourses about pornography and censorship were deployed in state parliaments. But in the early 1970s liberal and libertarian discourse came to dominate parliamentary debate, with conservative views occupying the margins. This trend was subject to a great deal of regional variation. In South Australia, for example, there was no evidence of the rampant sexual libertarianism which was such a marked feature of the debate in New South Wales and Victoria. The Labor government in South Australia deployed a discourse about the need for a calm and pragmatic, administrative response to the issue of pornography. In 1973 the Premier, Don Dunstan, welcomed 'the new approach to censorship that has emerged in Australia over the last few years'. He argued that the old censorship laws were patronising and paternalistic and struck 'at the basis of a person's moral autonomy by taking away rational choice in the selection of reading material. Moreover, the very existence of censorship implies the possibility of its use for sinister purposes'. On the other hand, Dunstan argued, it was necessary to address problems which arose from the relaxation of censorship controls. Citizens were entitled to be protected from the 'public flaunting' of material which was personally offensive to them; also children, whose judgements were immature, needed to be protected (SAPD 1973–74: 1688). This sort of approach was very similar to the balanced or modified liberal approach to censorship mooted by Don Chipp in the Commonwealth parliament in 1970.

In Victoria and New South Wales (where the Labor Party was in opposition), parliamentary debate on the classification of pornography ranged much more widely around this modified liberal approach, with both extreme libertarianism and extreme conservatism being evident.[8] Libertarian parliamentarians argued that 'adults should not be told by a law that they cannot read certain material', and that everyone should have the freedom to read what they wanted to read *even* if that was pornography (NSWPD 117: 4585). In the New South Wales parliament one of the most notable exponents of the libertarian position was the Member for Illawarra, George Petersen. He argued strongly against the 1973 Obscene and Indecent Publications Bill and cited several reasons (NSWPD 102: 3908–13). In the first place, he suggested that the proposed legislation would deny a large number of people the freedom to read what they wished without furnishing proof that this material was in any way harmful. 'Girlie magazines' were said to be sold mostly in working-class suburbs because, in middle-class suburbs, people with a 'middle-class morality' pressured their newsagents not to stock these publications. But the suppression of such magazines was represented as 'legislation for the enforcement of sex according to conventional standards'; that is, sex in marriage and sex in the missionary position only. Thus, Petersen regarded the proposed legislation as a means of suppressing both working-class sexuality and other forms of unconventional sex.

In the second place, Petersen argued that the bill was 'totalitarian and authoritarian' and 'authoritarian power goes with sexual repression'. He contested the (conservative) view that society needed self-denial and self-discipline in sexual matters:

> Disciplined sex! Who would discipline the most wonderful thing in the lives of all men and women – the magnificent life-extending relationship, whereby one person can make contact with another. Quite frankly, there is only one way to enjoy sex: that is, to enjoy it on a basis of non-exploitive mutuality. But unfortunately, this conflicts with the competitive, elitist and authoritarian mores of capitalist society and, indeed, of all authoritarian societies.

As has already been suggested, this representation of sex as an essentially good and healthy activity (although vulnerable to capitalist corruption) was a characteristic feature of libertarian discourse. Claims for de-censorship were, then, premised on what was seen as the need to liberate essentially good and healthy human endeavours.

Finally, Petersen argued that the bill was 'contrary to the growing liberality of public attitudes to censorship laws' and would represss the free publication of material of intrinsic worth. This was not, however, a completely coherent position. On the one hand, he argued that girlie magazines such as *Ribald* and *Kings Cross Whisper* 'have very little social value; in fact they simply reinforce the existing stereotyped idea of the male society's domination of women ... [and] they simply reinforce existing norms of sexuality'. On the other hand, however, Petersen defended the right of publishers to produce such 'rubbish' (with the qualification that 'it shall not be forced on any one') on the grounds that some articles of value were being published in these magazines. The examples he gave included a recent issue of *Ribald* in which there was 'a frank description of how a male can restrain orgasm until the female achieves it in their sexual relations'. Similarly, he said that in the latest issue of a 'serious homosexual publication', *Camp Inc.*, there was a beautiful satire called 'The Twilight World of the Heterosexual' which he thought was particularly instructive for heterosexuals. In Petersen's view, then, there was a danger that the proposed legislation would be used to suppress material which had value for society. But his approach contained a clear problem; if pornography did participate in the oppression of women (and of non-hetero sexualities) the main value of permitting the free flow of girlie publications would accrue to heterosexual men.

Libertarian members of parliament tended to refute the suggestion that there was a link between the circulation of sexually explicit material and anti-social behaviour or sex crimes (VPD 312: 5397, 5413;

NSWPD 116: 4579). Both the United States Commission on Obscenity
and Pornography (Lockhart 1970) and a report of the British Arts
Council were cited in support of this position by libertarian parliamentarians in Australia. Libertarians also tended to associate the liberalisation of Australia's censorship laws with a much broader process of
intellectual maturity and social progress. As one member of the Victorian parliament argued:

> Censorship is near and dear to the Australian way of life. There has always
> been a strong vein of authoritarianism running through the Australian
> temperament from the time of the first settlement. ... censorship was like
> quarantine, high tariffs and the white Australia policy – very much part of
> the Australian mystique ... just as there were tariffs or immigration barriers
> to keep immigrants out, there was a kind of censorship barrier which kept
> ideas out [VPD 312: 5400].

In this view, the dismantling of existing censorship barriers would be
conducive to the formation of a healthier, more open and less authoritarian society. As a result of past censorship regimes, Australia was said to
be a long way behind countries such as Denmark where the people have
'fewer sexual hangups' and a lower incidence of all sorts of 'mental
instabilities' such as suicide and alcoholism. One parliamentarian
suggested that since censorship had been abolished in Denmark 'people
didn't worry about looking for obscene things' because 'once the awful
tensions, mysteries and forbidden lure are taken away from crutches,
pubic hair, nipples ... and bottoms they cease to be part of a dank, dark
world apart and merge into the general scene' (VPD 312: 5403).

Within libertarian discourse, then, the display of (women's) bodies
and the consumption of pornography was associated with notions of
moral and sexual health. It was also firmly linked to the production of
a healthy, modern, body politic. In the New South Wales parliament
during 1973 Neville Wran argued that people should be 'free to make
a choice as to the moral path and standards they would adopt' and that
the attempt to maintain strict controls on the consumption of pornography by adults was a 'grotesque step backwards', one 'born of a
misjudgement of what is the current level of tolerance in the community for the views of others'. In his view, the main customers of sex
shops were not 'freaks, kinks, weirdos' but 'ordinary members of the
community who patronise them constantly, regularly and without any
inhibition in order that their lives and pleasures may be all the better'
(NSWPD 102: 3856, 4374–5, 4381).

In a new development for Australian political discourse, the ordinar-

iness of those who patronised sex shops and consumed pornography
was frequently emphasised by libertarian parliamentarians in the early
1970s. There was now said to be a mass market for 'girly magazines and
papers' with more than one hundred thousand such publications
being sold in New South Wales each week. As one parliamentarian
argued, this indicated that there was a public demand for sex publications and it was 'inconceivable' that all such readers were sexual
perverts (NSWPD 103: 3856). Various members of the New South
Wales parliament argued that 'ordinary, decent people read porn'
(NSWPD 116: 4578) and that this was becoming an integral part of
'normal' sexual relations. Ducker, for example, argued:

> By far the majority of husbands and wives live normal, happy and contented
> married lives, sometimes assisted by the sort of technical and detailed mate-
> rial that is now available. No one should be ashamed of it; it is of benefit to
> people in respect of their own development and fulfilment in marriage
> [NSWPD 116: 4396].

For the first time, then, pornography and sex aids were represented in
parliamentary debate as compatible with the ideals and practices of
modern, companionate marriage. Moreover, the ordinary people who
purchased pornography were now seen to have rights as pornography
consumers. These were rights which some libertarian members of the
Labor Party were prepared to represent (NSWPD 116: 4579).

However, the idea that the main consumers of pornography were
normal married couples was not accepted by all parliamentarians – or
even all Labor parliamentarians – at this time. For example, the
member for Bankstown, Nicholas Kearns, argued in 1973 that the
proposed New South Wales legislation failed to address the entrepreneurs who made huge profits from sex shops and from the sale of
pornography. In his view, this sort of capitalist businessman simply
exploited the immature, those with sex 'hang-ups' and those who were
'sexually different from what is normal' (NSWPD 102: 3922).

The growing power of liberal and libertarian approaches to pornography and censorship meant that conservative discourse was now less
dominant. However, in all state parliaments conservatives rejected the
primary role of individual rights in censorship decisions and emphasised the need to preserve a common good. From this perspective it
was the community's duty, via its elected government, to screen out
destructive ideas and pornography which 'fouled the social nest'. This
process was likened to a farmer controlling the growth of noxious
weeds on his property or a housewife keeping a clean home (NSWPD

103: 3683). As the member for Swan Hill argued, there was nothing wrong with censorship. The community had an extensive system for supervising the quality of food production and distribution, housing construction, etc., and there was 'no reason why [obscene material] … should not be treated in the same way as the jerry-built house, the dirty shop, the adulterated sausage or anything else that is below accepted community standards' (NSWPD 103: 5408). In the clearly conservative view of the member for Northcote in New South Wales, Jim Cameron, pornography destroyed the 'ethical climate' of our culture. Its first victim was said to be 'femininity, that distinctive blend of qualities and attributes which have evoked since the beginning of time the special regard and admiration enjoyed by womenfolk. … I believe that regard for womenfolk is the natural response of ordinary males' (NSWPD 103: 3865). Cameron thought that the second 'victim' of pornography was the family and the community at large, for 'progress and licence have never gone hand in hand'. People should not, therefore, be regarded as free to do 'their own thing' in relation to the consumption of pornography (NSWPD 103: 3865, 4576). Children needed to be protected from the corrupting influence of pornography, as did various 'fringe adults'.

The view that, in the first instance, pornography degraded women (and initiated a downward slide which involved the whole community) was also argued by other conservative parliamentarians at this time (see NSWPD 103: 3925, 4383; 116: 4475). Some members of the Labor Party also agreed that pornography 'appalled women' and was generally directed against them. (However, the only proposal for dealing with this was that three of the seven members of the State Advisory Committee on Publications should be women.) However, some Labor members directly refuted the suggestion that pornography destroyed families. They argued that the family was not as vulnerable as conservatives made out. The family was instead represented as a tough and resilient social institution which harboured discerning and intelligent people whose capacities should not be underestimated (see for example NSWPD 103: 4396–7).

As in the 1960s, conservative discourse emphasised the dangers of sexuality. In this view, even 'a man who was normally balanced and decent from the sexual point of view' could be led into the commission of a sex crime by reading 'the wrong type of literature or looking at the wrong type of picture' (VPD 312: 5604–5; see also NSWPD 116: 4575). People had no way of knowing if, like a drug addict with opium, they would be susceptible to the influence of pornography – thus ruining their own lives and the lives of those who came in contact with them (VPD 312: 5405).

According to conservative parliamentarians, 'the majority of Australian citizens' regarded sex as 'something sacred and personal'. It was
not 'animalistic' or obsessed with sexual deviation and violence as most
pornography was (NSWPD 116: 4575). Thus: 'Rightly used, rightly
represented ... the human body is God's artistry and deserves
to be treated as such. When it is ill-treated, misrepresented and
perverted, the devil comes into the scene' (VPD 312: 5406). Because
'real' sex was 'personal' it was not to be 'flaunted' in public; therefore,
the open display of pornography could be represented as a 'gross invasion of privacy' (NSWPD 103: 3914). Pornographers were simply businessmen who destroyed 'the last bastion of privacy, that is, private
sexual life' and exploited 'the weakness and physiological problems of
human beings' (NSWPD 116: 4575).

While libertarian discourse had a significant effect on public policy
in the 1970s, the vast majority of parliamentarians held more moderate
(liberal) views that looked like Don Chipp's balanced approach. In the
New South Wales parliament, for example, one Labor member argued
that both the extreme libertarian and extreme conservative views were
flawed. In his view the conservative approach to erotic and/or pornographic material projected a too pessimistic view of human beings and
human society, one that was also 'patronizing and paternalistic'. On
the other hand, extreme libertarianism should also be rejected because
of the need 'to protect the young and impressionable and to ensure
that the public is not subjected to an invasion of their privacy by material that is salacious or offensive to them' (NSWPD 103: 3855). The
classification of pornography – rather than an outright prohibition –
was now regarded as the best way to achieve a (liberal) balance
between individual rights, the protection of children and the preven-
tion of public offence.

Going It Alone: The Queensland Approach

Queensland was the only state or territory in the early 1970s which did
not adopt a regulatory scheme for the classification of pornography. The
Queensland legislature continued to support a regime of strict prohibition on pornographic material. This was most likely a consequence of
the dominance of conservative discourse in Queensland politics and of
the activities of both the Literature Board of Review (established in
1954) and the Films Board of Review (established in 1974).

Several authors have commented that any manifestations of sexual
libertarianism were strongly suppressed in Queensland during the late
1960s and early 1970s (Thornton 1986; Dutton and Harris 1970). One
example of this was the political response in 1971 to the distribution of

a sex education pamphlet by members of the Women's Liberation Movement. The pamphlet, titled 'Female Sexuality and Education', contained explicit instructions on how to masturbate and was handed to schoolgirls outside several Brisbane high schools. A 20-year-old female arts student was eventually arrested and the Brisbane Women's Liberation Movement had its postal facilities withdrawn (*Courier Mail*, 9 October 1971).

This incident produced cries of outrage in the Queensland parliament. The Member for Toowong, Charles Porter, said that the pamphlet was 'so obscene, so lewd, and such an outrage of unmodesty as to make a hardened whore blush'. The people who distributed this pamphlet were not women 'in the proper sense of the term'. As the girls who received the pamphlets could have sustained 'lasting scars' the Women's Liberation activists were represented as pornographers, 'child molesters' and 'mental rapists' (QPD 257: 821–2).

The Premier, Joh Bjelke-Petersen, indicated the government's intention to take action and amendments to the *Vagrants, Gaming and Other Offences Act* relating to both prostitution and obscene literature passed through the Queensland parliament in December 1971. These provided for indecent as well as obscene publications to be outlawed, increased the penalties for printing and publishing obscene and indecent matter, and introduced new penalties for the distribution of such material to children.

There were to be no further legislative changes in Queensland addressed to obscene and indecent literature during the 1970s. However, the Literature Board of Review was active in prohibiting the distribution of all publications which it deemed to be objectionable. From an average of fewer than four prohibition orders per year in the 1960s, the board began to issue large numbers from 1972 onwards; in the 1970s overall there was an average of forty-six prohibition orders per year.

Initially, the board said that this increase was due to the adoption of new censorship policies by the Commonwealth under the auspices of the Minister for Customs, Don Chipp (QLBR 1971–72: 2). However, the advent of the Whitlam government and the 'abandonment of threshold censorship by the Commonwealth' had produced a significant increase in the board's activities and 'large scale prohibitions' (QLBR 1973–74: 2). The vast majority of the publications which attracted prohibition orders at this time were hard-core sex magazines with titles like *After School Orgy, Sex on a Water Bed, Two Girls and a Vibrator* and *Filthy Rich Nympho*. However, the upmarket and soft-core *Australian Penthouse* was also prohibited in the 1970s, as were several nudist, horror, crime, detective and martial arts publications.

In its annual reports during the 1970s the Literature Board of Review repeatedly deplored the fact that 'objectionable' publications were available in Australia. The main problem was described as 'soft-cover, hard-core pornography magazines, explicitly displaying sex and degrading women' (QLBR 1974–75). Sex was treated as a mere 'spectator sport', with all sorts of sexual perversions represented as 'a normal way of life'. Such publications were said to 'present to all of us (and there is none of us immune from these depravities) the degradation of humans taking their sex as animals' (QLBR 1973–74: 2). As suggested above, this representation of sex as a social danger was characteristic of conservative discourse.

After the election of the Whitlam government, Queensland also came to adopt a different approach to the issue of film censorship from the other states. For the Queensland government, the increasingly liberal censorship practices of the Commonwealth meant that it was essential for the state to have its own censorship laws. The proliferation of violent and sexually explicit films – and their release under an R certificate – was said to be a social danger which would increase sexual promiscuity, venereal disease and sex crimes (QPD 263: 1525–8, 1729). Pornography that 'was once the province of the commercial brothel' was now said to be generally available (QPD 263: 1528), for many R-certificate films depicted 'extremes' rather than 'real life behaviour'. Thus, young people could get a false sense of what was 'normal'. Many R movies were said to have excessive sex scenes that were almost devoid of tenderness; 'the sex idea is shown as only brutal, unlovely and animalistic'. As one member of the Queensland parliament argued, sex should be represented as 'wonderful and beautiful, but ... associated with married life' (QPD 263: 1728–9).

In 1974 the Queensland government established the Films Board of Review, which was to examine all films being distributed in Queensland (including those that had already been passed by the Commonwealth film censor) and to prohibit those which it considered objectionable. The definition of an objectionable film was to be made by reference to similar criteria as an objectionable publication (see Chapter 3).

The government argued that the establishment of the Films Board of Review had been made necessary by the breakdown of negotiations with the Commonwealth on film censorship. The last straw was said to be the decision of the federal Attorney-General, Lionel Murphy, to overrule the Commonwealth censor and release two Swedish movies under an R certificate. One member of the Queensland government argued that since Whitlam had come to power an 'eccentric, permissive, lunatic fringe' had gained a hold on the 'public instrumentalities that mould people's minds'. R-certificate films were blamed for the increasing levels of sex crime and the 'moral pollution' which had recently afflicted Australian society. The Labor Party was accused of wanting freedom for pornographers and those who, like men who lived on the earnings of prostitution, made money from 'visual prostitution … visual pimping and poncing'. Many modern films that were passed by the Commonwealth censor were said to depict 'abnormal' sexual behaviour; people who wanted to see such films were 'maladjusted in their sex life'. As one member of parliament argued, it was necessary to 'ensure that our films depict normal behaviour in the community …sexual relations, certainly between male and female, are normal, but … they are also private' (QPD 264: 3080, 3092, 3119, 3761, 3085, 3760).

As expected (given Labor policy on censorship) the Queensland Opposition voted against the Films Review Bill. One Labor parliamentarian argued that history was 'littered with people and organisations who attempted to ban sex; but, as always, human nature triumphed' (QPD 264: 3763, 3092). Thus, censorship controls on adults were represented as an attempt to 'ban sex'. However, in general, there were no outspoken statements of sexual libertarianism in the Queensland parliament at this time.

Between 1974 and 1978 the Queensland Films Board of Review issued prohibition orders against 106 films. While several mainstream and art films – such as *Julia*[9] and the Louis Malle film *Pretty Baby* (about child prostitution) – were banned in this period, the majority of the films subject to prohibition orders had titles like *Love Hungry Girls*, *Hot Sex in Bangkok* and *In Love With Sex*. They were described by the board as 'cheap sexploitation films made on a low budget, with little skill in production and featuring actors and actresses of doubtful "acting" ability' (QFBR 1974–75: 2). Several films which adopted a sham documentary approach were also prohibited in this period – for example, a film called *Sex Aids and How to Use Them*. A small number of horror movies were also prohibited – for example *Northville Cemetery Massacre* (QFBR 1974–75: 2).

In its annual reports between 1974 and 1975 the Films Board of Review frequently deplored the fact that films were 'becoming more and more explicit in displaying violent, horrific and sexual scenes' and also that 'they are presenting concepts and behaviour, which previously have been regarded in society as undesirable, in an attractive and desirable manner'. Drug-taking and lesbianism[10] were said to be particularly subject to this type of misrepresentation (QFBR 1974–75: 2). On the other hand, married couples were frequently depicted as 'unattractive, quarrelling, frustrated alongside happy free lovers' (QFBR 1976–77: 2). Films were said increasingly to be propaganda vehicles for the sexual

revolution – they advocated increased sexual activity and sexual experimentation with no address to the responsibilities and consequences of
this. Thus:

> rarely, if ever, do any of the participating women ever become pregnant, or
> does either party become emotionally involved, contract venereal disease,
> etc. There is a continuing depiction of men and women, but more particu-
> larly women, as being solely the objects of sexual gratification. ... Board
> members are yet to hear in the exploitation films either the male or female
> at any time during the sexual act use the words 'I love you' or any other
> term of endearment [QFBR 1976–77: 2].

While this was not a consideration in deciding whether a film was
objectionable under the terms of the Act, the board argued that it was
necessary to draw these matters of concern to public attention. Young
people in particular needed to be made aware that films were propaganda vehicles and 'that there is a soft, and sometimes a hard, sell in
many films' (QFBR 1976–77: 2). While the board agreed that there
was no simple relationship between film trends and changes in human
behaviour, it had noticed a coincidence between the increasing
number of women involved in criminal activity in Queensland and
'the increase in the number of films in which women are shown in
more aggressive roles not only in legitimate activity but mainly as the
initiators of violence, sexual assaults and other offences' (QFBR
1974–75: 2). There was said to be 'a considerable body of overseas
research' which showed that mass media portrayals of violence
produced a predisposition to violent behaviour in the community
(QFBR 1974–75: 3).

It will be apparent, then, that conservative discourse was dominant
on pornography and censorship among members of all political
parties in the Queensland parliament and within the statutory authorities assigned to review the suitability of film and literature. This meant
that Queensland did not move with the other states to a regulatory
scheme for the control of pornography.

Prostitution Debates in the Early 1970s

In the early 1970s prostitution began to assume a new role in political
debate. This occurred as a result of several factors. First, during the
early 1970s, there was a visible proliferation of massage parlour prostitution in all Australian capital cities. This produced calls for official
action and, in most states, new laws to cover massage parlour prostitution. But the increasing prominence of liberal and libertarian

discourse in Australian parliaments during the late 1960s and early 1970s also began to have an impact on the *type* of political approaches pursued by governments in relation to the prostitution industry. Some states – such as Queensland – continued to extend the criminal sanctions against prostitution, thus continuing a trend well established in other parts of Australia during the late 1950s and 1960s (see Chapter 4). But in other states – most notably South Australia and Western Australia – existing politico-legal approaches to prostitution began to be called into question in the early 1970s.

Queensland

In the early 1970s the Queensland government initiated two separate amendments to the prostitution laws. Both of these significantly extended the ambit of the law and/or increased the penalties which could be applied by the courts for prostitution-related offences. In 1970 an amendment to the *Vagrants, Gaming and Other Offences Act* ensured that both males and females were liable to prosecution for living on the earnings of prostitution. This was similar to legislation enacted earlier in other states, and related to the Commonwealth's intention to become a signatory to the United Nations *International Convention for the Suppression of the Traffic in Persons and of the Exploitation of Others*. In parliament, however, the Opposition noted the coincidence of this amendment with revelations on Brisbane television by Dr Bertram Wainer (a Victorian abortion activist) that police were protecting prostitution and pornography operations in Brisbane brothels (*Courier Mail*, 14 March 1970).

In 1971 another amendment to the *Vagrants, Gaming and Other Offences Act* provided new penalties for massage parlours, photographic studios and saunas which offered prostitution services. As in 1970, this legislation was passed amid allegations that police were involved in the protection of prostitution in Brisbane and had perjured themselves at the National Hotel Royal Commission in 1963–64 (see Chapter 4). The 1971 legislation also significantly extended the law in relation to soliciting in a public place. All soliciting for the purposes of prostitution (whether carried out by a known prostitute or not) as well as homosexual soliciting (whether for the purposes of prostitution or not) was prohibited, and fines were increased 400 per cent. Police powers in relation to the searching of brothels and massage parlours were extended and penalties for living on the earnings of prostitution and for loitering in, near, or within view of a public place for the purpose of prostitution were significantly increased (QPD 258: 2514–16).

As in other Australian states, the Labor Opposition in Queensland vehemently opposed the extension of police powers to be included in the new Act and argued that the police already had adequate powers to control prostitution. However, a member of the government, Don Lane, contended that the legislation would facilitate police action against soliciting. Until 1971 police had to prove that a person was both soliciting and was a known or reputed prostitute before a conviction could be obtained. The unsubstantiated claim by police witnesses that a female defendant was a prostitute had not been regarded by the courts as sufficient evidence to achieve convictions in this regard. Lane, therefore, supported the new measures and argued that they would give police more adequate powers to deal with the 'dens of vice' known as massage parlours (*Courier Mail*, 2 September 1971). He also argued against the reintroduction of 'legal' prostitution in Queensland (see Chapters 2 and 3) and suggested that legal suppression was the only way for governments to adequately address the problems associated with prostitution. He said that the presence of prostitution in a community encouraged crime and had no effect on reducing the incidence of sex offences; it also effectively divided the female population into two categories 'one ... of decent women who must be protected by law from sex deviates and perverts, and another category that would be licensed to suffer these people' (QPD 258: 2520).

In parliamentary discourse, then, there was to be no return to a system of tolerated prostitution in Queensland. However, evidence presented to the Fitzgerald Inquiry during 1987–88 suggests that the heavy criminal penalties for all prostitution-related activities established in Queensland facilitated the establishment of an extensive system of police graft and corruption during the 1970s. In 1990 Don Lane was gaoled for corruption.

South Australia

During the early 1970s there was a visible proliferation of massage parlours and health studios in Adelaide. The Opposition called for action (SAPD 1971–72: 1269; 1972: 1163) and in 1972 the Dunstan government drafted the Massage Establishments Bill. However, this bill was never presented to the parliament because it was seen to have 'unsatisfactory definition provisions' which would make it ineffective (SAPD 1976–77: 1971). Given the liberal inclinations of the government at this time (for example, its response to the *Portnoy's Complaint* case and its general approach to the issue of pornography) it is likely that there was also some reluctance to increase the criminal penalties on an adult, consensual sexual activity such as prostitution, particularly where there was no question of public offence.

The South Australian government did, however, amend the *Police Offences Act* during 1972. This appears to be in response to a Commonwealth request that the offence of living on the earnings of prostitution should apply to both men and women because the Commonwealth intended to become a signatory to the *International Convention for the Suppression of the Traffic in Persons and of the Exploitation of Others* (SAPD 1972: 545).

During the mid-1970s the Opposition was unremitting in its criticism of what it termed the government's non-action on prostitution. The member for Mitcham, Robin Millhouse, was particularly active in this regard. Until his membership on the Select Committee of Inquiry into Prostitution during the late 1970s, Millhouse was a strong advocate of a licensing system for brothels and massage parlours. (In the 1970s he was also a high-profile and conservative anti-pornography campaigner in the parliament.) However, most other Opposition members urged the adoption of stronger controls on massage establishments and on the advertising of massage and prostitution services (SAPD 1972: 374).

Premier Dunstan resisted both of these approaches. He rejected the suggestion that a licensing system would be 'effective as a means of suppression' (SAPD 1976–77: 640), and said that the existing law was already being used to achieve prosecutions. In 1975, for example, the Vice Squad made 959 visits to massage parlours; as a result 49 people had been reported and 13 convicted for prostitution-related offences (SAPD 1975–76: 584). It is obvious from questions in parliament over the following year that this police blitzing of massage parlours continued for some time.

In the parliament Dunstan argued that a 'close watch' was being kept on criminal activities associated with the prostitution industry and that there was no evidence of a general public health problem arising from massage parlours. Complaints of public nuisance caused by the establishment of parlours in residential areas were being referred to the relevant local government authority to be dealt with under ordinary zoning laws (SAPD 1976–77: 640). It appears, then, that the government was concerned to address the already illegal aspects of the industry as well as issues of public health and public nuisance. But it was not concerned to establish blanket prohibitions on new forms of prostitution (such as massage parlours), especially when that took place in non-residential areas and when there was no question of a 'public harm'.

Western Australia

In the early 1970s the Liberal Party Opposition in Western Australia began to use the issue of prostitution in its campaign against the Labor government. Questions were raised in parliament about the number of prosecutions for prostitution-related offences and about the government's 'inaction' in the face of a burgeoning number of massage parlours and escort agencies in Perth. As in South Australia, however, the government indicated that it did not intend to introduce any special legislation to address massage parlours and argued that the police were able to use the existing laws to achieve prosecutions against those who were involved in massage parlour prostitution (WAPD 198: 94, 333).

After the state election in 1974 it was the turn of Labor to pressure the Liberal government of Charles Court on the issue of prostitution and it was the long-standing police policy of containing (rather than suppressing) prostitution which came into political focus. There were intimations during 1974 and 1975 that certain madams and premises in Perth had police immunity and that the prostitution trade in Kalgoorlie was directly controlled by the police. But Premier Court assured the parliament that the prostitution industry in Western Australia was being effectively policed (WAPD 203: 292; 204: 768; 205: 2589, 2874).

During 1975 parliamentary pressure continued to build in the wake of allegations (by individual police officers and members of parliament) about police corruption and misconduct and at least one prostitution-related murder. The Civil Liberties Association also called for a public inquiry into police activities in relation to prostitution. This pressure for official action was not abated by amendments to the *Police Offences Act*, introduced in 1975, which generally tightened the law in relation to prostitution and increased penalties for prostitution-related offences.[11]

As a result of the continuing political furore, the government appointed a Royal Commission of Inquiry (under the direction of Judge J. G. Norris) in October 1975. The report of the commission – tabled in the parliament in June 1976 – found no conclusive evidence to support allegations that there had been police improprieties in the administration of the law relating to prostitution. The Commissioner rejected the allegation that police policy and practice were based on an illegal and improper 'toleration' of prostitution. He argued that the methods employed by the police were aimed at controlling prostitution and were 'by no means ineffective'. In his opinion, there was no evidence to support the allegation that police policy and practice in relation to the containment of prostitution was a conspiracy to prevent or defeat the execution of statute law. If the practice of containment had continued in disregard of a specific ministerial directive then it could be said that the police had acted improperly. As no such direction had been received (and police did not inform their minister about this practice) the Commissioner found that no impropriety had been committed. Moreover:

> No suggestion that prostitution can be eradicated was made during the hearing. That being so, I find it difficult to see what other system could be employed. ... The existing statutory provisions do furnish an effective means of [prostitution] control. The discretionary but not capricious manner of enforcement adopted has kept the state of Western Australia relatively free from the evils which may be associated with prostitution [Western Australia 1976: 163].

As, in the Commissioner's opinion, prostitution could not be eradicated, the system of containment was an appropriate and useful means of policing the prostitution trade. After this, containment became official policy in Western Australia. However, several brothels were closed down; ten only were permitted to remain open in Perth and Kalgoorlie (see CJC 1991).

Early Initiatives for the Decriminalisation of Prostitution

Outside parliament, there was a push to decriminalise prostitution. In New South Wales members of civil liberties associations had been advocating reform of the laws against prostitution since the late 1960s (see Buckley 1968). But it was the emergence of the Women's Liberation Movement – and renewed feminist interest in prostitution – which gave additional impetus to the civil liberties campaign during the 1970s. American second wave feminists, such as Kate Millett (1971), argued: 'Women have the right to dispose of their bodies as they see fit ... prostitution is not a transaction in the public domain ... police intervention here is an invasion of privacy.' From this liberal perspective, the ownership rights that women had in their own bodies meant that they should be free to choose prostitution if they so wished.[12] A liberal distinction between public and private behaviour – that would be called into question in the 1980s by feminist theorists such as Carole Pateman (1983a) – was also seen to determine the legitimacy or illegitimacy of state intervention.

This analysis of prostitution was soon being deployed by Australian feminists. At the 1974 national conference of the Women's Electoral Lobby, for example, a motion was passed calling for the decriminalisation of prostitution (that is, the repeal of all laws pertaining to it) in both state and federal jurisdictions. In the mid-1970s the feminist debate about prostitution also took a particular national turn as a result of the publication of Anne Summers's *Damned Whores and God's Police* (1975). This was a widely read and influential feminist book in Australia during the 1970s.

Summers developed an analysis of contemporary Australian society that was premised upon its historical roots in prostitution. She argued that in the early days of European settlement in Australia, all women – convict women, free settlers and Aboriginal women – were subject to an 'enforced whoredom'; that is, they were forced to trade sex in exchange for food, clothing and shelter. Summers contended that Australian women were still mostly in this position. However, after the early days of convict settlement, women were increasingly separated into 'bad' or 'good', damned whores or God's police. It was, Summers argued, the assigned role of 'good' women (a category that included married women, celibate spinsters and feminists) both to discipline and to divert 'bad' women from their evil ways. But the overall effect of this process was to divide women, to classify them as 'either maternal figures who are not ... sexual or as whores who are exclusively sexual'. Summers argued that stereotypes like these disciplined *all* women, for they ignored or actively repressed 'good' women's sexuality while all sexually active women were represented as 'bad' (like prostitutes). It was in the interests of all women for these stereotypes of sexual behaviour to be broken down, so she suggested that 'good' women should refuse their policing function; feminists needed to identify publicly with those who were designated as 'bad' women – a category that clearly included prostitutes.

The influence of feminist and liberal/libertarian approaches to the issue of prostitution are also evident in the findings of the Royal Commission on Human Relationships (see above). Among a series of recommendations relating to abortion, family planning and homosexuality, the report argued for complete decriminalisation of prostitution. It suggested that the activities of prostitutes should be regarded as a criminal offence only to the extent that they caused public nuisance or annoyance, and that soliciting, being on premises used for the purposes of prostitution, permitting premises to be used as a brothel, and living on the earnings of prostitution should be removed from the criminal law. The continuation of some prostitution laws was regarded as necessary only in order to protect minors, to prevent public nuisance, and to protect sex workers from exploitation and coercion. A further recommendation was that brothels and other prostitution premises should be subject only to such restrictions as were required by planning laws relating to business premises or by-laws relating to public health and safety.

Conclusion

In the early 1970s the sex industries became an important focus of political debate in Australia. This occurred as a result of two main factors. First, there was a visible expansion in the sex industry as both the number and range of pornographic publications on the Australian market increased and as massage-parlour prostitution proliferated. This expansion was clearly related to a number of important changes in the sexual culture, most notably the growth of an international pornography industry and the increasing power associated with sexual discourses which emphasised the liberatory potential of sex.

Second, at the same time as this expansion in the pornography and prostitution industries occurred, traditional political approaches to controlling these industries were increasingly being called into question. Influential sections of the electorate argued against the censorship of publications and films designed for an adult audience and, to a much lesser extent, against the imposition of new penalties against (private) prostitution. This combination of factors produced a new political problem – how to control the sex industries without resorting to comprehensive prohibitions which might be unpopular with the electorate.

As a result, most states moved away from politico-legal approaches which emphasised the prohibition of pornography. In their place regulatory systems were established which extended new rights and privileges to adults in relation to the legal consumption of pornography (although I am not suggesting this represents a 'liberation').[13] Within political discourse, libertarian approaches became more influential; these represented the consumer of pornography as a normal citizen and pornography itself as a modernising influence. In Queensland, however, conservative discourse remained politically dominant. This, together with the significant role played by the Films and Literature Boards of Review, was a major reason why Queensland did not adopt a regulatory scheme for the control of pornography in the early 1970s.

Queensland's enactment of new anti-prostitution laws in the early 1970s appears to be the continuation of a long-term trend in which prostitution was increasingly marked out in law as a deviant and abnormal sexual practice (see Chapter 4). In both South Australia and Western Australia there was considerable resistance by Labor governments to new anti-prostitution measures, despite intense political pressure. This resistance was clearly related to the importance of political discourses which emphasised the essential privacy of all sexual behaviour conducted by consenting adults and the desirability of sexual freedom. Increasingly, the resort to prostitution, like the use of pornography, was conceptualised as a private sexual activity in which government interference was illegitimate. Thus liberalisation of the laws addressed to pornography and the decriminalisation of prostitution were regarded by a growing number of parliamentarians as related aspects of an overall strategy which aimed to eliminate the legal sanctions on all private, consensual sexual behaviour between adults.

PART THREE

After the Revolution

CHAPTER 6

New Sexual Politics, 1975–88

In the period after 1975 prostitution and pornography became an important object of public and political debate in Australia. A number of important inquiries took place into both prostitution[1] and pornography,[2] and several significant legal reforms were instigated in these areas. In the late 1970s and early 1980s new laws were introduced to prohibit child pornography and to control the distribution of hard-core pornographic videotapes which combined sex and violence. At the same time, legislation which aimed to decriminalise aspects of the prostitution trade was debated in three states, New South Wales, South Australia and Victoria. In New South Wales soliciting for the purposes of prostitution was formally removed from the statute books in 1979. While new anti-soliciting laws were introduced in 1983 and 1988, some street soliciting still remained legal. In South Australia a bill designed to decriminalise brothel prostitution failed in 1980. In Victoria in 1984, brothel prostitution was decriminalised for premises with a valid town-planning permit.

In this chapter I look at the way in which new issues associated with the sex industries came onto the mainstream political agenda in the late 1970s and 1980s. I am interested in how and why law reform was seen to be necessary in this period (and not before), and in the type of reforms that were seen as appropriate. In the first section of this chapter I examine several key features of the political and sexual culture – in particular the wide deployment of feminist discourse in mainstream political institutions in this period.

In the second and third sections of this chapter I look at two important turning points in debates about the regulation of pornography. In the late 1970s child pornography became an important political issue throughout Australia. This led to the introduction of new controls on pornography designed for adults and, therefore, to a partial retreat from the libertarian principle that adults were entitled to read and view whatever they wished. This trend was reinforced during 1983–84 when heated debates occurred in state and federal parliaments about the regulation of video pornography which depicted explicit sexual violence.

In the final section of this chapter I examine the shift to a decriminalisation of prostitution in New South Wales and Victoria and to the beginning of a contemporary trend away from prohibition as the norm of prostitution law in Australia. As in previous chapters, I also look at how parliamentarians (in New South Wales, Victoria and South Australia) spoke about prostitution transactions and connected this to the argument that decriminalisation was now an appropriate approach for governments to take in their dealings with the prostitution industry.

Sexual and Political Cultures

In the late 1970s and early 1980s socio-economic conditions in Australia continued to deteriorate and unemployment levels remained high. Many of the trends noted in the previous two chapters also remained evident. For example, changing patterns of marriage, divorce and family formation continued to impact upon the intimate relations of men and women. While there was a substantial increase in the number of single women and women with children living on welfare benefits, women in general continued to improve their economic and political power in relation to men. While women's average weekly earnings relative to men's increased only marginally, their overall participation in the paid workforce increased by 26.5 per cent between 1975 and 1986; men's increased only 7 per cent across the same period (O'Donnell and Hall 1988: 20).

The number of women in parliaments around Australia also increased significantly in this period. Sawer (1990) reports that between 1972 and 1989 the number of women MPs in Australian parliaments rose from 2 to 11 per cent; many of these new MPs were members of the Labor Party, which adopted an affirmative action policy in 1983. As a result of an increasing feminist engagement in Australia with state institutions and formal public decision-making (Watson 1990; Sawer 1990) – in parliament, in political parties and in the bureaucracy – many new legal and policy initiatives, designed to improve the situation of women, were implemented. These included initiatives addressed to child care, women's health, sex discrimination, and rape and domestic violence (Sawer 1990; Simms and Stone 1990; Watson 1990).

Feminist arguments about prostitution and pornography also began to appear on mainstream political agendas in this period. In the second half of the 1970s, Australian feminists began to take up many of Anne Summers's arguments about prostitution (see Chapter 5). Jackson and Otto (1984), for example, argued that the dichotomy between damned whores and God's police was 'a form of social control of female sexuality' which made the support of prostitutes by other women 'a matter of self-interest rather than a moral imperative'. However, this sort of approach was also seen to present a significant dilemma; feminists needed to provide effective support for prostitutes in the short term without compromising their overall opposition to the sexual exploitation inherent in prostitution. This dilemma could be resolved by a focus on prostitution as work and on prostitutes as sex workers (Aitkin 1978; Jackson and Otto 1984). Prostitutes were simply women who worked in the sex industry, and feminist support could be confined to areas of immediate concern to prostitute women such as wages and working conditions. The decriminalisation of prostitution and (for some authors) the unionisation of the prostitute workforce was a necessary precondition for improvements in prostitutes' working conditions (Aitkin 1978; Jackson and Otto 1984).

Elsewhere (Sullivan 1995) I have argued that the conceptualisation of prostitution as work has some strategic disadvantages for feminists and has failed to resolve a fundamental (and probably irresolvable) tension within feminist politics around sexual issues like prostitution. If prostitution is to be regarded wholly as work (rather than sex) then the primary object of analysis remains the prostitute rather than the client. As in traditional analyses of prostitution, then, the client disappears. This means that the sexual desires and aspirations of clients – and the ways that these reflect broader cultural practices and patterns of masculinity – tend to be both de-emphasised and assigned to the realm of 'natural' male sexual needs (that is, problematic but inevitable). This point has been emphasised by Overs (1989), while Carpenter (1994) has recently argued that the focus in contemporary feminist work on prostitutes – rather than clients – tends to replicate and reconstitute biological accounts of men's sexuality in ways that are positively detrimental both to women and a broader feminist project. However, it is also apparent that the conceptualisation of prostitution as work had some clear political advantages for Australian feminists in the political environment of the late 1970s and 1980s. In particular, it made possible broad feminist support for measures designed to decriminalise prostitution.

From the mid-1970s onwards a feminist opposition to pornography also gained significant grassroots support within Australia, although this never assumed the same dimensions as in the United States. In 1977 the Women's Electoral Lobby in New South Wales began organising around the issue of pornography with the formation of a study group on 'The exploitation of women in pornography' (*WEL-Informed*, July 1977). By the early 1980s other feminist groups, such as the Women Against Violence and Exploitation (WAVE) had advanced radical critiques of pornography that were strongly influenced by the work of American anti-pornography feminists such as Dworkin (1981) and Morgan (1980). Feminist theory in general was beginning to emphasise the role of men's violence in the construction of women's oppression (A. Edwards 1987), and pornography was clearly located on a continuum of practices such as rape and domestic violence.

In the early 1980s some Australian feminists began to call for tougher laws against pornography (Jones 1984), although others argued against a pro-censorship stance and questioned the increasingly central role that pornography was occupying within feminist theory (Pringle 1981). However, it was feminist anti-pornography discourse that was to have the most impact upon mainstream political debate, particularly in the early 1980s.

Conflicts about Child Pornography, 1976–77

The issue of child pornography burst on to the political agenda during 1976–77 and provided an important initial impetus to the formation of new anti-pornography discourses within Australian parliaments. In all states (except Queensland)[3] the issue of child pornography provoked a significant re-evaluation of the regulatory systems established in the early and mid-1970s for dealing with pornography. As I have demonstrated in Chapter 5, systems for classifying and regulating the distribution of pornography were designed to prevent public offence and to ensure that children were not able to obtain hard-core pornography. Adults, on the other hand, were regarded as entitled to purchase and consume whatever they chose. Child pornography – which depicted children naked or in explicit sexual activity with other children and with adults – appeared on the Australian market in commercial quantities in the mid-1970s. Although children were the actors in this type of pornography, it was clearly designed for adult consumers. Under laws established in the early and mid-1970s, child pornography needed to be classified but was then available to adults.

Concerns about the impact of child pornography were given wide press coverage during the visit of two visiting experts on child sexual abuse in 1977. Dr Judianne Densen-Gerber and Dr Michael Baden from the United States claimed that there was a larger range of child pornography available in Sydney than anywhere else in the world; they also specifically linked this material to a rising incidence of child sexual abuse. A public furore ensued and new laws prohibiting child pornography were enacted in state parliaments throughout Australia.[4] This marked a clear departure from the principle established in public policy during 1973–75 that the state had no legitimate right to interfere with the freedom of adults to buy and read whatever they wished. The issue of child pornography, therefore, brought about a significant re-evaluation of libertarian principles and of the regulatory systems established only a few years before.

In New South Wales, for example, an urgency motion was debated in 1977 on the issue of child pornography. Opposition members claimed that there was a significant problem with the existing regulatory scheme for classifying publications, particularly as the worst sorts of pornography (such as child pornography) could achieve classification even though that was as 'direct sale' only. Thus, it was said that material which 'incited child rape' was freely available in the community (NSWPD 130: 5224, 5254).

Initially, Premier Neville Wran was against the imposition of new censorship controls. He agreed that paedophilia was 'repulsive and repugnant', but sought to maintain a distinction between the act and its representation in pornography. Wran said there were 'provisions in the law more than adequate to deal with people who perform acts of indecency involving children'. Thus, there was no need for any new anti-pornography laws (NSWPD 130: 5237). The Minister for Planning and Environment, Paul Landa, took a similar view. He argued that children had been used in pornography throughout history and that refusing to censor material was not the same as condoning and applauding its content. Pornography, he said, appealed to a 'primordial force'; thus, ways would be found around any new restrictions which were imposed (NSWPD 131: 5647–8). This approach clearly attempted to maintain a libertarian distinction between actions and ideas; as in the early 1970s, while actions were regarded as an appropriate object of state laws, ideas (a category that was seen to include all publications) were not.

The strength of public and parliamentary opposition to child pornography did, however, force the Wran government to modify this approach. An amendment to the *Indecent Articles and Classified Publications Act* was passed in 1977 which added a new classification category – 'child pornography publications' – to the existing categories of restricted, unrestricted and direct sale. It became an offence to distribute, display or otherwise publish a publication classified as a child pornography publication (NSWPD 132: 6439).

Members of all political parties argued strongly in support of this legislation on the grounds that 'to be able to see and read [child pornography] means that a child has been debased'. The consumers of child pornography were represented not as normal citizens but as 'utterly depraved adults' (NSWPD 132: 6966). Even those parliamentarians who had adopted a strong libertarian position in the early 1970s rose to support the legislation against child pornography. For example, in 1973 and 1975 the member for Port Kembla, George Petersen, had argued against the censorship of adult literature although, as he indicated in 1977, he had always expressed some reservations about the rights of adults to see and read what they wished. As in 1973–75 Petersen suggested that pornography was a product of male domination and of a sexually repressed society. He also represented child pornography as 'children being exploited to produce material that incites violence and child rape' (NSWPD 130: 5242–4). However, in general, he thought there was:

> a great deal less harm in the free publication of pornographic material than in its censorship and restriction. ... I do not care how people get their kicks in their dealings with one another in equal relationships. I admit that a great deal of the pornographic material available indicates the exploitation of females by males. ... But [child pornography] is ... reprehensible, to a degree that far exceeds other forms of pornography. In fact, *I am hesitant really about calling it pornography*. It is an incitement to rape children, an incitement to violence and an incitement to despoil and degrade. One should contrast that with a great deal of the other pornographic material that is being published, indicating mutual relationships between men and women and men and men. Because the form of pornography dealt with by this bill is of concern to all people who have any decency, and involves children who are our responsibility, it cannot be tolerated in any circumstances. We cannot tolerate rape and violence against children. That is the reason why I support this legislation [NSWPD 132: 6969, emphasis added].

Thus, child pornography was problematic because it involved sexual acts that were not equal, mutual or consensual. By law a child could not consent to any sexual activity with an adult. The specific absence of consent meant that child pornography was the representation of child rape; it was violent and could legitimately be prohibited. However, 'real pornography' was not violent; while it might be unhealthy and degrading to women it could somehow also be regarded as consensual (and involving mutual desire). For libertarians such as Petersen, then, the imposition of additional legislative controls on 'real pornography' was still illegitimate.

This indicates that, in mainstream political discourse, questions about violence, consent and mutuality in pornography were first raised in relation to child pornography. However, similar questions also began to be raised in relation to adult pornography. In December 1977 the member for Playford in the South Australian parliament, Terence McRae, reported that he had been consulted by a group of constituents – people who, in the early 1970s, had 'heartily agreed with the sale of pornography under [certain] safeguards' and had supported the dismantling of oppressive censorship controls. The issue of child pornography had 'jarred them badly' but they felt this was a problem which had been satisfactorily resolved by the imposition of new legal controls. In their view there was now another problem:

> They came to believe that pornography is a violation of the rights of women. They found that the majority of all this material is based on treating women not as persons but as things, and on degrading and humiliating women. ... they found that what they had once supported or tolerated was, in fact, the brutal exploitation of women, an exploitation being conducted in the cause of giant profits. They found that 90 per cent of purchasers of this material were men. They concluded that the very existence of this traffic in the degradation of women in our city was a giant step backwards in what has been the gradual emancipation and liberation of women over the last century [SAPD 1977–78: 1292–3].

This speech indicates that some of the former advocates of pornography – and opponents of censorship – were now adopting feminist analyses of pornography which regarded the representation of women in 'adult' publications as fundamentally problematic. The actors and models who were photographed for pornographic publications were said to be members of a 'new breed of slave' and to have 'no choice' about the acts they performed (SAPD 1977–78: 1292). Thus, there was concern that – like the children in child pornography – the women who worked in the pornography industry were coerced and had not freely consented to the sexual activity which was represented.

But there was also concern that the consumption of pornography positively undermined public and private attitudes towards all women; according to McRae, this was 'linked to' (if not causally related to) the perpetration of various crimes of violence against women, most notably rape. He went on to suggest that there was now a political 'conflict of interests' between 'the dignity and liberation of women' and 'the liberty to purchase these pornographic books'. But there was no solution to this political dilemma apart from getting 'everyone in society to re-examine his [sic] attitude'; only broad community pressure would remove the pornography industry and 'maintain the dignity of all men and women'. More censorship was not a good idea because liberty was 'essential to any fair and decent society' and an important means of avoiding the totalitarianism of both fascism and communism. However, in McRae's view, violent pornography was a new and legitimate problem which the government needed to address. He called for the South Australian Classification of Publications Board to deal with violent pornography in the same way that it had with child pornography – that is, by refusing to classify it (SAPD 1977–78: 1292–3).

This was a call supported by conservative parliamentarians such as the member for Coles, Jennifer Adamson, who argued: 'The ready availability of pornography, including hard-core bondage material, has coincided with the rapid rise in the incidence of rape and sexual crimes in South Australia' (SAPD 1978–79: 1203). Feminists and conservatives increasingly agreed, then, on the dangers posed by violent pornography. Moreover, even those who were opposed to the imposition of additional censorship controls on 'adult literature', and remained unconvinced by feminist arguments about the role of pornography in the cultural oppression of women, could be convinced by arguments which focused on the non-consensual and exploitative nature of *violent* pornography.

In 1979 the South Australian government responded to this issue by amending the *Police Offences Act* specifically to prohibit publication and distribution of material which depicted sexually oriented acts of violence. The definition of indecent material was expanded so that, like child pornography, sadistic and masochistic publications were liable to prosecution. While speaking in support of this legislation, Premier Don Dunstan indicated that the representation in pornography of 'bondage without cruelty' – as recommended in Alex Comfort's best-selling advice manual, *More Joy of Sex* – would not fall within the ambit of the new legislation (SAPD 1978–9: 1984). Thus, as in the early 1970s with *Playboy* magazine (see Chapter 5), the prevailing standards of popular literature were used to determine the limits of acceptable sexual behaviour and legal regulation.

X-rated Video Pornography

The focus on sexual violence in adult pornography continued in the 1980s. This occurred as video technology became widely available, as the market for video pornography expanded, and as feminist anti-pornography discourse was more widely deployed in mainstream political institutions. During 1983 alone in Australia, home video ownership rose from 11 to 25 per cent of households. In the New South Wales parliament the member for Willoughby, Peter Collins, noted that the Australian market for video cassette recorders was 'the fastest growing of its kind in the world today'. Almost 25 per cent of the videotape market was said to be derived from pornographic videos (NSWPD 178: 4576).

In July 1983 a meeting of Commonwealth and state ministers responsible for censorship was convened to examine the need for uniform regulation of the videotape market. At this meeting it was agreed, with Queensland abstaining, that a new X classification for hard-core pornographic videotapes would be introduced. Such a measure was regarded as 'overdue' for several reasons. A formal discrepancy between federal Customs law and federal Customs practice – instituted by the Whitlam government in 1973 (see Chapter 5) – meant that there were few formal barriers to the importation of pornography (JSCVM 2: 332). The revolution in video technology and the activities of a vigorous international sex-video industry had also led to a significant increase in the number of hard-core pornographic videos entering Australia by the late 1970s and early 1980s. However, the legal status of video pornography was regarded as 'uncertain' because existing film censorship laws did not specifically address the distribution of videotapes designed for private home use. Consequently, the Australian market was virtually uncontrolled (JSCVM 2: 332–5). The federal government saw the introduction of a new video classification system as an important step towards the regulation of this market.

In February 1984, the Commonwealth government introduced a legislative package that was designed to begin the process of implementing a uniform classification scheme for videotapes.[5] As with publications in the early 1970s (see Chapter 5), regulation of the videotape market was to be achieved through a point-of-sale scheme which specified how various categories of material were to be distributed. The existing classifications for films were to be applied to videotapes, although an additional X classification was to be available for videotapes which were more sexually explicit than was allowed under the guidelines for R-rated films. At this stage it was proposed that classification for videotapes would not be compulsory.

Almost immediately, this scheme became the object of intense public and parliamentary debate. In New South Wales Premier Neville Wran announced that, despite his government's commitment to non-censorship, 'there are certain things that are beyond the pale'. In this category he placed 'extreme violence in association with sex acts' (*SMH*, 20 February 1984). Wran's position was strongly influenced by the opposition of the New South Wales Women's Advisory Council to the introduction of X-rated videos (NSWPD 178: 4572). In a definition that was obviously drawn from the work of American anti-pornography activists such as Andrea Dworkin (1981), the New South Wales Women's Advisory Council defined pornography as:

> the sexually explicit subordination of women, graphically depicted, whether in pictures or words, including showing women as things, commodities or objects and in scenarios of degradation, injury, abasement, torture, shown as filthy, or inferior, bleeding, bruised or hurt in a context that makes these conditions sexual [cited in NSWPD 178: 4571].

Two days after Wran's speech to the parliament, the Labor member for Rockdale, Frank Walker, initiated an urgency debate in the Legislative Assembly on the following motion:

> Whilst acknowledging the powers of the Commonwealth Government in respect of bringing into the country video movies, this House calls on the New South Wales Government to examine closely the type and nature of certain classes of such movies becoming available under an X-rating with a view to action being taken to protect women and children from exploitation [NSWPD 178: 4570).

Walker said that the problem posed by X-rated videos had been brought to his attention by women members of his Labor Party branch. There was obviously significant grassroots opposition within the Labor Party and within the broader community to video pornography. Moreover, many women's organisations 'from the extreme right to the extreme left of the spectrum have a strong policy attitude to this issue, for it degrades women and children' (NSWPD 178: 4570–1).

Walker defined pornography as 'degradation, domination, humiliation, objectification, violation, annihilation and violence mixed with sex'; it was a cultural practice which associated sex and violence with the exploitation and subordination of women and children. He said that under the new videotape regulations many videotapes which contained 'an unacceptable and horrifying level of violence' would be legally allowed into Australia. According to Walker, this would create several new problems, including the protection of women and children from exploitation in the preparation of video films and dealing with the effects (on both adults and children) of viewing these videos. Walker argued that the incidence of rape would increase in the future if children grew up thinking that the type of activity depicted in X-rated videos was normal and acceptable. He called upon the New

South Wales government to look at the whole issue of X-rated videos with a view 'to seeing whether some form of control or rating can be imposed on these movies so as to provide protection for individuals and the society at large' (NSWPD 178: 4571–3). Thus, New South Wales positioned itself to refuse the X classification.

During March and April 1984 motions for the disallowance of the new regulations covering X-rated videos were debated in the Senate. These disallowance motions were moved by an Australian Democrat as well as by conservative members of the Liberal and National Parties. The ensuing debate encompassed many different approaches to the issue of video pornography. For example, conservative members identified X-rated videos as a symptom of the breakdown of society and as an issue that could be dealt with only by strong legal prohibitions (see, for example, Senate 102: 1222). However, some members who were not otherwise identified with conservative politics, also clearly regarded video pornography as problematic, albeit in quite different terms from their conservative counterparts. As Democrat Senator Colin Mason argued: 'we are talking about videotapes that go beyond showing explicit sex to showing cruelty, violence and sadism with sexual association. Such material typically uses the humiliation, the degradation and even the torture of women as its central theme' (Senate 102: 1162).

Thus, it was not the breakdown of society that was a problem or even the representation of explicit sexual scenes. It was the combination of sex with violence that was regarded as dangerous, particularly for women. Mason cited the concern that adults (as opposed to children) were vulnerable to the effects of 'video nasties' and that they might, therefore, be driven to act out sex crimes that they saw depicted on videotape (Senate 102: 1164–5).

This approach was rejected by the Attorney-General, Senator Gareth Evans, who argued that legislative changes and the X classification were necessary: video pornography was already widely available in the community and the police were unwilling to use obscenity laws against it because they knew 'community standards and attitudes had changed to the point where people wanted that kind of X-rated material to be available for home use'. This was, Evans argued, both a 'practical desire' and an 'appropriate' extension of a citizen's privacy. While X-rated videos would never be certified for public screening, their use was 'appropriate in the privacy of people's own homes if they wish to see them' (Senate 102: 1178–81, 2073). As the existing Customs regulations which applied to video pornography were said to be both unenforceable and easily circumvented, regulation needed to focus on the point of sale rather than the point of importation.

It was, then, the regulation of the market that was the government's main concern; the content of videotaped films was not regarded as problematic for a private, adult audience. Censorship, Evans contended, had ceased to be a major political issue in Australia for, since 'the Dark Ages of intolerance in the 1960s', 'a pretty broad consensus about the approach to be adopted' had been established amongst members of the Labor Party, the Liberal Party and the Australian Democrats. All that remained now was 'to complete the process of the rationalisation of administration, the clarification of classification standards and ... to bring the law and practice into line particularly so far as ... Customs practice is concerned' (Senate 102: 1178).

As Evans suggested, a new political consensus on censorship *had* been established in the 1970s (see Chapter 5). From this consensus position the starting-point for all censorship decisions was:

> that adults should be entitled to read, hear and see what they wish and in public subject to two things: first, adequate provisions to ensure that persons will not be exposed to unsolicited material offensive to them and second, by adequate provisions to prevent conduct which will exploit or which is detrimental to the interests of children [Senate 102: 1178].

However, in 1984, it was clear that there were now some new issues which needed to be taken into account in the censorship area. Under intense public and parliamentary pressure the Attorney-General sought to modify his formerly hard-line position. He suggested that while the 1970s consensus position was still valid, there were now 'a couple of additional principles' which needed to be addressed in the development of censorship guidelines. These were, firstly, 'the consumer protection principle'; he said that consumers needed to be given as much guidance as possible about the type of pornography they were purchasing. It appears that, once again, the consumers of pornography were normal, ordinary citizens and consumers with rights as consumers (see Chapter 5).

The second new principle said to be involved in the formulation of censorship decisions was described by Evans:

> there is a general view that quite apart from the situation of children there is in principle something extremely offensive, and justifying bans in particular cases, about material which is exploitative in a highly significant way or involves the brutalisation of adults, be they men or women [Senate 102: 1178].

This statement, while somewhat vague and ambivalent, is clearly derivative of feminist arguments made in relation to pornography, sexual violence and social power. Although the Attorney-General saw the issue in terms of the brutalisation of adults, 'be they men or women', debate in the Senate during 1984 particularly focused on the appropriate classification to be given to filmic representations of rape and sexual violence against women.

The government had proposed that an X classification be given to material which depicted explicit sexual activity between adults except where that was of 'an *extreme* sexually violent or cruel nature'. Representations of extreme sexual violence were to be refused classification, as were child pornography, materials which depicted bestiality, and instruction manuals for terrorism or hard drug use. Material refused classification automatically assumed the status of a prohibited import.

Under intense pressure and questioning as to when sexual violence could be designated as extreme, the government again sought to reformulate its position. Evans agreed to reword the guidelines for the X category to exclude all sexual violence against *non-consenting* persons (JSCVM 2: 12–23), a change that was suggested by the Commonwealth Chief Censor, Janet Strickland. Notably, this made censorable the representation of non-consent rather than the representation of sexual violence *per se*.

This was a liberal solution to a liberal dilemma. While feminist concerns about pornography could not remain completely unaddressed at this time, the consumption of pornography was already defined in parliamentary discourse as a private activity of 'persons' which needed to be defended against illegitimate state interference. Because liberal polities accepted the absence of consent and the visibility of demonstrable harm as suitable indicators of the need for legitimate constraint by law, representations of rape and sexual violence could appear in the parliamentary arena as problematic representations.

There were, however, a range of feminist concerns about pornography which could *not* be made visible in parliament because they did not fit dominant liberal values. These included concerns about the nature of normal sexual relations between men and women and the relationship of these, and pornography, to women's cultural subordination. Because the consumption of pornography was already defined in parliamentary debate as an idea, rather than a practice, and as a private activity of people rather than as a distinctly gendered practice (of men), many feminist questions were rendered invisible.

The problems here are evident in the continuing focus on public offensiveness as the main determining criterion for censorship decisions on material which was 'innocent' of non-consensual sexual violence. Evans argued that there was no possible justification for banning 'hard sexual material', that is, material which contained no violence, 'simply on the ground that you or I might find [it] distasteful or offensive'. This was in spite of the fact that 'most people in the community may well find [it] revolting, distasteful, vulgar or unacceptable' (Senate 102: 1183). It appears, then, that notions of a common good (and of a community's right to prevent the circulation of material which was merely offensive to it) had little purchase in Australian parliaments by 1984, although this had been one of the main premises of the debate on censorship in the early 1970s. Individual rights, as opposed to a balance between individual rights and the common good, were now the main foundation for censorship policy.

At the same time, in 1984 (but not in the early 1970s), there was universal agreement in the Commonwealth and state parliaments that some form of censorship was needed. While the representation of explicit sex and/or violence in X-rated videos – and the dividing line between videos which were to be given an X classification and those that were to be refused classification – was the object of sometimes heated parliamentary debate, there were *no* parliamentarians in 1984 who advocated the complete abandonment of censorship. Child pornography, as well as material which represented extreme violence or sexual violence, was now considered to be 'beyond the pale', even by those who were otherwise committed to an anti-censorship position.

In 1984 it was the representation of sexual violence that was the main focus of concern in Australian parliaments. The explicit representation of sex alone (in what is now frequently termed non-violent erotica) was not regarded by most parliamentarians as problematic. Indeed, it was only when the sexual was sullied by its collapse into the realm of violence that representations which were merely offensive became both extremely offensive and illegitimate. This suggests that the sexual itself could be regarded as an unproblematic category although – as the analysis of the 1971 censorship debate in Chapter 5 showed – the sexual is always deeply imbued with assumptions about the nature of 'normal' men, women, and 'normal' sexual relations. So even non-violent erotica can act as a political discourse with effects and consequences, perhaps undermining some of the gains women have made in the public sphere over the last three decades.

In 1984 libertarian parliamentarians still suggested that cultural representations such as film merely mirrored life. As one member of the Queensland parliament argued, pornographic images 'reflected' rather than 'created' a gendered social reality (QPD 296: 3033). The continuing emphasis on public offensiveness also tended to maintain a

distinction between ideas (a category that included films and publications) and actions, although there was now said to be strong scientific
evidence to suggest that films which represented explicit sexual
violence could have real anti-social effects. As one feminist member of
parliament argued, real women are often 'pressganged' into
performing in pornographic films, while 'men's attitudes and behaviour towards women are seriously damaged' by the availability of this
sort of material, linking pornography with later actual violence
(NSWPD 185: 3022).

Other parliamentarians argued that non-violent, hard-core pornography was unproblematic. The Commonwealth Attorney-General, for
example, argued that the licensing of X-rated video movies was a 'practical desire', for the majority of this material 'demonstrates both partners having a joyous and pleasurable time as distinct from a brutalising
or humiliating time'. In addition, pornography was seen to have 'a very
real utility' for those who are 'too ugly, too physically unattractive, or
ill, or incapable as a result of paraplegia-inducing accidents ... to be
able to enjoy normal sexual relations'. For such people, there was real
benefit to be obtained from 'living out, perhaps in a fantasy kind of
way, experiences which are perhaps available to others of us in the
community' (Senate 102: 1179, 1185). This is reminiscent of the category of 'persons' that, in 1971, 'couldn't get a beaut bird into bed' (see
Chapter 5).

Arguments about the socially disadvantaged nature of clients and
customers are frequently used to explain the persistence of both prostitution and pornography in these sexually liberated times, but it is clear
that they hold little credence. Consumers of pornography, like the
clients of prostitutes, are largely indistinguishable from the rest of the
population, although a recent survey in Australia has indicated that
male university graduates, with an average age of thirty-nine, are
proportionately larger users of porn videos (*Weekend Australian,* 20–21
January 1996). Hite (1981: 1123) found that only 11 per cent of her
sample of American men never looked at pornography while 26 per
cent were 'infrequent' consumers. The majority (57 per cent) of the
men that she interviewed were either 'regular' consumers (36 per
cent) or said they 'sometimes' (21 per cent) looked at pornography.
Thus it seems that, far from being an activity which only the ugly or the
disabled indulge in, the consumption of pornography is a normal male
activity in the present period.

There are other obvious differences between the censorship debates
that took place in the early and mid-1970s and those that occurred
around the introduction of the X classification in 1984. In 1971 only
one female parliamentarian took part in the censorship debate and

her contribution cannot be distinguished from that of her male colleagues (SAPD 1971–72: 2074–5). By 1984, however, significant numbers of women had entered parliament at both state and federal levels; during parliamentary debates they often identified themselves as feminists and as parliamentarians who represented the specific interests of women (see, for example, Ann Symonds, NSWPD 181: 836).

The feminist critique of pornography clearly had a significant impact on both conservative and libertarian positions within the debate about X-rated videos. While the argument that pornography degraded women had been used by some conservative parliamentarians during pornography debates in the early 1970s, it was widely deployed by conservatives during 1984.[6] However, in 1971 conservative parliamentarians were more likely to argue that pornography threatened the family, while in 1984 it was the sexual bond between men and women that was seen to be most at risk.[7] As one member argued, The exploitation of women in pornography 'is destroying and degrading the relationship between man and woman which has been the basis of society. It develops a lack of respect between man and woman which will break down our society for generations' (NSWPD 185: 3025). Similar anxieties about changes in the nature of real relations between men and women were made manifest across the political spectrum during the debate about X-rated videos. It was not, however, a feature of the R-certificate debates in 1971. This indicates that both sexual relations and sexual representation had become increasingly politicised within Australian culture by the mid-1980s.

In 1984 feminist critiques of pornography also posed a considerable challenge to the libertarian position, particularly as they brought into focus some of the masculinist assumptions implicit in libertarian discourse. Feminists argued that the pornography industry could not be dealt with by a gender-neutral regulatory framework because (in the main) it was representations of women's bodies that were being marketed to a male viewing public. From this perspective, men and women had a different relationship both to the pornographic images available on the Australian market and to projected modes of regulation; it was said to be women's citizenship which was most in danger.

Libertarians dealt with this sort of feminist challenge in several ways. First, as has been suggested, it was dealt with by a 'purging' of the sexual so that illegitimate acts of violence were firmly located outside the realm of appropriate freedom; pornography which depicted extreme sexual violence would be refused classification but non-violent pornography would be permitted. This strategy did not, in fact, address the basis of many feminist arguments against pornography, but it did appear to deal with some of the most urgent and compelling aspects of the pornography issue (sexual violence) for both feminists and libertarians. Second, feminist arguments were undermined by a strategy of divide and conquer. Gareth Evans, for example, argued that extreme feminists who argued against the X classification were part of a 'new puritanism' which also characterised right-wing politics in Australia. Thus, feminists were divided into extreme and moderate with the extreme position being located as both politically suspect and prone to an element of 'sexual repression' (Senate 102: 1183).

Feminist parliamentarians who were opposed to censorship and yet deplored some of the excesses of contemporary pornography were also called in to publicly support the case for the X classification. For example, Senator Susan Ryan, who was Minister assisting the Prime Minister on the Status of Women, assured Australian women that under the revised guidelines 'the most offensive material – the [sexually violent] material that was giving most concern to women and women's organisations – will be excluded from Australia' (Senate 103: 2370–1). Another female Labor Senator argued that sexist attitudes towards women were pervasive in our society and existed 'in a much wider context ... than just in X-rated movies'. In Queensland, Ann Warner, a well-known feminist member of parliament, argued:

> Pornography is not a problem in itself; it is a manifestation of a distortion of sexual relations. Violence in pornography and pornographic images do not in themselves produce rape; they simply translate the existing power imbalance between men and women into an image that reflects rather than creates ... There are really more pressing problems that should be attended to in relation to the exploitation of women [QPD 296: 3033].

From this perspective, education and information were preferred to 'banning and an increase in censorship'. In a libertarian variation of the domino theory it was also argued that censorship could be used against pornography today and feminist material tomorrow (Senate 102: 1224–5). This suggests that women – as well as men – had something to be concerned about if the censorship debate was 'lost'. It could be argued, however, that the new X classification was an extension of the liberal rights of male pornography consumers rather than a measure designed to 'increase censorship'. The argument that moderate feminists did not oppose the introduction of the X certificate and that pornography was not a cause but merely an effect of women's oppression was of immense strategic importance in this process. By permitting (some) feminist concerns to be both addressed and set aside, the federal government facilitated the introduction of the X classification.

While the X classification became a new legal category for video-tapes in the Australian Capital Territory and Northern Territory, it was (and continues to be) rejected by all state parliaments. As indicated by the earlier discussion of the move against the X classification in New South Wales, feminist arguments against pornography appear to have had a significant impact at state level, converging with a conservative push (especially in states like Queensland) against both the federal Labor government and a liberalisation of censorship laws. The result was the appearance of a new and significant disparity between the Commonwealth and territories on the one hand, and the states on the other. Over-the-counter sales of X-rated videos became legal in the Australian Capital Territory and Northern Territory but not elsewhere in the country. Consequently, a thriving (and legal) mail-order industry has become established in the Australian Capital Territory to service interstate customers.

Decriminalising Prostitution

Street Soliciting in New South Wales

From the early 1970s onwards in New South Wales some feminists and civil libertarians called for reform of the laws against prostitution (see Chapter 5). In 1976 this cause was significantly advanced by the election of a Labor government which was publicly committed to various social justice issues, including the need for legislation to combat sex discrimination and for law reform in the area of so-called victimless crimes (such as vagrancy and prostitution).

Pressure on the Wran government to tackle the issue of prostitution was immediate and sustained. In 1976 a general meeting of the Women's Electoral Lobby (WEL) passed the following motion: 'That prostitution be decriminalised and that a copy of this motion be sent to Premier Wran and Attorney-General Walker reminding them of election promises on victimless crimes. Plus WEL support of the government's intentions and promises' (*WEL-Informed*, August 1976: 3). The New South Wales branch of WEL had already been organising on this issue for some time. In 1977 a discussion group on prostitution was formed and members actively lobbied individual members of the government to reform prostitution law. This group also prepared a submission for the public seminar on victimless crime that the government organised in 1977 (*WEL-Informed*, February 1977: 27).

In 1976–77 the New South Wales branch of WEL presented motions for the decriminalisation of all victimless crimes – including abortion, prostitution, homosexuality, vagrancy and drunkenness – to local branches of the Labor Party and to the Labor Party's Women's Conference (*WEL-Informed*, March 1977: 10). In 1976 the NSW Labor Women's Committee resolved that 'prostitution is not an offence and should not in any legislation be regarded as other than acts between consenting adults' (cited in Women's Advisory Council Report, NSWPD 141: 30).

This suggests that prostitution was starting to be conceptualised in terms of a private sexual activity between consenting adults, that is, one which should not be liable to undue government interference. While privacy arguments had been applied for some time to homosexuality, abortion, and the consumption of pornography (see Chapters 4 and 5) they had not previously been applied to prostitution by central political actors within mainstream political institutions.

In its first annual report to the parliament in 1978, the NSW Women's Advisory Council presented a position paper on prostitution and argued for a decriminalisation of various prostitution-related offences. In particular, the council advocated the removal of laws against soliciting or loitering for the purposes of prostitution. The practice of arresting and fining street prostitutes, the council argued, was discriminatory (because it targeted street prostitutes as opposed to other sorts of prostitutes and because 'only female prostitutes are charged and not their male clients'); it was also ineffective as a deterrent, expensive in its use of police and court resources, an encouragement to police corruption, and left the state open to the charge that it lived on the earnings of prostitution. The council also recommended the strengthening of legal sanctions against those who exploited prostitutes (as cited in NSWPD 141: 31). *Discrimination* and *exploitation* were, therefore, key words in this approach to prostitution law reform.

The government's principal response to this was the 1979 Prostitution Bill (later Act). This legislation was part of a larger cognate bill which repealed the notorious *Summary Offences Act.* It contained no provisions to outlaw public soliciting for the purposes of prostitution, which meant that soliciting was effectively decriminalised in New South Wales. Any 'truly offensive' soliciting in a public place was now to be dealt with under the general laws against offensive conduct (as prescribed under the new *Offences in Public Places Act*).

The repeal of the *Summary Offences Act* also removed the offence of being a reputed prostitute on premises habitually used for prostitution. To some extent, this increased the rights of prostitutes to work in brothels and from their own homes. However, under the *Landlord and Tenant Act*, landlords retained the right to evict tenants who carried out prostitution and, under the *Disorderly Houses Act*, police retained the right to apply to the Supreme Court for brothels to be declared a disorderly house, which meant that persons found on those premises were guilty of an offence. Under the 1979 Act sanctions were also continued for procuring, living on the earnings of prostitution, and using premises for the purposes of prostitution which were 'held out' as available for massage, sauna, photographic studios, etc. The government described living on the earnings of prostitution as one of the 'more repugnant aspects of prostitution' and 'a classic situation of exploitation ... one that should continue to be condemned by criminal sanctions' (NSWPD 146: 4923). As in the past, owners, operators and receptionists in brothels were vulnerable to these laws, as were the lovers and adult children of prostitutes. The 1979 *Prostitution Act* also introduced new sanctions for advertising that premises were used or that a person was available for prostitution.

The effects of the 1979 reforms were, therefore, rather mixed. As Marcia Neave (1994: 78) commented: 'Not surprisingly, the retention of provisions directed at brothels, coupled with the ban on advertising and the decriminalisation of street prostitution, led to an increase in street prostitution. Virtually every interest group was critical of the legislation.' Sex workers complained that the new laws did not go far enough and that they were being applied arbitrarily by the police. In March 1981 complaints from local residents about a deteriorating situation in the Kings Cross and Darlinghurst areas were reported at length in the *Sydney Morning Herald*. Residents claimed that since the repeal of the *Summary Offences Act* in 1979 prostitution had spread out of its traditional domain in the Cross and into surrounding residential areas. Prostitutes and their clients were said to be creating a major public nuisance, by conducting their business virtually in public – in cars and laneways – and by littering the area with used condoms. Residents accused the police of inaction and corruption, while the police responded with claims that the new *Offences in Public Places Act* did not provide them with sufficient powers to control street prostitution (*SMH*, 6, 20 March 1981). In fact, the Police Union clearly campaigned against the 1979 laws by advertising in the *Daily Telegraph* that it could no longer guarantee safety on the streets (Neave 1994: 79).

The Attorney-General agreed that there had been a spread of prostitution from the 'accepted areas' of Kings Cross. He reported that more younger people were now involved in prostitution and that there were more male and transvestite prostitutes (*SMH*, 6, 19 March 1981). However, the government rejected the claim that police had insufficient powers to control street prostitution. Complaints continued from local residents, business people and local council members.

The Sydney City Council responded to the problem by closing streets and installing special amber street lights. According to council engineers, these lights would make the faces of prostitutes appear yellow and their lips black:

> It was hoped that potential customers in passing cars would be dissuaded from stopping if they saw the girls like this. ... People don't like to spend a lot of time down there choosing a girl, and if they all looked alike, it was hoped that people wouldn't use the area for picking up prostitutes (*SMH*, 2 December 1982).

This plan was said to have failed because there was no reduction in the number of women soliciting or in the number of cars and male pedestrians cruising the area (*SMH*, 2 December 1982).

The *Sydney Morning Herald* called on the government to re-criminalise soliciting in residential areas and to give the Sydney City Council more effective town-planning powers to deal with brothels in residential areas (*SMH*, 10 December 1982). This latter issue came to a head in February 1983 when the council failed in its bid, under the *Environmental Planning and Assessment Act*, to close down one of Sydney's most famous brothels, A Touch of Class. In a reserved decision, the Chief Judge of the Land and Environment Court, Justice McClelland, said that the use of these premises as a brothel was not prohibited by the relevant planning legislation. He argued that A Touch of Class was a 'well-conducted brothel' and that, anyway, the court was not designed to uphold morals (*SMH*, 9 February 1983).

In parliament the Opposition attacked the government for its failure to control prostitution. An Opposition bill, the Offences in Public Places (Amendment) Bill, was introduced in order to address what were seen as deficiencies in the existing law, 'particularly regarding street prostitution and street conduct in Darlinghurst and East Sydney'. It proposed to reinstitute the offence of soliciting for the purposes of prostitution in or within view of a public place and thus to make clear that soliciting was offensive conduct (NSWPD 174: 4785).

This Bill did not survive beyond its second reading debate. However, less than two weeks later the government introduced a Prostitution (Amendment) Bill, which aimed:

> to ensure that persons who reside in basically residential areas are not subject to the flagrant and unseemly aspects of prostitution which cause severe inconvenience. Prostitution is an activity that has traditionally been confined to commercial areas. The effect of creating an offence of soliciting

in the terms of [this bill] will be to redirect what is essentially a commercial
activity back into commercial and industrial areas [NSWPD 174: 5244].

The new legislation prohibited soliciting for the purposes of prostitution in public places that were 'near' dwellings, schools, churches and
hospitals. As Neave (1994: 79) commented, the 'imprecision' of this
amendment – together with changes to the *Offences in Public Places Act* –
'considerably expanded the powers of police'; these powers were used
against prostitutes rather than their clients.

In 1983 the government also announced its intention to set up an
inquiry into the public health, criminal, social and community welfare
aspects of prostitution. In the interim, however, the *Prostitution (Amendment) Act* was said to be a 'practical and commonsense' attempt by a
'caring and responsible' government to deal with the 'complex and
highly sensitive' issue of prostitution. Moreover, the government
remained committed to 'avoiding the gaoling option' (for prostitutes)
and to affording 'the minimum opportunity for prostitutes to be exploited by others' (NSWPD 174: 5244, 5459). There was, then, an
ongoing concern with issues of justice and equity as they applied to
prostitutes.

The Select Committee of the Legislative Assembly upon Prostitution
was appointed in March 1983 and tabled its findings in April 1986. As a
result of its assessment of the nature of client demand (arguably one of
the most original and outstanding features of its report) the committee
proposed that a reduction in the level of prostitution was both feasible
and desirable (NSWSCP: 75). This was premised on evidence which
suggested that the demand for prostitution could not be explained
wholly in terms of men's biological urges, particularly as considerable
changes in the size and nature of client demand had occurred over the
previous decade. Research conducted by the Select Committee indicated that in the mid-1970s:

> prostitution continued to thrive despite – rather than because of – 'sex
> freedom'. New clients were coming forward with new demands. ... The
> sexual revolution of the 1960s and 1970s – as packaged and sold in maga-
> zines such as *Penthouse* and *Playboy* – stimulated the demand for a variety of
> sexual partners and practices. Often this demand could only be met within
> prostitution [NSWSCP: 75].

The committee suggested, then, that if the demand for prostitution
services could be stimulated (by changes in the sexual culture), it
might also be reduced by specific legal and public policy initiatives
(NSWSCP: 75). As in the Neave Report in Victoria, the committee

argued that the overall aim should be a minimisation of prostitution. This aim was the basis of a series of recommendations for community education programs, restrictions on prostitution advertising, and restrictions on pornography (NSWSCP: 91).[8]

As a way of better managing the existing demand for prostitution services, the Select Committee recommended a policy of 'decriminalisation with controls'. The controls proposed included that brothels be subject to town-planning (rather than criminal) laws and that the ownership of brothels be subject to official supervision. The committee recommended the continuation of existing laws which prohibited public soliciting, but argued that changes to the *Prostitution Act* were needed to clarify the meaning of the offence of soliciting near certain premises. The committee also recommended that clients should be subject to the same enforcement of soliciting laws as prostitutes (and recognised the injustice of the double standard which protected clients from prosecution while criminalising prostitutes). It argued for the repeal of laws which prohibited living on the earnings of prostitution (except where violence, coercion or other forms of exploitation were applied) and suggested changes to social welfare arrangements which would 'make it less difficult for prostitutes to leave the trade and ... make prostitution less of an alternative to those who may be forced to consider it as employment' (NSWSCP: xxix–xxx).

The Select Committee's recommendations were never acted upon by the Labor government before it was voted out of office two years later, in 1988.

Brothel Prostitution in Victoria

In Victoria proposals to decriminalise brothel prostitution had a long history and assured cross-party support by the time a specific bill was presented to the parliament in 1984. The subject of prostitution, massage parlours in particular, produced questions in the Victorian parliament throughout the 1970s.[9] In March 1978 the (Liberal) Chief Secretary was taken to task by the Liberal Party State Council for the government's failure to act on the massage parlour problem in Melbourne. The council called for an inquiry into the prostitution industry preparatory to legislation which would legalise and control the prostitution trade in massage parlours (*SMH*, 6 March 1978).

While no inquiry was announced, the government passed the *Summary Offences (Amendment) Act* in 1978. This Act initiated substantial increases in legal penalties for soliciting and gutter-crawling, activities which the government claimed were causing rising concern in certain Melbourne communities. They said that many local residents, 'both male and female', were being accosted on the streets outside their own homes (VPD 341: 6295). The new amendment to the *Summary Offences Act* focused on street soliciting and did not address the issue of massage parlours. However, the government indicated at this time that it intended to seek a voluntary agreement with the media in an attempt to curtail advertising by massage parlours. In addition, the government said it had future plans for the licensing of massage parlours and a zonal system of regulation to be instituted by means of town-planning laws. This approach was described as a decriminalisation of prostitution 'with controls' and as a 'good solution' to the prostitution problem: 'Where prostitution is simply a moral judgement between two people it should be of no concern to the police. ... police attention should be confined to injurious and offensive matters' (VPD 341: 6961–2). Clearly, this speaker regarded prostitution as a private sexual transaction, although soliciting for the purposes of prostitution could still legitimately fall within the ambit of police attention. While several members of parliament applauded the suggestion that discreet forms of prostitution should be decriminalised in certain zones of the city, there was criticism from various Labor members of the decision to increase the legal penalties for soliciting. For example, the member for Ascot Vale supported the proposed zoning system but cited the findings of the recent Royal Commission on Human Relationships which found that, in many respects, 'the practice of soliciting is not offensive'. Edmunds argued that the law needed to distinguish between offensive and non-offensive soliciting because 'community attitudes to this type of human behaviour have changed'. Other Labor members argued that increasing the fines for soliciting would simply increase the level of criminal involvement in prostitution. They also argued for an all-party committee to investigate the prostitution industry, to ensure that homosexuals and prostitutes were not denied their human rights and to ensure that 'people involved in prostitution' were not harassed by police (VPD 341: 6959–62). The harassment of prostitutes was also a central issue in a report published by the Status of Women Policy Committee of the state branch of the Labor Party in December 1978. This report presented an explicitly feminist case for decriminalisation of prostitution (see *Bulletin*, 5 December 1978: 20–1).

By the early 1980s, the basis of the impetus to decriminalise brothel prostitution in Victoria was twofold. On the one hand there was a continuing (and expanding) concern that the law should be withdrawn from private, consensual sexual relations between adults. On the other hand there were new concerns with equality between the sexes and with issues of sexual exploitation. The nature of these twin concerns and the way that they intersected on the issue of prostitution first became visible in Victoria during debate on the *Crimes (Sexual Offences) Act* in 1981.

This Act sought to reform the law in relation to a whole range of sexual offences, including prostitution. It introduced new definitions of rape, outlawed rape in marriage, decriminalised private, consensual homosexual relations between men, and rendered prostitution law gender-neutral. Thus, the legal definitions of *prostitution* and of *brothels* were to apply equally to males and females; the laws against soliciting for the purposes of prostitution were also reformulated so that they applied equally to both. All penalties for this latter offence were increased (VPD 355: 4456–9).

It appears, then, that there was significant support for the view that laws addressed to sexual behaviour should not show any evidence of sex discrimination and should address only inherently public and offensive acts such as soliciting for 'immoral purposes' (homosexual soliciting)[10] or soliciting for the purposes of prostitution. Quite clearly, then, it was the public act of soliciting (but only by male homosexuals and prostitutes) and not acts of prostitution or homosexuality *per se* that was to be subject to prohibition. Clearly, too, part of the price for shifting the legal onus from public to private (and decriminalising private homosexual behaviour between adult men) was the imposition of heavier legal penalties on street prostitutes and cruising homosexuals.

The debate in parliament on this Act was notable for its focus on the issue of male homosexuality and the relative absence of concern with other male sexual practices (such as rape and prostitution). Perhaps this was because most members of parliament did not see (heterosexual) prostitution – or even rape – as particularly problematic. As the member for Ringwood argued, 'heterosexual activity is natural; homosexuality is not' (VPD 355: 5021).

While the Leader of the Opposition, John Cain, commended the moves to remove criminal penalties from consensual sexual acts between males and females, he suggested that this initiative was possible only because of the immense social changes which had taken place in Australia over the previous decade, particularly in relation to the role of women and relations between the sexes (VPD 355: 5010). Cain also cited the Wolfenden Report and the Royal Commission on Human Relationships in support of the argument that 'it should not be a criminal activity to engage in what are characterised as offences relating to prostitution, simply because money changes hands – unless there is some nuisance or annoyance caused to other persons' (VPD 355: 5103). Cain moved an amendment calling for the withdrawal of the bill and its replacement by one which abolished all 'consensual, adult sexual offences' except where such acts cause nuisance or annoyance or where the protection of children was required (VPD 355: 5011–14). This amendment was rejected by the government.

In 1984 the new Labor government in Victoria – headed by John Cain – introduced a Planning (Brothels) Bill (later Act). Originally this was called the Planning (Massage Parlours) Bill but the government acceded to Opposition pressure that the legislation should reflect its 'real contents'. The government said the bill aimed 'to regulate and control the location of brothels in Victoria and to enable them to have the opportunity of obtaining proper planning permits as brothels' (VPD 374: 4415). For brothels with a valid town-planning permit, most prostitution-related activities (such as managing a brothel, using or permitting premises to be used for the purposes of prostitution, soliciting within a brothel, consorting with prostitutes) would not attract criminal penalties. However, the legislation significantly increased the penalties to be applied to illegal brothels. In parliament the Government indicated that the new legislation was designed to improve the management of the prostitution industry and to address some specific problems. It signalled its intention to allow a twelve-month moratorium on the prosecution of illegal brothels and to hold a full inquiry into prostitution (VPD 374: 4416).

The report of the Inquiry into Prostitution (conducted by Marcia Neave) was tabled in the Victorian parliament in October 1985. Its thrust was clearly feminist. Neave argued:

> prostitution is an undesirable form of work often undertaken at personal or emotional cost. For many men and women the decision to prostitute themselves is influenced by poverty, lack of education or unemployment. ... [However] A society which, at least rhetorically, prizes sexual equality, human dignity and non-exploitative relationships should not regard prostitution as acceptable. The purchase of sexual services involves the treatment of human beings as objects. We believe it is symptomatic of sexual and economic inequalities which should not exist in a healthy society [Neave Report 1: 229].

The overall goal, therefore, was the minimisation of prostitution and, 'if possible', its eradication. To this end the Neave Report recommended a repeal of the criminal laws covering prostitution-related activities, except where their retention was necessary to prevent harm to prostitutes or those at risk of becoming prostitutes, and to protect the community from demonstrable nuisance caused by prostitution-related activities. Four main factors were said to have influenced this position – an increasing trend towards the abolition of criminal penalties for the private sexual activities of adults; the discriminatory operation of the law in relation to prostitution-related activities; the costs involved in the retention of criminal penalties; and the inability of criminal penalties to eliminate the harmful effects of prostitution (Neave Report 1: 230).

The Neave Report also recommended: the imposition of controls upon prostitution advertising; a decriminalisation of small-scale prostitution (that is, one or two workers operating alone); a limited decriminalisation of street soliciting; and greater emphasis in police practice on the apprehension of the clients of prostitutes (where they were committing offences under the *Summary Offences Act*). It generally supported the decriminalisation of brothel prostitution which had been established in 1984 under the *Planning (Brothels) Act* but recommended a range of specific reforms to this Act, including a provision that brothel operators be licensed.

In parliament the government said that it accepted the basic premise of the Neave Report (that prostitution was exploitative) and agreed that social policy should be directed towards the minimisation of prostitution. The 1986 Prostitution Regulation Bill adopted all of the recommendations for legislative reform made by the Neave Report except for the proposal that there should be a limited decriminalisation of street soliciting; this latter recommendation was said to be impractical (VPD 384: 1497). However, this bill was extensively amended in the Victorian upper house and the government did not proclaim much of the resulting *Prostitution Regulation Act*. As Neave (1994: 85) argued, the result was an 'irrational patchwork' of prostitution laws in Victoria, and the strategy proposed by her inquiry was 'effectively undermined'. Small scale prostitution – even where it involved a single worker operating from his or her own home – remained illegal (where this occurred without a planning permit) and continued to attract significant penalties. Local councils retained the right to veto planning permits for brothels, although this was still subject to a right of appeal. (Neave had recommended that councils should not be able to refuse planning permits for brothels.) Consequently, the procedure for establishing a legal brothel continued to be both lengthy and expensive because it invariably involved an appeal process; this tended to encourage the growth of illegal brothels. The 1986 reforms did not, then, offer any substantial solutions to the problems already identified in the prostitution industry in Victoria.

Parliamentary Debates about Prostitution

While New South Wales and Victoria adopted quite different legislative strategies in relation to prostitution from the late 1970s onwards, there were also some clear continuities in the way that the main issues and problems were conceptualised in parliament. In all three states where new prostitution laws were debated (including South Australia where reform legislation failed in both 1980 and 1986), the aim was to decriminalise various aspects of the prostitution industry. This was an aim which had been confined to political groups outside the parliamentary arena in the early 1970s (see Chapter 5). By the late 1970s, however, calls for the decriminalisation of prostitution were becoming part of mainstream political discourse.

Several specific arguments were deployed in parliament in support of decriminalisation proposals. In the first place, feminist arguments about the legal discrimination faced by women working in the sex industry were raised by parliamentarians in all three state parliaments (although to a greater extent in New South Wales and South Australia than in Victoria). As the New South Wales government argued in 1979, there was 'discrimination inherent in ... the laws relating to prostitution. The prostitute is fined; the client is not'. In the Legislative Council one male member described this as an example of a male 'chauvinistic double standard', while Dorothy Isaksen argued that the laws against street soliciting were 'a farce ... hypocritical and extremely discriminatory', particularly as escort agency advertisements appeared freely in at least one Sydney newspaper (NSWPD 146: 4921, 5003, 4846–8).

Similarly, in South Australia, members of parliament argued that there were 'major difficulties' with the implementation of prostitution laws (SAPD 1980–81: 1813), particularly as they 'grossly discriminated' against the prostitute. It was considered an injustice that prostitutes were frequently charged before the courts while their clients got off scot-free (SAPD 1979–80: 1046). These arguments were raised by both male and female parliamentarians but were clearly influenced by the increased numbers of women (and feminists) in State parliaments and on policy committees within the Labor Party.

The second argument used in Australian parliaments to support proposals for the decriminalisation of prostitution related to the inherent privacy of sexual behaviour. For some parliamentarians, prostitution was a private contract between individuals:

If individuals wish to make a contract between themselves for whatever purposes, where they are not going to cause any harm either to themselves or anyone else and they wish to take part in sexual or any other activity associated with sex, that is purely a matter for themselves. If they do not offend anybody then the law has no part in those arrangements. If it is to be done for money, that is a matter between the two individuals. ... I see nothing wrong with a person who is prepared to prostitute himself [sic] [VPD 355: 5028–9].

As prostitution was a private sexual arrangement, decriminalisation drew an appropriate line:

> between conduct that is properly a concern of the criminal law and conduct that falls into the area of private morality. ... In no way will [decriminalisation] condone prostitution in a moral sense ... Indeed ... to society as a whole prostitution is not acceptable. ... [But] moral condemnation should not necessarily be synonymous with legal condemnation, and this legislation will, quite rightly, leave the matter squarely with the individual to decide for himself or herself [NSWPD 146: 4945].

It was argued, then, that it was inappropriate for governments to be involved in policing the private sexual behaviour of individuals by means of laws against prostitution. While the parliament had a responsibility to protect the community's interests it should 'not ... legislate beyond that point' (SAPD 1979–80: 1048; 1980–81: 1813). As one member of the South Australian parliament pointed out, this was an important part of the approach advocated by the Wolfenden Report.

However, the Wolfenden Report had specifically advocated increased legal penalties on street prostitution because of its capacity to create public offence (see Chapter 4). While the decriminalisation proposed in South Australia and Victoria addressed private (brothel) prostitution, the New South Wales proposal specifically decriminalised street prostitution. This was clearly an effect of feminist arguments about sex discrimination and of a civil liberties approach which emphasised the need for a reduction in the range and type of street offences. In the NSW Legislative Council, Dorothy Isaksen reported that she had visited Kings Cross and observed the activities of street prostitutes and their clients. She reported:

> most of the girls were standing quietly in doorways, or leaning against the wall; I saw only four girls speak to or approach prospective customers. Many more men approached the girls and conversed with them. They then went quietly into a nearby hotel or residential. I considered some of the spruikers outside the blue movies or kinky sex shops to be much more offensive [NSWPD 146: 4846–8].

This approach contained, then, a specific critique of the idea that street soliciting was inherently offensive.

The argument that prostitution involved private sexual behaviour – and should therefore be decriminalised – had an important rationale. When the New South Wales government proposed to reintroduce penalties for soliciting in residential areas, it was suggested that prostitution was essentially a private, commercial activity which should be conducted only in commercial areas. There was, then, a split within the private sphere between the personal and economic (commercial) realms of private life. Moreover, it was not regarded as appropriate that the latter should infringe on the former, for 'every citizen is entitled to expect that what is essentially a commercial activity is not conducted in front of his or her house. This is not a matter of morals – it is a matter of environmental planning' (NSWPD 174: 5447). Thus, prostitution was illegitimate in residential areas where it could interfere with personal and family life and pose a health risk to children (NSWPD 201: 1338–9).

The third argument used in support of the proposals to decriminalise prostitution was managerial in nature. Members of parliament argued that, because prostitution was an inevitable feature of human society and could not be eliminated, the important thing was to adopt the most effective means of managing the particular problems which emerged around the industry. This approach reflected the growing importance of administrative reform discourses during the early 1980s (Yeatman 1990). It was particularly evident in Victoria but also appeared in New South Wales and South Australia. In 1984, for example, the Victorian government's main rationale for the *Planning (Brothels) Act* was almost entirely the pragmatic need for better management:

> The Government accepts that prostitution is a reality in our society and that brothels exist and will continue to exist in some form or another. These amendments will enable the decriminalization of prostitution to the extent that it occurs in brothels which conform with relevant town planning controls [VPD 374: 4415–16].

Thus, while prostitution was represented as a 'situation that exploits women or men' it was also important to 'face up to the reality of things as they are in the real world' (VPD 374: 4418–21). In this view prostitution was 'a fact of life', one which has been present in human societies for centuries (VPD 384: 2508).

According to Australian parliamentarians, one of the main problems associated with prostitution was that the laws encouraged problems such as police corruption while the trade itself attracted gangsters and drug traffickers (NSWPD 146: 4945). Decriminalisation was said to be a 'sensible, rational and reasonable' (VPD 374: 4422–3) approach to beginning to manage these problems in new ways. The identification of the HIV virus and its recognition as a potentially major public health problem was also influential from the mid-1980s onwards. Parliamentarians began to argue that decriminalisation would assist in the deployment of AIDS-prevention programs in the prostitution industry (see, for example, NSWPD 201: 1339; VPD 384: 2519).

Apart from addressing some of these problems, decriminalisation was also represented as a suitable strategy for organising the industry. As several members of parliament suggested, decriminalisation offered new rights for workers and 'some measure of protection' against exploitation. Decriminalisation did not mean that the parliament approved of prostitution; it simply acknowledged that the industry needed to be controlled in more efficient ways and in ways that were more acceptable to society (VPD 384: 2520).

Underlying these arguments about the need to decriminalise prostitution were, of course, specific views about the nature of prostitutes and their clients. In the late 1970s and 1980s the figure of the prostitute (at least in parliamentary debates) was still predominantly female, although the presence of male and transsexual workers was increasingly acknowledged. As in all of the previous periods examined in this book, prostitutes also continued to be subject to a set of contradictory discourses about their 'true' nature. Many parliamentarians, whether they supported decriminalisation or not, argued that prostitutes were driven into the industry by economic need (VPD 355: 5029; SAPD 1979–80: 1047) and that this was a direct effect of the harsh eco-nomic climate of the 1980s. Prostitutes, then, were 'more to be pitied than condemned' for they had 'an extremely unpleasant existence' (NSWPD 174: 4777–8). Other parliamentarians, but particularly those who supported decriminalisation, argued that sex workers chose their occupation. In New South Wales Elisabeth Kirkby argued: 'Not all prostitutes are forced into prostitution ... many women choose prostitution as a way of life. It is their democratic right to do so' (NSWPD 202: 2331). In this view women had the right to do with their bodies what they wished and prostitution was not necessarily a degrading occupation or a sign of social deviance. However, as in the Wolfenden Report, there was still some suggestion in parliament that 'predisposing psychological factors' were involved in a woman's decision to become a prostitute (SAPD 1979–80: 1048).

Evidence collected by various official inquiries into prostitution, conducted during the late 1970s and 1980s, indicated that not all (or even most) prostitutes felt exploited and degraded by their work. Sex workers reported that they often felt powerful in their interactions with clients and that 'the job they did was less degrading than ... many of the other options available' (SAPD 1979–80: 1458, 1047). Some parliamentarians also argued that prostitutes provided a 'necessary service as evidenced by the hundreds and thousands of people [*sic*] who call on their services every day' (NSWPD 202: 1341; also NSWPD 174: 5128). There was, therefore, no reason to scapegoat prostitutes by increasing criminal sanctions upon them; it was 'not the prostitutes but the noise, the offensiveness, the misbehaviour, the misconduct [and] the traffic congestion' that were the main problems associated with the industry (NSWPD 174: 4778). Many parliamentarians were sympathetic to the legal discrimination faced by sex workers. In general, the representation of sex workers in parliamentary debates during this period was more positive than in any other period examined so far. Clearly, feminist discourse played an important role in this change.

The parliamentary proponents of decriminalisation tended to represent the clients of prostitutes as men who were either 'victims of circumstances' or simply free agents pursuing their individual choices. For the former group, prostitution was said to provide 'a therapeutic service', particularly for elderly men, migrant men, men without the social skills to strike up a relationship with women, and men who were 'physically and mentally disadvantaged'. In this view men sought out the services of prostitutes because of 'personal or, more particularly, psychological problems. ... [Such a client] is unable to create a person-to-person relationship with a woman' (SAPD 1979–80: 1047).

In the New South Wales parliament Premier Neville Wran argued that:

> Every night on the streets of Sydney thousands of men who have been aboard ships for weeks at a time are unleashed. There are others who perhaps because of personality problems have no continuing association with a member of the opposite sex. They are persons who because of language or other difficulties have no relationship with a member of the opposite sex. It has always been recognised in great cities such as Sydney that prostitution is a safety valve for the protection of women in the community. So if what is really being debated here is eliminating prostitution, the question is what do we substitute for it? [NSWPD 74: 4780].

As in previous historical periods, then, clients were represented as men who – for various reasons associated with their work, health, marital status, or lack of good looks – were without sexual outlets apart from prostitution. But this view contains an explicit assumption about men's sexual needs; these are assumed to be biologically driven and probably irrepressible. From this perspective, it is notable that moves to decriminalise prostitution can be represented as a means of facilitating – and better managing – men's access to prostitutes.

The New South Wales Attorney-General argued that community ideals about appropriate sexual behaviour posed a major obstacle for government in dealing with prostitution:

> one of the things about prostitution that can blind us is our sexual hang-ups. Everyone would like there to be a warmblooded loving relationship between a man and a woman and would be saddened that something less must be found by some people – and found it must be, for if it is not found in that way, it may be found in other violent and tragic ways [NSWPD 174: 5460–1].

While the argument that men need sexual release of some kind has been reformulated here in terms of 'people', it clearly asserts the dangers of unserviced (probably male) sexual needs. The post-war norm and ideal of 'loving, warm-blooded' relations between the sexes is represented as the best sort of relationship but as one not available to everyone. From this perspective, the decriminalisation of prostitution could also be regarded as a rational means of managing irrepressible and dangerous sexual needs. Even in the 1980s, then, masturbation – or celibacy – was not regarded by politicians as a suitable substitute for (hetero)sexual intercourse. However, in the late 1970s and 1980s we also see the appearance of a tendency to represent clients as men who were free agents seeking to supplement their more normal sexual outlets. Thus, men were reported to go to prostitutes out of a desire for 'novel sexual contact' or because they wanted 'kinky sex' (SAPD 1979–80: 1459; VPD 384: 2503–4). Women were said to be 'deprived' of such sexual options. A suggestion was made to the South Australian Select Committee of Inquiry on Prostitution that something should be done to allow women the same advantage which men had in relation to the services of prostitutes (SAPD 1979–80: 1459).

From this perspective, men's sexual use of prostitutes was not inherently problematic; any 'sex discrimination' could be overcome by extending men's 'freedom to use prostitutes' to women. However, as in the 1960s and early 1970s (see Chapters 4 and 5), there was also the suggestion from several quarters that men who went to prostitutes were *not* normal men: 'Anyone who uses a brothel in this age must have either a deep physical need, be desperately lonely or have some sort of psychological hang-up. ... Only a "desperate" or a fool would frequent brothels in this era of AIDS' (VPD 384: 2511).

Now that non-prostitute women were sexually available outside marriage, it was assumed that normal men did not need to seek out the services of prostitutes. According to one member of the Victorian parliament, men who regularly went to prostitutes were sexually maladjusted and probably the victims of 'sexploiters', that is, pornographers. Such men turned to prostitutes in order to be able to act out the sexual fantasies which they had acquired from the consumption of pornography, although such 'depersonalised sex reinforces a psychic maladjustment in which sexual gratification becomes separated from love, affection and responsibility. Pornography often aggravates the slide into even more bizarre forms of deviation and perversion' (VPD 384: 2504). In this view pornography was a form of prostitution advertising and positively undermined the acquisition of a normal pattern of masculine sexual behaviour.

In all three state parliaments under review there was also a significant level of opposition to the proposal that prostitution should be decriminalised. This was more evident in New South Wales (where the Liberal–National Party Opposition was vehemently opposed to the decriminalisation of street soliciting) and South Australia. In Victoria both Labor and Liberal Parties (but not the National Party) supported the proposal to regulate brothels under town-planning laws and to decriminalise prostitution-related activities which occurred in legal brothels. Conservative members of these parliaments argued that prostitution was wrong because it perverted 'the true role of sex' which was 'a mutual act, a sharing act, an expression of love' (SAPD 1979–80: 2220; see also VPD 384: 2503). Prostitution was a form of human slavery (VPD 384: 2502); it exploited and degraded men, women and children – but particularly women.

The conservative approach included an explicit critique of the idea that prostitution was a private sexual activity (and/or a victimless crime). In the South Australian parliament, for example, members argued that the effects of prostitution extended 'way beyond the boundaries of private morality' to disrupt the lives of individuals, families and the wider community (SAPD 1979–80: 2077–8). Prostitution was said to degrade all who were involved in it, clients and workers, because they were 'forced to subdue their own feelings and by so doing would be hardened towards other people' (SAPD 1980–81: 1817). In this view prostitutes (but not, apparently, clients) irretrievably damaged their future relationships: 'Once the commitment to take money has been made, the female has given up even the pretence of an emotionally valued relationship with a male' (VPD 384: 2503). As a result, sex workers 'turned against men' to become lesbians; they also took drugs and ceased to care about their families after working in the industry for any length of time. Similarly, the wives of clients were said to 'suffer neglect, perversion or venereal disease' (VPD 384: 2504). For conservatives, then, prostitution was not a private issue for its effects could not be confined to the individuals directly involved in the prostitution transaction (SAPD 1980–81: 1817).

Some women parliamentarians were also vehemently opposed to the decriminalisation of prostitution. In South Australia Jennifer Adamson, a member of the Liberal Party and Minister for Health, was the only woman to participate in the debate on the decriminalisation of prostitution in that state. Adamson cited the views of the League of Women Voters of South Australia and argued that decriminalisation meant that prostitution would be 'given the imprimatur of the South Australian community'. In her view it was offensive to suggest that prostitution should simply be subject to the normal laws governing business activity because prostitution was 'traffic debasing to human dignity' (SAPD 1980–81: 2078–9). Thus, in South Australia, but not in New South Wales, a conservative feminist discourse was deployed by a woman parliamentarian against the proposal to decriminalise prostitution.

Conservatives argued that it was necessary for the law to continue to exact heavy legal penalties on prostitution-related activities (NSWPD 174: 5450; VPD 384: 2493). In the view of one speaker in the Victorian parliament, it was only 'relativistic' and 'hedonistic' legislators who thought otherwise (VPD 384: 2500). Conservatives argued that legal sanctions were an effective deterrent to the growth of prostitution (SAPD 1980–81: 1817) and were an important means of asserting what was right and wrong for society as a whole.

Conclusion

In the late 1970s and 1980s the level of public and official concern with pornography and prostitution continued to increase. This is evident in the large number of government-sponsored inquiries into prostitution and pornography, and in various attempts at law reform addressed to the sex industries.

There are several reasons why this occurred. The most important factors were the increased number of women in politics, the wide deployment of feminist discourse within mainstream political institutions, and the emergence of new 'managerial' discourses which sought more efficient and equitable methods for managing the sex industries.

Most feminists in this period argued that the sex industry oppressed women (specifically sex workers, but also women more generally). From their new vantage points within political parties, policy committees and parliament, they were able to shape the direction of political debate and legal reform from the late 1970s onwards. For example, it was largely as a result of feminist anti-pornography arguments that the states refused the X classification for videotapes in 1984–85. While the crisis over child pornography in 1976–77 provided the first challenge to the regulatory systems established by state and federal governments in the early 1970s, it was feminist arguments deployed during the debate over X-rated videos which contested the dominance of liberal and libertarian perspectives on pornography. In 1984 a significant number of male and female parliamentarians argued that the consumption of pornography was detrimental to women's safety and civil status. As a result, feminist discourse came into headlong confrontation with liberal and libertarian discourses which tended to emphasise the harmlessness of pornography, the private nature of its consumption and the illegitimacy of government intervention.

In relation to prostitution, feminist and liberal/libertarian discourses were less at odds (although fundamental tensions were later to become more apparent; see Chapter 7). During the late 1970s and 1980s decriminalisation was posed as a modern, feminist and more efficient solution to some of the problems and 'social dangers' posed by the prostitution industry. The main political impetus underlying the shift to a decriminalisation of prostitution was twofold. In the first place there was the increasing and long-term importance of arguments about the private nature of all sexual relations between consenting adults. By the late 1970s, these arguments were seen to be relevant to prostitution (as well as to all the non-commercial sexual practices of adults). Thus, liberals, libertarians and feminists tended to agree that the state should not intervene in the private sexual affairs of citizens just because money was exchanged. In the second place, feminist arguments about the need to address the legal discrimination faced by women who were sex workers became increasingly important from the mid-1970s onwards. This was particularly obvious in the move to decriminalise street soliciting in New South Wales during 1979, but also played an important part in the shift to a decriminalisation of brothel prostitution in Victoria in the 1980s.

CHAPTER 7

Current Issues

During the 1990s pornography and prostitution have continued to attract significant public and political attention in Australia. Debates continue about the regulation of X-rated videos and, more generally, about the depiction of violence in film and television. A plethora of new laws and policies have also been applied to prostitution, with many more jurisdictions introducing some form of decriminalisation. Australia now has a greater diversity of laws addressed to prostitution – and has implemented a larger range of decriminalisation strategies – than any other country in the world. New laws have also been developed to deal with child sex tourism and to address the transmission of pornography via new computer-based information technologies.

In the first section of this chapter I examine the context in which these legal innovations have been generated, noting in particular the impact of HIV/AIDS on national and international organisation of sex workers and the diversification of feminist approaches to both prostitution and pornography. I go on to examine changes in prostitution law – in Queensland, the Australian Capital Territory, the Northern Territory, Victoria and New South Wales – and look again at how parliamentarians speak about both the problem of prostitution and the range of appropriate solutions. Significant changes are now evident in both of these areas. In the final section of this chapter I examine some of the current Australian debates about pornography and new measures to control its transmission through information technologies.

Shifting Political and Sexual Cultures

In the late 1980s and 1990s economic issues and the consequences of economic recession have been a central concern of Australian governments. The theories and terminology of economics, economic rationalism and managerialism have come to dominate political life. Despite this, concerns about gender equity have not disappeared from the political scene. Indeed, the argument could be made that gender equity has now become a part of mainstream political culture in Australia. Rhetorically at least, governments of all political persuasions now find it necessary to address the situation of women citizens. This shift is evident at both federal and state levels – for example in the extension of laws designed to deal with sex discrimination. While many problems of gender inequality remain, significant policy interventions have occurred over the last decade in relation to women's health, child care, sexual harassment, rape and domestic violence (see Commonwealth of Australia 1992).

During this same period sexuality and sexual practice have also emerged as important public issues. In large part, this has been a direct consequence of the increased governmental focus on gender equity and of influential feminist approaches which link women's secondary status to the deployment of many 'normal' male and/or heterosexual practices. So, for example, the feminist call for better laws to deal with rape and sexual harassment have led to discussions (in both public and private spheres) about what coercive sexual practices might look like, that is, how they might be recognised by both men and women. Discussions like this have necessarily drawn attention to the details of sexual practice, leading individuals to scrutinise their own practices in the light of (what appear to be) new categories of proper and appropriate sexual behaviour.

Feminist critiques have also raised the issue of the sexual abuse of children. Most jurisdictions in Australia have introduced new laws (or tightened existing laws) in relation to both child sexual assault and pornography or prostitution involving children. In 1994 the Commonwealth parliament also passed the *Crimes (Child Sex Tourism) Amendment Act* which prescribed tough penalties for Australian citizens or residents who engaged in sexual activities with children while travelling overseas. Notably, this was the first occasion on which the Australian government sought to make a law pertaining to behaviour outside its territorial jurisdiction. Although this latter aspect of the legislation was controversial, there was widespread support among parliamentarians for a tougher approach to sex tourists (and sex tour organisers) who sought contact with children. The appearance of new international concerns about the sexual exploitation of children was also evident recently at the first ever World Congress Against Commercial Sexual Exploitation of Children in Stockholm. Delegates from 126 countries adopted a declaration and plan of action to address what was described as 'a billion-dollar industry that entraps 2 million young people around the world' (*SMH*, 20 August 1996).

Other factors have been significant in the production of an increasingly visible public concern with sexuality and sexual practice in Australia in the present. The sex industries, for example, have maintained an important presence in political and sexual culture over the last decade. Changes to prostitution laws (discussed below and in Chapter 6) have been widely debated in the community and have tended to make prostitution – and prostitution advertising – more visible. Pornography and other adult products continue to be available in sex shops (and in many newsagents, supermarkets and petrol stations) throughout the country. Since the Goss Labor government dismantled the Films and Literature Boards of Review, this national trend has also become manifest in Queensland.

In the 1990s explicit attempts have been made to create and service a pornography market for women with the establishment of separate sex shops and marketing lists for female customers.[1] At the same time, there have been ongoing public debates about the regulation of pornography, the depiction of sexual violence against women and, more generally, about the consequences of pervasive violence in film and television. Organisations like the Eros Foundation – which represents distributors of various adult products and services, including X-rated videos – have lobbied hard over this period for more amenable laws, particularly in relation to what they call non-violent erotica. The Eros Foundation argues for a stricter censorship of violence (in films classified as M, R and X) and a more liberal approach to films which depict sexually explicit but non-violent erotica. On occasion, the Eros Foundation has also threatened to seriously embarrass Australian politicians. For example, it promised to release taped evidence of Liberal–National Party MPs shopping for X-rated videos (and a copy of an X-rated video made by a former Liberal Party staffer) if the coalition parties carried out their threat to ban X-rated videos (*Weekend Australian*, 23–24 January 1993). The federal coalition government elected in 1996 has yet to act on its campaign promise to ban the distribution of X-rated videos out of Canberra, although the Attorney-General, Daryl Williams, has indicated his intention to proceed with this (*Canberra Times*, 14 September 1996).

During the 1990s we have also seen the appearance of strong and persuasive claims for equal citizenship rights by gay, lesbian and transsexual groups in Australia (see Burgmann 1993). Moreover, one effect of the HIV/AIDS epidemic has been to transform the relationship between the state and various 'sexual outlaw' groups. As in the late nineteenth and early twentieth centuries, the spectre of sexually transmitted disease has tended to focus public and political attention on sexual practice. In its governmental concern to foster safe sex, the

Australian state has entered into new modes of cooperative engagement with homosexual communities (Ballard 1992) and with sex
worker organisations. In 1986 Victoria became the first government to
directly fund a prostitute organisation – the Australian Prostitutes
Collective – for the provision of health and welfare services to prostitutes (Perkins 1991: 369). Other states and territories have since
followed. The main aim here has been to protect the public health by
instigating and monitoring the deployment of safe practices in the
prostitution industry. But state funding has also tended to consolidate
sex worker organisations and, consequently, to facilitate some political
lobbying in favour of decriminalisation proposals.

At local, national and international levels prostitutes' rights groups
have been more active and visible than ever before. Sex worker organisations now exist in all capital cities and in many regional areas. In
1988 the Prostitutes Collective of Victoria organised a first national
conference on prostitution; a second national conference was held in
Adelaide in 1989 and the Scarlet Alliance, a national forum for prostitute organisations, was formed. In 1991 the Australian Institute of
Criminology organised a conference entitled 'The Sex Industry and
Public Policy', which brought together a range of sex industry workers
and employers, academics, politicians, pornography distributors,
censors, police and tax officers (see Gerull and Halstead 1992). In all
of these arenas demands for – and convincing evidence in support of –
decriminalisation have been advanced.

On the international stage sex workers and their organisations have
also begun to develop a strong political voice. In 1984 the International Committee for Prostitutes Rights was formed and a first World
Whores Congress was held in Amsterdam in 1985 with participants
from North America, Europe and South-East Asia. It produced a World
Charter for Prostitutes' Rights which included a specific demand for
the decriminalisation of prostitution (see Phetersen 1989; Delacoste
and Alexander 1988). The Network of Sex Work Projects, an international non-government organisation supported by the World Health
Organisation (as part of its Global Program on AIDS), is presently
advocating internationally for the advancement of the rights of sex
workers. For example, this organisation – as well as a network of
Australian sex worker organisations – lobbied for sex workers and an
address to sex work issues to be included in the United Nations Fourth
Conference on Women in Beijing.[2]

Since the 1980s there has also been increasing international and
feminist concern with sex tourism and trafficking in women (Enloe
1989; Truong 1990; Barry 1995). Feminist activists like Kathleen Barry
(1995) tend to deal with all prostitution as if it is sexual slavery and to

elide important differences between various sexual practices often lumped together and called prostitution (Sullivan 1995).[3] They usually, therefore, look to the abolition of prostitution[4] and press for stronger anti-prostitution laws. This has tended to undermine the growth of international support for decriminalisation strategies although, at the 1994 International Conference on Traffic in Persons, in the Netherlands, the 'right of an individual to decide to work as a prostitute' was upheld as was the right to safe, legal working conditions. Recognising prostitution as a form of work was seen as a way of reducing the vulnerability of prostitutes and others to trafficking.

Alongside these shifting national and international approaches to prostitution are important changes in the conceptualisation of prostitution within various academic literatures. The conceptualisation of prostitution as sex work – the dominant position within feminist and sex worker groups in the 1970s and 1980s – continues to be influential. However, in the 1990s a greater diversity of approaches to prostitution is now apparent among feminists and sex workers. Some sex workers have begun to represent themselves as a sexual minority rather than as a group of oppressed workers. This has occurred in the wake of increasing gay and lesbian visibility and amidst the flourishing of a Queer politics which is broadly critical of both 'normal' heterosexuality and identity politics (Butler 1993; Sedgewick 1993). Sex worker activists like Andrew Hunter have argued in favour of what he calls a pro-sex view of prostitution; prostitution is simply 'an expression of sexuality – an expression which in itself is good'. This means that sex worker groups should 'look for allies amongst other groups of people who were stigmatised because of their sexuality and sexual expression' (Hunter 1991: 111).

However, the voices of prostitutes who oppose this pro-sex position – who are anti-pornography and refuse the label sex worker – have also recently appeared in the international literature (Wynter in Delacoste and Alexander 1988). The group WHISPER (Women Hurt in Systems of Prostitution Engaged in Revolt) argues that prostitution is a crime of coercion, degradation and exploitation, committed by men against women. This approach, which has clearly been influenced by the discourse of Barry concerning sexual slavery, has not been influential among Australian sex worker groups.

Over the last decade, feminist approaches to prostitution and pornography have clearly undergone profound changes. Some feminists continue to oppose pornography explicitly and/or to support censorship (see for example Russell 1993). Some male theorists and theorists of masculinity have also recently adopted aspects of this approach (Kimmel 1990; Kendall 1995). However, Queer and pro-sex feminist approaches to pornography have become increasingly important over the last decade (see for example Caught Looking Inc. 1988 and Harwood *et al.* 1993), proffering powerful critiques of the anti-pornography feminism of the 1980s (see Brown 1995; Cornell 1995). Writers from this camp often assert the importance of sexually explicit representation – including pornographic images – in the constitution of a new cultural politics positioned to oppose a dominant and oppressive, heterosexual culture. In Australia this position has been taken up by various gay and lesbian (including lesbian feminist) groups. The lesbian magazine *Wicked Women*, for example, contains explicit representations of lesbian women in various sado-masochistic poses.

It appears that Queer theorists, pro-sex and post-structural feminists have had less to say about prostitution than about pornography. But it is clear that feminist approaches to prostitution have changed significantly over the last decade. The focus on prostitution as work and as a practice which exists on a continuum of other sexual-economic practices which women engage in (see Chapters 5 and 6) has largely disappeared from feminist theory. Moreover, a much stronger anti-prostitution line has become apparent (see for example Jeffreys 1985; Shrage 1989; Overall 1992), with some feminists (Pateman 1988) mounting an explicit critique of the notion that prostitution should be treated as work. Elsewhere (Sullivan 1994, 1995) I have discussed this shift in feminist approaches in more detail and argued against the propensity of theorists like Pateman, Shrage and Overall to mount a principled feminist opposition to prostitution grounded in essentialist claims about prostitution transactions. For the purposes of this book, however, I am more interested in the impact that changing feminist approaches have had on the formulation of new law and public policy addressed to the sex industries. I will return to this issue in the next sections and in the conclusion of the chapter.

Prostitution

In Chapter 6 I discussed the decriminalisation of prostitution in New South Wales and Victoria – and its failure in South Australia – during the late 1970s and 1980s. Since then two further attempts at decriminalisation have failed in South Australia (the most recent in 1995), while in Queensland new anti-prostitution laws were introduced in 1992. However, in four other jurisdictions – the Australian Capital Territory, the Northern Territory, Victoria and New South Wales – some new form of decriminalisation has been introduced. In the Australian Capital Territory brothels are now legal if they are registered and located outside residential areas. In the Northern Territory escort agencies are subject to licensing but are otherwise legal (brothels remain illegal). In 1995 Victoria extended its system of regulated brothels to include escort agencies, and New South Wales established clearer grounds for the legal operation of brothels.

This means that there are now marked differences in the laws pertaining to prostitution across Australia (see Neave 1994). While different types of decriminalisation have taken place in some jurisdictions, in South Australia, Tasmania and Western Australia the law pertaining to prostitution is virtually unchanged since the beginning of the century.[5] In Queensland there is now a more extensive regime of criminal penalties attached to prostitution than in any other state at any other time. But there also appears to be a general shift to broader definitions of prostitution (regardless of whether decriminalisation has also occurred). In both the Australian Capital Territory and Queensland, for example, the law now specifies that prostitution can include acts of masturbation and sexual voyeurism (that is, where no physical contact occurs).

In the next sections I examine the transformation in politico-legal approaches which occurred in the 1990s in Queensland, the Australian Capital Territory, the Northern Territory, Victoria and New South Wales.

Australian Capital Territory

A far-reaching reform of prostitution laws took place in the Australian Capital Territory in 1992. Reform was first recommended by the Legislative Assembly Select Committee on HIV, Illegal Drugs and Prostitution in its interim report of 1991. The chair of this committee, Michael Moore, then introduced two private member's bills which aimed to decriminalise prostitution. Although both of these bills were defeated, they became the object of much community and cross-party consultation. A modified bill (with tougher health requirements) was subsequently passed.

The stated objectives of the *Prostitution Act* of 1992 were to safeguard public health; to promote the health and occupational health and safety of prostitutes; to protect the social and physical environment of the community by controlling the location of brothels; and to protect children from exploitation in relation to prostitution. The Act requires the operators of brothels and escort agencies to notify the Registrar of Brothels and Escort Agencies within seven days of the commencement of business; failure to register can attract substantial fines ($10,000 for an individual or $50,000 for a corporation) or imprisonment. The Act also prohibits the operation of brothels outside certain prescribed areas; this means that legal brothels are confined to the industrial suburbs of Fyshwick and Mitchell. Solo operators (prostitutes who work on their own) and escort agencies are required to register, but they do not need to work from or in a prescribed area.

This system of registration is quite different from the licensing systems in Victoria and the Northern Territory. In Victoria, both brothel premises and (since June 1996) the operators of brothels are required to undergo an extensive vetting procedure prior to the granting of a licence. In the Northern Territory both escort workers and the operators of escort agencies are required to submit themselves to police scrutiny before they can operate legally. In the Australian Capital Territory registration simply consists of a notification to a public authority of the names and addresses of those persons (including, where relevant, directors and shareholders) who run a prostitution business. During debate in parliament the Attorney-General was keen to draw out the distinctions between this registration scheme and the more cumbersome system of licensing in Victoria. The Victorian approach was seen to have 'failed' largely because it was inefficient and so complicated that operators tried to avoid it (and operate illegally). The government argued that 'we should know who is in the industry, but we should not license' (ACTLAD, 18 November 1992: 3184).

The ACT *Prostitution Act* completely prohibited public soliciting for the purposes of prostitution and prescribed a fine of $2000 for this activity (or three years' imprisonment where a child is involved). Tough new penalties were established for encouraging, permitting, or participating in child prostitution and, in the case of brothels and escort agencies, having children on the premises without reasonable excuse.

New penalties were also established for those who coerced others into providing commercial sexual services – whether by the threat of violence, false representation, or the supply or offer to supply a drug of dependence. In a break with tradition, the Act makes no provisions for the prosecution of those who live on the earnings of (adult) prostitution. So sex workers in the Australian Capital Territory are now able to spend their money as they see fit and lovers, spouses, etc. are not liable to criminal charges (as they still are in most Australian jurisdictions).

Health provisions established under the new Act are more mixed. The operators of brothels and escort agencies are required to take reasonable steps to ensure that prostitutes do not have a sexually transmitted disease; medical practitioners for this purpose are to be designated by the government. This means that prostitutes – at least those who work for brothels and escort agencies – are subject to compulsory medical examinations by the state, a scenario which formally re-enacts a practice heatedly debated in the early twentieth century (see Chapter 1). In the parliament several members pointed to research that showed that safe sex was already the norm in commercial sex transactions in Canberra and that sexually transmitted disease was less likely to be acquired in a brothel than in any other sexual situation. Michael Moore argued that medical examinations should be an individual responsibility of workers, but he was unable to convince others of this. It seems that the spectre of disease is an inevitable feature of parliamentary debates about prostitution and will be used to justify the application of draconian measures to sex workers even in the absence of reasonable grounds.

To some extent, though, the Act breaks with this tradition by laying some responsibility for the maintenance of sexual health on clients. So, for example, the new law prohibits 'persons' from providing or *receiving* commercial sexual services while infected with a sexually transmitted disease.[6] It also prohibits providing or *receiving* oral, anal or vaginal penetration unless a condom is used. The Australian Capital Territory is the only jurisdiction in Australia which has enacted such a measure (although several other jurisdictions claim it is implied in general work safety legislation). In parliament, the government referred to this as a 'safe sex obligation' on all participants in prostitution transactions. It clearly addresses both the health of clients and the occupational health and safety of workers in the industry. It also clearly increases the power of workers – in negotiations with clients and with operators of brothels or escort agencies – to insist on safe sex.

To all appearances the *Prostitution Act* works extremely well. A consultative committee – composed of sex workers, brothel owners, the AIDS Council, the Health Department and the Australian Federal Police – provides ongoing review and recommendations to the Attorney-General. There are few, if any, illegal brothels (although a large number of solo workers are probably unregistered) and very little street soliciting. It is clear, however, that this situation was not suddenly brought into being by the 1992 Act. The Interim Report of the Select Committee on HIV, Illegal Drugs and Prostitution (1991) indicated that a policy of 'toleration and control' in relation to prostitution had already been in place for some time. Since 1970, prosecutions for prostitution-related offences had required the consent of the (federal) Attorney-General. In 1984 the Commonwealth Director of Public Prosecutions, with the consent of the Attorney-General, adopted a prosecution policy based on aggravating circumstances. This meant that a prosecution for a prostitution-related offence would not proceed simply because there was a *prima facie* case; prostitution premises had to be the object of public complaint, be situated in a residential area, be employing juveniles, be using and distributing drugs, or otherwise posing a threat to public health (ACT 1991: 13–14). Consequently, very few prosecutions were initiated in the two decades prior to law reform.

So it appears that these measures – and judicious policing – had already established the main contours of the prostitution industry in the Australian Capital Territory long before the 1992 Act formalised this situation. The good relations which prevail between the industry, police, the government and the public attest to this and are probably unique in Australia. Only in Canberra do brothels organise well-attended public open days (complete with barbeque) and host contemporary art shows. This history, together with the absence of a strong conservative voice in the House of Assembly (and the relative homogeneity of the electorate), clearly assisted passage of the 1992 *Prostitution Act*. Debate in the House around this legislation was notable for a lack of controversy and for high levels of cross-party agreement; only one member spoke against the bill and he was also the only member to vote against it. A similar situation is unimaginable in any other Australian jurisdiction.

Queensland

Prostitution has been a hot political issue in Queensland since the mid-1980s. In 1985 the Sturgess Report was scathing of police failure to address prostitution adequately, although these findings were mostly ignored by the Bjelke-Petersen government. In 1987 two investigative journalists exposed the activities of gambling and prostitution rackets in Brisbane. Phil Dickie's articles in the Brisbane *Courier Mail* and Chris Masters's 'The Moonlight State', shown on national television in May 1987, both presented clear evidence of ongoing police corruption associated with gambling and prostitution (see Dickie 1988). On the day after 'The Moonlight State' went to air, Acting Premier Bill Gunn ordered a full-scale public inquiry into the connections between prostitution, illegal gambling, drugs, political party donations, policing practices, and several identified 'organised crime' syndicates. Tony Fitzgerald QC was appointed to conduct this inquiry.

The Fitzgerald Inquiry ran for eighteen months and, almost from the beginning, heard sensational evidence of police corruption associated with prostitution (see Dickie 1988). The Fitzgerald Report was released in June 1989. Among a plethora of specific suggestions pertaining to institutional and administrative reform, Fitzgerald advised that, unless there was further research and inquiry into prostitution, the reform process in this area would simply create more problems

(Fitzgerald Report: 190). While he refrained from any specific suggestions about prostitution law reform, Fitzgerald did indicate that he thought a system of regulated prostitution would be the best way of managing many of the problems associated with this industry (Fitzgerald Report 1989: 192–3).

Six months after the Fitzgerald Report was handed down, the first Labor government to be elected in Queensland for thirty-two years took office. The Goss government instigated a series of institutional and policy reforms (see Stevens and Wanna 1993) and asked the Criminal Justice Commission (CJC) to report on the best options in regard to prostitution law reform.

The CJC report, titled *Regulating Morality? An Inquiry into Prostitution in Queensland*, was released in October 1991. In summary it recommended the establishment of a regulatory framework for the management of prostitution, including a Registration Board to examine applicants for brothel licences and establish guidelines for the operation of small brothels and escort agencies (involving two to ten people). Larger operations were to be prohibited, while solo workers (never illegal in Queensland) could continue to operate legally from their own homes. The report also recommended strengthening the criminal law in relation to several areas – street soliciting, prostitution which involved children or disabled groups, procuring which involved coercion or intimidation, and explicit and offensive advertising.

However, even before the CJC report was released, Premier Goss announced his opposition to any form of decriminalisation of prostitution in Queensland. This clearly constrained the future direction of the reform process. The report was considered by the Parliamentary Criminal Justice Committee, which published its own report in November 1991. It supported recommendations for tougher penalties on street prostitution, for prostitution involving children and disabled groups, and for procuring which involved coercion and intimidation; it also supported a continuation of the legal status of solo workers. However, a majority of the committee did not support recommendations in the CJC report regarding a regulatory framework.

When the Goss government introduced the Prostitution Laws Amendment Bill in 1992 it was clear that it took a very different tack from the one proposed by the CJC and would stand against the trend towards the decriminalisation of brothel (or escort agency) prostitution being established elsewhere in the country. In what the government described as a measure designed to deal with 'organised prostitution', the new *Prostitution Act* significantly expanded the range and scope of the penalties that could be applied to prostitution and prostitution-related activities. In his speech, the Minister for Police, Paul Braddy, said:

> The Government recognises that prostitution will not be eliminated from our society, nor would it be appropriate to embark on a moral crusade to attempt to do so at the expense of other problems in our society. However, the Government acknowledges that organised prostitution is debilitating and detrimental to our society [QPD 323: 684].

The government argued that the decriminalisation of prostitution would not reduce or eliminate the criminal activity and exploitation associated with organised prostitution. The aim, then, was generally to minimise prostitution and to have a more enforceable law, one which would target 'the pimps and parasites of organised prostitution' and enable the imposition of 'significant terms of imprisonment' for the organisers of prostitution (QPD 323: 685).

The new *Prostitution Act* introduced much tougher penalties for procuring for the purposes of prostitution; these measures applied to all procuring (even where this involved adults) but specified particularly tough penalties where coercion was involved or where the person was a child or an intellectually impaired person. New or substantially new provisions were introduced against advertising prostitution (previously there were no specific laws against this) and against knowingly participating in the provision of prostitution. This latter offence now included those who drove prostitutes or their clients to assignations,[7] those who received or redirected telephone bookings for prostitution, and those who provided financial resources for the establishment of prostitution services.

New provisions were introduced against being found in places reasonably suspected of being used for prostitution. This provision significantly expanded the power to arrest those found in brothels. Certificates of discharge were to be available to those who gave evidence against other offenders. So the new provisions also significantly expanded the ability of police to gather evidence for a prosecution.[8] The new Act also enabled the confiscation of profits earned from illegal prostitution.

While these measures all targeted organised prostitution, other measures apparently aimed at solo workers were also introduced. For example, the new Act significantly tightened the law addressed to street soliciting for the purposes of prostitution, an activity which is usually undertaken by independent workers looking for customers. The maximum penalties for street soliciting were increased, and a graduated scale for repeat offences was introduced. These provisions were to apply equally to males and females, prostitutes and their clients, as well as to persons acting for either prostitutes or clients. Interestingly, this move was justified by reference to public opinion surveys (conducted by the CJC) which showed that a majority of Queenslanders – 83 per cent – thought it should be against the law to solicit in a public place for the purposes of prostitution. But the CJC also found that a majority of Queenslanders (63 per cent) thought it should not be against the law to sell sex from a brothel, while 53 per cent thought it should be illegal to sell sex from home (Queensland 1991: 58–65). So public opinion on these matters ran contrary to the other 'reforms' introduced by the Goss government.

The new *Prostitution Act* did preserve (and even extend) the legality of solo workers working from their own homes. This was contrary to the trend being established elsewhere in the country (for example in Victoria and the Northern Territory) but was clearly in line with the government's concern to eliminate organised prostitution and permit private, small-scale prostitution. Under the old laws, solo workers were not illegal; if they owned their own premises, they were relatively safe from police harassment. However, solo workers who rented premises were liable to eviction. Sex workers reported that police frequently informed on them to landlords, who could then be prosecuted if they knowingly let premises for the purposes of prostitution. Under the new Act, landlords did not have to evict prostitutes; they were liable only when two or more workers were operating from premises. So the new laws did increase the housing security of solo operators. On the other hand, extra provisions were introduced to address sole operators who caused unreasonable annoyance or disruption to the privacy of others.

The new prostitution laws proved to be extremely controversial. Some commentators were critical of the government's failure to close down solo operators. Others decried the failure to introduce some form of decriminalisation of brothels. Elsewhere (Sullivan 1993) I have argued that the new configuration of prostitution laws established ideal conditions for racketeering and police corruption, and rendered prostitutes more vulnerable to violence and legal discrimination. It is notable that after the new Act was proclaimed, the Queensland government introduced a bank of policy and funding initiatives addressed to the sex industry; no other jurisdiction in Australia spends as much money in this area. The new measures, largely funded via SQWISI (Self-health for Queensland Workers in the Sex Industry), have supported health education and retraining programs, the employment of outreach workers, and the establishment of an 'exit house' for workers who wish to leave the industry. This is an excellent policy package, but it cannot really make up for increased dangers and legal sanctions presently being borne by sex workers in Queensland (see Sullivan 1993).

Northern Territory

Until 1992, the Northern Territory had a *de facto* system for the regulation of prostitution. Escort agencies, but not brothels or street soliciting, were tolerated and subject to a rigorous police surveillance. Police conducted formal interviews with prostitutes who wished to be employed by escort agencies; they were photographed and their background checked for criminal, particularly drug, offences.

By the early 1990s such informal methods of controlling prostitution had fallen into disrepute right around Australia. This was largely a consequence of the sensational evidence of police corruption associated with tolerated prostitution presented to the Queensland Fitzgerald Inquiry. Prostitution law reform was given further impetus in the Northern Territory by an official inquiry into the police investigation of drug dealing. While Mulholland QC found no evidence of corruption in the police, he criticised the lack of a statutory basis for the police regulation of escort agencies.

In 1992 a new *Prostitution Regulation Act* became law. It established a system for the regulation of escort agencies but maintained criminal penalties on brothels and public soliciting or loitering for the purposes of prostitution. The prohibitions in relation to brothels also applied to individual prostitutes working from their own premises. However, a hotel room used for prostitution does not constitute a brothel where the arrangements for this transaction have been made elsewhere. As Neave points out (1994: 88), this means that hotel-keepers cannot be prosecuted for brothel-keeping if their rooms are used by escort agency workers, but freelance prostitutes who take clients to their own premises are guilty of an offence.

The Act established an Escort Agency Licensing Board with the power to grant, renew and cancel licences to the operators of escort agencies. To operate legally, operators must obtain licences and renew them annually. Sex workers are not required to be licensed but must obtain a certificate from the Commissioner of Police; this is designed to insure that escort agency workers are not under-age[9] and do not have convictions for violent offences or for specified drug offences in the preceding ten years. It is an offence for an escort agency to employ a person who does not have a certificate.

The new Act made it an offence to advertise to induce persons to seek employment as prostitutes and placed some controls on the advertising of prostitution services. It is no longer an offence to live on the earnings of prostitution (except in the case of child prostitution) although new penalties have been created to prohibit the coercion of adults into prostitution.

There are clearly some good aspects to this legislation. The designation of a zone of legal prostitution is advantageous for workers who wish to avoid arrest and imprisonment, and the formalisation of licensing procedures reduces (but does not eliminate) the police discretion which can lead to corruption and abuse. The repeal of measures which might be used to harass the lovers or spouses of prostitutes who live on earnings is also clearly advantageous for workers. However, escort agency prostitution is not the safest type of prostitution; escort workers are far more vulnerable to violence from clients than prostitutes who work in brothels. Because legal prostitution is confined to escort agencies, agency operators also retain considerable control over sex workers. Moreover, while the Escort Agency Licensing Board is formally independent of the police, police involvement in certification still 'gives them information about and power over prostitutes, which may be abused' (Neave 1994: 89).

Victoria

In Chapter 6 I discussed some of the problems associated with the 1986 Victorian *Prostitution Regulation Act,* a measure which has been widely referred to as a 'failed experiment'. Official inquiries (Queensland 1991), academics (Hancock 1992; Neave 1994), sex worker groups (Dobinson 1992) and brothel owners (Richardson 1992) all identified serious problems with the regulation of the prostitution industry in Victoria. Because whole sections of this Act were never proclaimed, provisions for controlling the ownership and management of brothels were never in force. Prostitutes could not work legally from their own homes (as they could in Queensland, the Australian Capital Territory and New South Wales). The lengthy and often involved procedure for obtaining permits drove most small operators out of the legal market and led to the establishment of a few large, expensive brothels[10] with enormous power over the wages and working conditions of the prostitutes they employed. While workers in large legal brothels complained of harsh working conditions and low wages, workers in the (expanding) illegal industry were exposed to tougher criminal penalties and/or to more dangerous work in escort agencies.

In 1992 the Labor Party lost the state election in Victoria and a Liberal–National Party government, under Jeff Kennett, came to power. The new government instigated a review of prostitution and a new *Prostitution Control Act* became law in June 1995. This Act

re-enacted many provisions of the 1986 legislation (for example in relation to child prostitution, living on the earnings of illegal prostitution,
and forcing a person to remain in prostitution). The 1995 Act established the Prostitution Control Board and (as in the Australian Capital
Territory) an Advisory Committee. It does, however, set out much
more extensive conditions for administering licence applications and
renewals and approving managers. The board is required to monitor
the operations of 'prostitution service providers' (which now specifically includes escort agencies as well as brothels); to liaise with police
and instruct police to investigate complaints (including those from
prostitutes); to refer relevant matters for investigation by the Occupational Health and Safety Authority, the Australian Taxation Office etc.;
to assist organisations involved in helping prostitutes leave the
industry; to develop educational programs for magistrates, police and
community workers; and to disseminate information about the dangers
inherent in prostitution, 'especially street prostitution'.

The size of all *new* brothels was restricted by the 1995 Act. Solo or
duo operators (who occupy premises with a valid planning permit) are
not required to be licensed but are required to register their business
with the Prostitution Control Board. These small brothels do not have
to pay the hefty registration fees required of larger brothels but must
remain outside residential areas.

The Act also significantly increased penalties for unlicensed prostitution service providers, that is, prostitutes working illegally and the
owners and managers of unlicensed brothels and escort agencies. New
provisions outlaw being in, entering or leaving an unlicensed brothel
(and re-enact the offence of being in a proscribed brothel). These
latter provisions clearly apply to both clients and prostitution service
providers. Tighter provisions also now relate to the advertising of prostitution services (including escort agencies).

The 1995 Act introduced significantly higher penalties for street
prostitution and for prostitutes who solicit (or loiter and accost) in the
vicinity of churches, hospitals, schools or public places regularly
frequented by children and in which children are present at the time
of the soliciting. However, the same activities by clients now attract *twice*
the penalty units incurred by workers (but the same gaol terms for
repeat offences). When considered in the context of previous prostitution law, this strategy is truly remarkable. It reverses the historical trend
for clients on the street to be outside the law (see Chapters 1 and 2), or
to be dealt with much less severely than prostitutes (see Chapter 4).
The Act aims to punish and dissuade clients more than prostitutes for
the same activities, that is, street soliciting. (Of course, it remains to be

seen if clients are actually arrested under these provisions and if they are prosecuted to the same degree as workers; even where laws are gender-neutral, more women and workers get arrested than clients.) In another significant departure from tradition, the Act also specifically prohibits offensive behaviour towards prostitutes in or near a public place. This is tantamount to a prohibition on the public vilification of prostitutes.

An extensive set of regulations, designed to increase the occupational health and safety of workers, were also attached to the *Prostitution Control Act*. These set in place requirements for safe sex practices; enable a prostitute to refuse, or stop providing, sexual services when he or she believes a situation is unsafe; prohibit a manager or receptionist from misrepresenting the qualities of a prostitute or negotiating on behalf of the prostitute the sexual services to be provided; require brothel licensees to provide alarm buttons in rooms; require escort agencies to provide communication devices for escorts (or otherwise ensure their safety); and prevent managers from using prostitutes as cleaners.

It is too soon to evaluate the operation of these laws in Victoria. The new health and safety regulations – as well as the provisions which prohibit public vilification of prostitutes – appear to be of significant benefit to workers in the (legal) industry. However, it is also clear that the Act will not deal with some of the major problems already identified with the operation of the old Act. For example, the new Act does not deal with the reluctance of local councils to issue planning permits to brothels. The Neave Report had recommended that local councils should not have the right to refuse planning permission to brothels outside residential areas. But councils retained this right in both the 1986 and 1995 legislation. As the planning application and appeal process remains complicated (also lengthy and expensive), it is likely that many brothels and massage parlours will continue to operate illegally. The new Act, like the old one, makes no provision for prostitutes to work legally from their own homes; it also increases the penalties for street prostitution. Most workers in the industry will, therefore, continue to work illegally but will be subject to higher criminal penalties. As in the previous Act, penalties continue for living on the earnings of prostitution (except, as before, in the case of money earned in respect of legal premises). The new Act does not allow local governments to decide on any limited decriminalisation of street prostitution (as recommended in the Neave Report) despite the fact that at least one local council, St Kilda, has now said it is ready to accept some form of decriminalisation (*Sunday Age*, 21 May 1995).

New South Wales

Soon after its election in 1988, the new Liberal–National government under Premier Nick Greiner moved to extend and tighten the laws addressed to prostitution. It repealed the *Prostitution and Offences in Public Places Act* and replaced it with a *Summary Offences Act*. This Act increased the penalties for all existing prostitution-related offences (reintroducing gaol sentences in some cases); and it continued to limit, but still did not completely prohibit, public soliciting for the purposes of prostitution. Two new offences appeared in the Act – behaving 'in an offensive manner in or near, or within view or hearing from a public place or school', and engaging in an act of prostitution in a public place.

The new provisions regarding offensive behaviour relied more heavily on the judgement of police officers and did not, therefore, resolve the legal ambiguity attached to street soliciting. As Neave (1994: 80) commented, 'because of their breadth and uncertainty', the new provisions in relation to offensive behaviour increased 'the scope for selective enforcement and police corruption'. The new provisions regarding public acts of prostitution were explicitly addressed to 'each of the persons taking part in an act of public prostitution' which meant that both clients and workers were liable. (In 1985 the parliament was informed that 'for a number of years' the Vice Squad had been operating on the assumption that the *Prostitution Act* did not permit the arrest of the clients of prostitutes: NSWPD 185: 7132). As one Liberal member of the parliament argued, this measure addressed the discrimination faced by prostitutes, not by removing the offence from the statute book (the strategy adopted by the Labor government in 1979), but by making both parties equally liable (NSWPD 201: 1163). The government argued that it had 'crossed the Rubicon ... by making the customer liable' and that it 'would be both illogical and discriminatory to only apply legal sanctions to one person [the prostitute] where both persons were taking part in mutual acts of prostitution in public' (NSWPD 201: 1180, 1339).

This clearly signalled an ongoing commitment to end the discrimination faced by prostitutes, although the sex equality envisioned could subject both prostitutes and their clients to significant new penalties (up to six months in gaol or a $1000 fine for acts of public prostitution).

Later in 1988 the Greiner government moved to prohibit all advertising for the employment of prostitutes. New measures were also passed to strengthen existing laws against child prostitution and against the employment of children for pornographic purposes.

However, the 1988 reforms – like the 1979 reforms – left brothel and escort agency prostitution in a legal grey area (Neave 1994: 80).

Living on the earnings of prostitution continued to be illegal as did using premises held out to be for other purposes (massage, etc.) for the purposes of prostitution. Brothels were also unable to advertise for staff and could be closed down as 'disorderly houses'.

In 1995 this situation attracted intense public and political attention as the Wood Royal Commission (like the Fitzgerald Inquiry in Queensland) uncovered evidence of widespread police corruption associated with prostitution. The new Carr Labor government moved to deal with this via an amendment to the *Disorderly Houses Act.*

Under the existing law, all brothels were disorderly houses and were therefore liable to be closed down. The Attorney-General – like Commissioner Wood – argued that such laws enabled police corruption. They also brought about the closure of well-run brothels, thus forcing prostitutes 'back onto the streets'. This was 'unsuitable and undesirable' because street prostitution was generally offensive and street prostitutes posed a greater health risk to themselves and to the community (NSWPD, 19 October 1995: 2040).

The 1995 reforms did not establish a registration or licensing scheme for brothels. The *Disorderly Houses (Amendment) Act* simply sets out the grounds on which a complaint may be brought against a brothel in the Land and Environment Court. Councils can make an application for the closure of a brothel when they have received 'sufficient complaints' from local residents or occupiers. The Act sets out the criteria which are to be applied in this judgement: whether the relevant brothel is operating near, or within view of, a church, school, hospital, or any place frequented by children; whether the brothel causes a disturbance in the neighbourhood; whether sufficient off-street parking has been provided; whether the operation of the brothel interferes with the amenity of the neighbourhood. The Attorney-General argued that the 'overriding consideration' was that a brothel should operate 'in a discreet manner consistent with the amenity of the neighbourhood' (NSWPD, 19 October 1995: 2040).

The 1995 amendments also provided that 'persons who are in a legitimate commercial relationship with a prostitute are not guilty of the offence of living off the earnings of prostitution'. New penalties were, however, provided for inducing another person to commit an act of prostitution or surrender the proceeds of prostitution.

How Parliamentarians Talked about Prostitution in the 1990s

In the 1990s some significant changes were apparent in the way that parliamentarians talked about prostitution. One of the most obvious changes is that parliamentarians in all jurisdictions now frequently use the terms *sex worker* and *sex industry* when referring to prostitution. This suggests that feminist rhetoric deployed in the 1970s and 1980s, which represented prostitution as work and prostitutes as sex workers, has been widely taken up in mainstream political institutions. The view that prostitution is an industry – with employers, workers and clients – tends to challenge simplistic representations of prostitution as a moral problem and to point to the need for interventions which enable better management of the industry. In the New South Wales parliament one feminist speaker (Meredith Burgmann) argued that 'for many women in Australia prostitution is a legitimate choice of work' while a Green MP said he would like to see 'all laws pertaining to prostitution ... removed from the criminal statutes on the ground that sex work ... should be treated as a legitimate industry' (NSWPD, 14, 15 November 1995: 3074, 3149).

Many parliamentarians, however, rejected this approach and argued that prostitution should not be regarded as ordinary work (see for example QPD 323: 970). This approach was most likely to be deployed by conservatives and by members of parliament in jurisdictions where decriminalisation was *not* being considered by the government (for example, in Queensland). But even those who used the terminology of work and industry and supported decriminalisation were usually not prepared to deal with prostitution as if it was the same as any other sort of work or industry. The Attorney-General in the Australian Capital Territory, for example, argued that prostitution was 'an industry that needs perhaps, at least in the early stages, to be dealt with more cautiously than any other lawful industry' (ACTLAD, 18 November 1992: 3165).

One significant change in the 1990s was that the argument that prostitution should not be treated as work was now also put forward by some feminists. This was most evident in the Queensland parliament, where feminist members of the Labor Party argued in favour of the government's proposals for stronger anti-prostitution laws. Jan Power, for example, argued that prostitution should not be seen as work because it was a matter of male power and the sexual exploitation of women. The terms in which she argued this were remarkably reminiscent of the work of Carol Pateman in her book *The Sexual Contract* (1988). Indeed, in places, it appears that Power was directly quoting Pateman's work. She says that the presence of prostitution 'serves to continually remind men and women that men have the right of access to women's bodies' (QPD 323: 971). Pateman (1988: 199) argues: 'The general display of women's bodies and sexual parts, either in representation or as live bodies, is central to the sex industry and continually reminds men – and women – that men exercise the law of male sex-right, that they have patriarchal right of access to women's bodies'.

In the 1970s and 1980s feminists argued strongly in favour of the position that prostitution should be regarded as work (and, therefore, strongly in favour of decriminalisation). In the 1990s, it appears that feminist speakers in Australian parliaments argued on *both* sides of the debate about whether prostitution should be regarded as work. Some were opposed to or ambivalent about this approach (and, therefore, tended to be opposed to or ambivalent about decriminalisation). This feminist ambivalence was well described by Power:

> Prostitution is a subject which causes considerable difficulty for many women. It is also a subject which causes many women to feel a high degree of ambivalence. On the one hand, a desire exists to ensure that the women who are working as prostitutes are not stigmatised and isolated within the community. On the other hand, there is a pressure to respond decisively to the knowledge that prostitution involves the exploitation and domination of women by men [QPD 323: 969].

In the 1970s and 1980s this dilemma was resolved by a feminist insistence on prostitution as sex work (see Chapter 6). By the 1990s it appears that this sort of resolution was less possible for feminists. Elsewhere (Sullivan 1995), I have argued that this change reflected a general shift in feminist theory in the late 1980s and 1990s, one which tended to close down the possibility of feminist support for the decriminalisation of prostitution.

The Prostitute

In all jurisdictions in the 1990s the prostitute is still seen, primarily, to be a female figure, although many more parliamentarians now refer also to male prostitution in their deliberations on reform proposals. Indeed, for some, it is the spectre of male prostitution which is now most threatening, particularly as male homosexuality is seen to be directly connected with the spread of HIV/AIDS (QPD 323: 976). As in previous periods, prostitutes are still subject to a range of contradictory discourses in parliament. They are represented on the one hand as bad or mad, and on the other hand as helpless victims of circumstances.

In their bad or mad mode prostitutes are frequently characterised by parliamentarians as drug addicts and/or as single mothers fraudulently supplementing their welfare income. Despite evidence to the contrary (Harcourt 1994), they are also still seen as a major danger to the community in terms of sexually transmitted disease. At the same time, many parliamentarians continue to represent prostitutes as victims of circumstances who require some degree of state protection. In the 1990s two new themes have emerged as important in this area. With high levels of youth unemployment in the 1990s, young people – particularly young women – were seen to be more vulnerable than ever before to exploitation in the prostitution industry (NTLAPR 34: 3823, 3829). In the 1990s child abuse – and particularly sexual abuse – became a significant public issue. In parliament it was directly linked to the issue of prostitution. One speaker in the Northern Territory parliament, for example, argued that because prostitutes were more likely to have been sexually abused as children, they needed more legal protection, because 'The way in which they have been abused ... has led them to an occupation where that role of victim is perpetuated and they are subject to similar treatment repeatedly' (NTLAPR 34: 3774). The conclusion to be drawn here perhaps is that prostitutes continue to be seen by parliamentarians as worthy of both punishment and protection.

The Client

In previous chapters I have argued that in the post-war period the clients of prostitutes have increasingly come to be designated as objects of political scrutiny and as problematic men with deviant sexual proclivities. The trend towards an increasing visibility of clients has continued in all jurisdictions in the 1990s. In the debates which preceded law reform in Queensland, the Australian Capital Territory, the Northern Territory and New South Wales, clients were regularly mentioned by parliamentarians (although, as in previous periods, the main focus is still on prostitutes rather than clients).

The trend towards representing clients as men with problematic sexual proclivities is, however, now declining. In those jurisdictions where some form of decriminalisation was being debated (the Australian Capital Territory, the Northern Territory, Victoria and New South Wales), the sexual and other activities of clients were less likely to be represented as pathological. In the Australian Capital Territory, for example, little was said about clients except that they should be equally responsible with workers for obeying the law and practising safe sex. In New South Wales Ann Symonds pointed out that clients usually 'escape scrutiny' in official inquiries, but also commented that 'the profile of clients of prostitutes has been assessed as neither the disabled nor lonely but as an average married man, usually in his 30s or 40s' (NSWPD, 14 November 1995: 3042). Thus, clients were represented as ordinary, normal men. In many respects this strategy was indebted to feminist approaches which offered a strong critique of normal masculinity and normal male sexual practices. There was, then, feminist resistance to the notion that clients should be regarded as particularly deviant and pathological men.

However, in Queensland – where no decriminalisation was planned by the government – clients were still represented as both dangerous and outside sexual and social norms. One speaker argued:

> We do not want our quiet family areas to be subjected to the nuisance of prostitutes' clients coming to the wrong address or, indeed, to the right address. We do not want our children growing up next door to prostitutes and the sorts of people who are their clients [QPD 323: 906].

The new provisions in Victoria – imposing higher penalties on clients than on prostitutes for street prostitution – also suggest that clients are increasingly being marked out by law-makers as worthy of tougher criminal penalties.

Living on Earnings

In the 1990s a significant change is evident in the way that those who live on the earnings of prostitution are represented in parliamentary debate. In previous chapters I have shown that people (but particularly men) who lived on the earnings of prostitution were widely denounced by law-makers as pimps and bludgers worthy of tough criminal penalties. In the 1990s parliamentarians began to distinguish between various categories of living on earnings and to acknowledge that workers had the right to dispose of their income earned in prostitution as they saw fit. In many jurisdictions, new distinctions were drawn between those who profited from large-scale prostitution and those who were simply the lovers or spouses of sex workers. In the Northern Territory parliament, for example, one speaker argued that there was a need to change the laws against living on earnings because 'prostitutes should be able to spend their earnings as they choose' and 'the present law fails to differentiate between those who exploit prostitutes financially and those who may benefit from prostitution in an unexploitive way' (NTLAPR 34: 1307). As indicated above, several jurisdictions changed their laws in the 1990s to reflect this new approach. In Queensland, the Northern Territory, New South Wales and the Australian Capital Territory laws against living on earnings have been repealed (at least for legal prostitution); in several jurisdictions new or stronger laws have been introduced against coercing a person into prostitution. This suggests that law-makers are increasingly distinguishing between those who coerce and exploit prostitutes and those who, at the invitation of workers themselves, simply share in the financial benefits of prostitution. This shift is clearly connected to the success of other arguments that prostitutes should have the same rights and benefits as other tax-paying citizens.

The Act of Prostitution

In terms of understandings of the act of prostitution, it is clear that most parliamentarians in the 1990s still conceive of prostitution as a problematic sexual practice (regardless of whether or not they also view it as work). The argument that prostitution should be regarded as a victimless crime – which was a mainstay of the case for prostitution law reform in the 1970s – is not apparent in any jurisdiction; indeed, this argument is specifically rejected by several parliamentary speakers (see QPD 323: 685, 970). For many parliamentarians prostitution is exploitative, degrading and demeaning (QPD 323: 903; NTLAPR 34: 3830). Interestingly, the degradation of prostitution transactions is now said by many to be attached to both prostitutes and clients. In the past, it was usually only prostitutes who were seen to be degraded by their occupation, while male clients were represented as doing what came naturally.

There are, however, two arguments which cut across this approach. First, several parliamentarians made the argument that prostitution was not *necessarily* degrading or exploitative. In the Northern Territory parliament, for example, one speaker argued that prostitutes were not always demeaned by their work. He said 'there are people who work very willingly and happily in this industry' (NTLAPR 34: 3830), people who would 'take great offence' at the view that their work was degrading. In a speech reminiscent of feminist and libertarian arguments made in the 1970s and early 1980s, one female member of parliament argued:

> We all use our bodies in one way or another to earn money and, if it is the decision of prostitutes, male or female, to use their bodies in a certain way to earn money, that is their decision. Parliamentarians use their bodies to make money, as do mannequins and carpenters. We all use our bodies to make money [NTLAPR 34: 3767].

This approach was tied to strong notions of the free will that prostitutes were said to exercise in their decision to work in the sex industry. It is also apparent in an increasing resort to the language of commerce and contract in relation to prostitution. In the Australian Capital Territory, for example, the new legislation specifically defined prostitution as 'the sale of commercial sexual services' and set in place the legal conditions under which contracts for the provision of such services can be made. In the Northern Territory parliament too, there was a specific acknowledgement that the decriminalisation of escort agencies represented a 'move to a different view of the contract for sexual services' (NTLAPR 34: 3758). Such language was probably commonplace in debates about the regulation of other industries but was quite new in relation to prostitution.

The main advantage of the contract approach was that it conferred new legal rights on prostitutes as workers, as well as some new obligations (particularly in relation to taxation). In those jurisdictions where this approach was practised, sex industry employers also assumed new obligations in relation to ensuring the occupational health and safety of prostitutes. This was specifically sought and acknowledged by various members of parliament (NTLAPR 34: 3774; ACTLAD, 18 November 1992: 3168).

The second argument which cut across the view that prostitution was degrading for both prostitutes and clients focused on the power of men and the sexual exploitation of (female) prostitutes by male clients. In the Queensland parliament, for example, Jan Power argued that the problem with prostitution was that it involved 'the use of a woman's body by a man for his own satisfaction. It is not a mutual, pleasurable exchange of the use of bodies, but the unilateral use of a woman's body by a man in exchange for money' (QPD 323: 971). Moreover, prostitution was not simply a matter of sex. It was 'a matter of the power of one individual over another' and, as such, was 'abhorrent' (QPD 323: 966). This approach clearly resonated with the particular feminist view that prostitution – like rape and sexual harassment – was primarily about men's sexual power and the maintenance of a system of gender exploitation (see Mackinnon 1987) from which men, but not women, derive direct benefit.

In previous chapters I showed how arguments about men's biological sexual needs often drove debates about prostitution. Surprisingly, in the 1990s, this sort of explicit argument disappears from Australian parliaments. However, the implicit version remained: parliamentarians still frequently described prostitution as 'inevitable' without specifying the reasons why they thought this was so (NTLAPR 34 : 3783; QPD 323: 685).

In the 1990s a specific (and feminist) critique of the idea that men's behaviour was driven by hydraulic sexual needs also appears in some

Australian parliaments. In Queensland, for example, Power challenged the belief that prostitution has always existed and is inevitable. This approach, she argued, leaves the demand for prostitution unexamined:

> which means that men's behaviour in making the demand is neither examined nor condemned as legally or socially unacceptable. Further, that belief implies that men display biologically driven demands which must be met. That theory ignores any effects which social conditioning may have in shaping male attitudes to sex. Although biological determinism has now been discredited in every other sphere of social research, it remains central to the issue of male sexuality in the context of the debate on prostitution [QPD 323: 970].

It is probably fair to conclude, then, that while there is no consensus among Australian parliamentarians about how the act of prostitution should be understood, it is now more discussed than in any other period of history. This discussion has involved the elaboration of specific (and often conflicting) analyses of the relative social, economic and political power of men and women and the degree of social change which is possible.

The Government's Role

Not surprisingly perhaps, this discussion has also indelibly marked debates about how governments should deal with the prostitution industry, that is, what the appropriate approach of government should be. In Chapter 6 I discussed the establishment of decriminalisation as the driving force behind prostitution law reform in the late 1970s and 1980s. In the 1990s this trend has continued in Victoria, New South Wales, the Australian Capital Territory and the Northern Territory. As in the previous period, decriminalisation has been represented as a better, more efficient way of managing the problems associated with prostitution. A common approach in those jurisdictions introducing decriminalisation was to suggest that because prostitution could not be eradicated, and because laws prohibiting prostitution had failed to eliminate or control prostitution (ACTLAD, 18 November 1992: 3166; NTLAPR 34: 3764), governments should adopt more effective surveillance and control strategies. In the Australian Capital Territory, for example, the Attorney-General argued that the new system for registering brothels represented a 'mature' and 'intelligent' approach to a problem which 'has been part of society for as long as recorded history'. History, he said, had shown that: 'attempts to outlaw it [prostitution] will simply never work and, therefore, we are better to accept the reality of commercial sexual services, without condoning that, and to ensure that it operates in a manner which is controlled and in the public interest'. In the government's view, moralising about prostitution simply got in the way of practical efforts to deal with the problem. The best approach was:

> to remove the criminal laws based on an outdated and failed policy of prohibition and to replace them with laws designed to ensure that the community is protected from harm in relation to public health and in respect of children and to ensure that people in the industry meet appropriate standards in respect of health and other matters [ACTLAD, 18 November 1992: 3166].

It is notable, however, that significant differences have emerged between Australian jurisdictions about what a good and appropriate decriminalisation process looks like. Some jurisdictions have opted to license escort agencies and maintain criminal penalties on brothels (Northern Territory) while others have moved to register (Australian Capital Territory), license (Victoria) or otherwise decriminalise (New South Wales) brothel prostitution.

In Queensland, of course, decriminalisation was specifically rejected as an appropriate politico-legal strategy. Most parliamentarians in that state argued that decriminalisation was not the way to go. Jan Power, for example, argued that decriminalisation had been a failure in Victoria and that it was anyway 'undesirable to create a system which institutionalises men's rights to commercial sexual relations'. In her view: 'The creation of a regulatory framework institutionalises the existence of prostitution. It represents an acceptance of prostitution by the State, and an acceptance by society that prostitution is an acceptable role for women' (QPD 323: 971–2). The best approach was to make sure that the laws applied equally to prostitutes and clients and to ensure that social policy was in place to support prostitute women.

Interestingly, many of the arguments used in Queensland to justify the introduction of tougher criminal laws against prostitution were used in other jurisdictions to justify decriminalisation. In Queensland, parliamentarians argued that tougher laws against prostitution would help minimise some of the problems associated with prostitution. In other jurisdictions parliamentarians argued that decriminalisation would achieve this same result.

This suggests that, regardless of the specific approach adopted – decriminalisation or further criminalisation – there were significant areas of agreement among parliamentarians about what the problems associated with prostitution were. In all jurisdictions, for example, parliamentarians argued there was a need to minimise street prostitution and to increase criminal penalties in this area. Even parliamentarians who supported the decriminalisation of brothels did not speak in support of more liberal laws in relation to street prostitution. In the Queensland parliament, for example, Peter Beattie (chairman of the parliamentary CJC committee and a supporter of decriminalisation) argued that because many streetwalkers were hard drug users and because street work was so dangerous, this practice should be discouraged by the implementation of tough laws (QPD 323: 898). In the 1990s many parliamentarians argued that the law should be used (both punitively and protectively) to discourage certain prostitution practices, particularly street prostitution. We no longer see arguments (such as those made in New South Wales during the late 1970s and 1980s) about the non-offensiveness of street soliciting and the special discrimination faced by street prostitutes.

There are many other prostitution-related issues which now appear to attract widespread consensus among Australian parliamentarians. In the late 1980s and 1990s parliamentarians spoke strongly in favour of tougher laws against child prostitution, regardless of whether they also sought decriminalisation or increased criminal penalties for adult prostitution. In all jurisdictions there were also widespread calls for laws which were not discriminatory regarding gender (QPD 323: 883, 969; NTLAPR 34: 3823). In the late 1970s and 1980s, arguments about the discrimination faced by prostitutes were commonplace (see Chapter 6). In the 1990s this was still the case although the solutions to this problem could now be proposed in terms of decriminalisation or (as in Queensland) making sure that both men and women, clients and prostitutes, were equally liable to the law. In Victoria, the instigation of tougher penalties on clients than on prostitutes (for the same activities) was not seen to be incongruent. Clearly, then, arguments about the sex discrimination inherent in prostitution law could be used to justify both decriminalisation and the promulgation of more extended prostitution laws.

In all jurisdictions there was also widespread agreement that laws addressed to prostitution needed to make 'sensible provisions' in relation to sexually transmitted disease and public health. Education rather than forced compliance was seen to be the way to ensure that HIV/AIDS was not spread through the community via the sex industry. Even in Queensland the parliament refrained from enacting laws which might compromise or inhibit safe practices in adult prostitution (for instance, the possession of condoms was specifically excluded as evidence of prostitution activities).

In all jurisdictions widespread support was now expressed for the view that prostitutes should have equal access to the law and should not face discrimination in court cases (see for example NTLAPR 34: 3168; QPD 323: 904). This shift was probably a direct result of the work done by various feminists, sex worker organisations and femocrats in relation to violence against women; prostitutes were identified as particularly vulnerable to rape and assault in their working lives (Hatty 1989). Trenchant critiques were also mounted of some court decisions involving prostitutes. In 1994, for example, the federal Attorney-General, Michael Lavarch, publicly rebuked the Commonwealth Director of Public Prosecutions for saying it was a greater crime to rape a nun than a prostitute. This rebuke was prompted by criticism from leading women lawyers who argued that the impact of rape on victims should not be assessed using sexual stereotypes (*Canberra Times*, 24 April 1994).

In all jurisdictions there was also continuing acknowledgement of the need to prevent the attachment of organised crime and police corruption to the prostitution industry. In both Queensland and New South Wales clear evidence of police corruption associated with prostitution was an important factor in the initiation of law reform in the 1990s. In other jurisdictions anxieties about the possibility of police corruption were frequently used to support prostitution law reform (NTLAPR 34: 3764). Once again, however, it is notable that arguments about organised crime and police corruption were used to justify both decriminalisation (for example, in the Northern Territory) and the promulgation of tougher anti-prostitution laws (in Queensland).

Pornography, Violence and Cyberspace

As discussed in Chapter 6, one result of the censorship changes which occurred in 1983–84 was that a significant disparity opened up between the states and territories in relation to X-rated videos. While the sale or hire of these videos is legal in the Australian Capital Territory and the Northern Territory, it remains illegal in all other jurisdictions. However, the interstate sale of videos by mail is not illegal.

Since 1988 there have been various unsuccessful attempts to change this arrangement. In 1991, for example, the parliament of the Australian Capital Territory debated and defeated measures designed to outlaw the sale and hire of X-rated videos. Attempts by the government there to impose a tax on the distribution of these videos were ruled illegal by the High Court.[11] In 1994 the Kennett government in Victoria was forced to close a loophole in that state's laws which meant that the sale of X-rated videos could not be policed. (*The Age*,

11 February 1995, reported that unclassified material was also available in Melbourne at this time.)

Various unsuccessful attempts have also been made to extend the application of the X classification or to revamp it. The Joint Select Committee on Video Material – which reported to the federal parliament in 1988 – investigated all aspects of the video industry. Its terms of reference also required it to explore the availability and use of pornographic and violent videos in the community and to 'investigate the likely effects upon people, especially children, of exposure to violent, pornographic or otherwise obscene material' (JSCVM 1: xix–xx). The report – in two volumes presenting majority and minority reports – noted 'basic philosophical disagreements' that were 'not on party lines'. The report recommended the introduction of a new restricted video classification category for non-violent erotica and the incorporation of material currently classified as X into this new category. However, a significant section of the committee was opposed to this recommendation (the final vote was six for and five against). The dissidents argued that the introduction of this category would entrench hard-core pornography in the community and was 'counter to the overwhelming burden of evidence submitted to the Committee concerning the harmful effects of this material'. They suggested that material in the existing X category (said to contain violent but degrading pornography) should be refused classification by the Commonwealth (JSCVM 1: 302–3). In his dissenting minority report the chair, Dick Klugman (a consistent libertarian since the 1970s), argued that 'adverse effects upon adults and children of exposure to material containing various degrees of violence, pornography or obscenity have not been clearly demonstrated'. In his view, then, there was no basis for increased censorship controls (JSCVM 2: 622–3) or, we might gather, for maintaining restrictions on the distribution of tapes of non-violent erotica in the areas of state jurisdiction.

While the recommendation for the new category was presented to the Commonwealth parliament in 1988, there were no substantive moves to implement this recommendation. Indeed, it appears that there is now less public and political support for moves to extend the availability of pornography. As in the 1980s, much of the current debate focuses on the impact of representational violence on children and adults, as well as on the censorship of sexual violence against women. In the 1990s some new pornography-related concerns have emerged, particularly in relation to information technologies such as computer games, bulletin boards and the Internet.

Many of the issues here were apparent in the debate which took place in the Commonwealth parliament in 1994 on the *Classification*

(Publications, Films and Computer Games) Act. This Act was the first significant piece of censorship legislation to be debated by the Commonwealth parliament since the introduction of the X classification in the
mid-1980s (see Chapter 6). For our purposes, then, it is a useful point
at which to look again at how the discussion about pornography, and
its appropriate regulation, has changed over time.

In 1995 the federal Labor government argued that there were two
main issues which the new *Classification Act* was designed to address.
First, there was now perceived to be a need for laws to govern the classification and distribution of computer games; since the mid-1980s
these had become extremely popular among children and teenagers.
Second, the Attorney-General argued that the lack of a uniform classification system in Australia created administrative difficulties and some
inefficencies both for government and industry. New arrangements
had been recommended by the Australian Law Reform Commission in
1991 and the changes proposed by the new legislation had been
prepared in consultation with the states and territories (HofR 196:
1381–84).

The 1995 Act established the framework (a statute to be applied to
the Australian Capital Territory) for a uniform national system for the
classification of publications, films and computer games; the latter had
not previously been included in censorship legislation. Under the
proposed scheme, all jurisdictions in Australia would use the same
criteria and system for classification. They would accept the decisions of
the Commonwealth Classification Board (replacing the existing Censorship Board) and the judgements on appeal of the Classification Review
Board (replacing the existing Film and Literature Board of Review).

State and territory governments were, however, to retain some independent powers over censorship. They were still to be responsible for
governing the legal arrangements under which various categories of
publications, films and computer games were to be distributed. This
meant that the states and territories would still have the final say on
what material could be legally circulated in their jurisdictions and how
breaches of the law were to be prosecuted.

While the government argued that the 1995 Act was 'essentially
procedural in nature' (HofR 196: 1382) and simply reflected the
current approach to censorship being adopted by the Commonwealth,
states and territories, it is clear that the new Act significantly extended
governmental powers. It made continuing provision for the compulsory
classification of all films and videos, but replaced the existing voluntary
scheme for publications with a 'partially compulsory one'. The aim
here was to get more publications submitted for classification and to
enable the Classification Board to call in what it saw to be 'submittable

publications'. In effect, this extended the surveillance and classification powers of the Commonwealth in relation to print publications.

A new MA classification for films (located between the existing categories of M and R) was introduced; children under the age of fifteen were not to be admitted to MA films unless they were accompanied by an adult. There was also a general tightening of the existing guidelines for M and R films and videos, in order to reduce the violence, sex and coarse language to which children might be exposed.

The most significant change, however, was the introduction of a classification system for computer games. Three categories were established – G, M, and MA (no provision was made for R or X games). Any computer game which was deemed 'unsuitable for a minor to see or play' was to be refused classification. These new provisions were, then, much tougher than those which already applied to film and video. This was a direct consequence of lobbying by feminist and conservative politicians and by the Senate Select Committee on Community Standards (*SMH*, 19 August 1995). The action against computer games followed the controversy in 1992–93 over the Sega game 'Night Trap', in which scantily-clad women could be drilled through the neck and mutilated by sharp electric instruments.

Parliamentary Debates

Although the 1994 Classification Bill sought to significantly extend governmental powers in relation to censorship, this generated little comment in the parliament. Indeed, the lack of controversy is remarkable, especially compared to the debates in 1971, when the R classification was introduced, and 1984 when the X classification was introduced (see Chapters 5 and 6). In both 1971 and 1984 fundamental disagreements were voiced by parliamentarians about the problems posed by pornography and about the proper role of government in regard to its control. While many of the same conservative, liberal and feminist arguments that appeared then were visible in 1994, these were now couched in much less extreme language. Libertarian arguments – widely deployed in both the earlier debates – were absent from the 1994 debate. We do not see parliamentarians defending the rights of pornography consumers or suggesting that the use of pornography is a harmless and/or legitimate expression of a citizen's privacy (as the Attorney-General had claimed in 1984). No parliamentarian suggested (as a number did in 1984 and 1971) that pornography is a useful outlet for those who are handicapped or too ugly to aspire to normal sexual relations. Also missing is the argument – central to libertarian discourse in 1971 and still deployed in 1984 – that because representations are ideas rather than actions, reflecting rather than constructing the world, they should not be subject to government controls.

The pervasive tone of the 1994 debate was one of calm pragmatism and general agreement on the approach to be adopted. Indeed, we might say that a new political consensus was apparent on censorship matters. The main contours of this consensus were traced by the Attorney-General, Michael Lavarch. In the first place, he said :

> material will still continue to be classified on the basis of the principle that adults should be able to read, hear and see what they want, that children should be protected from material likely to harm or disturb them, and that everyone should be protected from exposure to unsolicited material that they find offensive [HofR 196: 1382].

This 'first principle' was, of course, also the foundation of censorship regimes established in 1971 and 1984. In 1994 Lavarch argued that there was also: 'a new principle, namely, the need to take account of community concerns about depictions which condone or incite violence, particularly sexual violence, and the portrayal of persons in a demeaning manner' (HofR 196: 1382). This was exactly the issue which had caused so much controversy in the parliament during 1983–84. The then Attorney-General, Gareth Evans, had argued that 'community' and feminist-inspired concerns about the representation of sexual violence should not override the general freedoms established by the first principle. As we saw in Chapter 6, Evans and his supporters were eventually forced to back down on this issue. In 1994, however, it appeared that Michael Lavarch's 'new principle' was no longer controversial; most parliamentarians accepted that representations of violence, particularly sexual violence, needed to be subject to stringent censorship guidelines. This new consensus around sexual violence clearly reflects the ongoing impact of anti-pornography feminism on Australian political discourse.

In previous chapters I have shown that the concern to protect children (from various dangers) has been an ongoing theme of Australian censorship debates in the post-war period. In 1994 this is clearly present in the concern to regulate computer games and tighten the classification guidelines for films and videos. Indeed, it can be argued that 'first principle' considerations about the freedoms entitled to adults were seen to have no place in the debate about computer games. The new classification system made no provision for R or X ratings for computer games and not one parliamentarian raised this as a problem.

Some speakers did raise concerns about the non-application of the legislation to computer bulletin boards, CD-ROMs and the Internet (HofR 196: 1385). There appears, however, to have been widespread acceptance both that the distribution of computer games needed to be regulated and that much tougher laws were appropriate for this medium.

The main reason for this was that computer games were seen to be almost the exclusive province of children and adolescents (although distributors have recently contested this view).[12] The games themselves were described as 'violent, sexist and racist, providing negative role models for children'; they were also said to 'encourage emotional detachment' and to 'promote questionable values and unacceptably negative responses in real-life situations'. Young males, in particular, were seen as liable to be 'desensitised to sexual brutality' through their use of computer games and to be 'more aggressive and callous towards women, more willing to believe that women are responsible for their own rapes' (HofR 196: 1383–9).

Similar arguments were, of course, made in relation to comics and pulp novels in the 1950s (see Chapter 3). In the 1990s, the production of appropriate patterns of sexual behaviour and of appropriate relations between the sexes is clearly also of political import. But in the 1950s adults could easily achieve surveillance of the films and reading material aimed at children; no special skills were required. In the 1980s and 1990s new inter-generational differences have opened up between adults and children in relation to computer-based technology. As one member of parliament argued, many children are now 'highly skilled in the use of computers' while many parents 'do not have the knowledge required to even see what their children have access to, let alone to make an evaluation of its content' (HofR 196: 1390). The incapacity of adults in this regard was clearly generating new political anxieties.

The interactive nature of computer games was another reason why they were seen as worthy of tougher censorship guidelines than films and videos.[13] In the House of Representatives, Janice Crosio argued that the active participation required in computer games made a stricter classification scheme 'relevant'. She cited the example of a game called 'Mortal Kombat', 'where the player pushes the opponent off a ledge and impales him on a sharpened spike, having the option of electrocuting the opponent and then either ripping out the still beating heart or tearing off the head and holding it aloft with the spinal cord dangling' (HofR 196: 1387). Quite apart from the violent nature of some computer games, then, there was seen to be a new problem caused by the active participation of players who were required to choose between various scenarios. As one member of parliament argued, it was 'one thing to watch a violent video; it is another thing altogether to be invited into the violence' (HofR 196: 1391).

Policing the Internet

The focus on children and the protection of children was also evident in public concerns during the 1990s about the transmission of pornography – particularly child pornography – on the Internet. In 1994 an 18-year-old male was charged in the Perth Children's Court with attempting to procure child pornography on the Internet (*Age*, 18 July 1994). The following year two men – one in Western Australia and one in Victoria – were charged and convicted of possessing child pornography (obtained via the Internet). The Western Australian man was prosecuted under state obscenity laws, while the Victorian man was charged under the *Classification of Film and Publications Act*. In both cases, these individuals were traced by 'Internet vigilantes', that is, Internet users who informed the Australian police that someone in their jurisdiction was looking for child pornography. In the Western Australia case no evidence was actually found by the police, but the man admitted he had downloaded photographs of naked children and a pre-pubescent Asian girl having sex with an adult from a bulletin board in Mexico. He estimated that these images had been on his computer screen for about 10 minutes. He was found guilty of possessing child pornography but no conviction was recorded (*Canberra Times*, 1 April 1995). In the Victorian case 500 printouts of child pornography, as well as a large collection of child pornography stored on the hard drive and several videos, were discovered by police. The man was sentenced to four months' gaol, suspended for two years, and fined $4000 (Adelaide *Advertiser*, 20 June 1995).

These cases suggest that existing laws can often be utilised to deal with pornography on the Internet. In the last few years, however, governments around the world have begun to look at regulating this area. German authorities are presently considering criminal penalties for the transmission of neo-Nazi material on the Internet while, in February 1996, US President Bill Clinton signed telecommunication reform legislation which banned the distribution via computer networks of indecent or obscene material to minors and of abortion information.

In Australia, the proposed strategy for regulation in this area has three key elements (Commonwealth of Australia 1995b):

- A self-regulatory framework will be set up, incorporating a code of practice and a complaints handling procedure. Self-regulation

means that there will be no attempt to classify material accessed
through on-line information services.

- A comprehensive education program will assist parents and teachers
  to protect children from unsuitable material.
- New offence provisions will be introduced to provide sanctions
  against persons who 'deliberately breach community standards' in
  relation to on-line services. (In July 1995 Commonwealth, state and
  territory ministers responsible for censorship agreed on the introduction of new laws to deal with offensive or restricted material
  accessed through on-line computer services, including bulletin
  boards and the Internet.)

The shift to self-regulation in this area is an important and historic
development. Notably, it moves away from the system of classification
and controls which still apply to publications, film and video and
computer games.[14]

Conclusion

Over the last decade there have been several significant changes in
the politico-legal regimes attached to both prostitution and pornography in Australia. The shift to a decriminalisation of some prostitution-related activities in several jurisdictions is particularly notable.
This appears to be the result of several distinct (and often contradictory) factors, such as the impact of feminist discourse and of
increasing numbers of women parliamentarians; the impact of HIV/
AIDS on concerns about public health; and the influence of new citizenship claims by sexual minority groups such as homosexuals and
prostitutes. While the shift to decriminalisation has probably brought
some advantages for workers in the prostitution industry, it has also
resulted in higher levels of official surveillance (for example, the
implementation of tough new health regulations for legal sex workers
in the Australian Capital Territory) and a demand for increased levels
of self-surveillance (in order to comply with the many new rules and
regulations). In those states and territories where registration or
licensing is a condition of the legal operation of sex businesses, new
bureaucratic machinery now operates in addition to a more extensive
criminal law.

In previous chapters I have identified a trend towards increasing
discussion and politicisation of prostitution transactions. In the 1990s,
prostitutes are still the main focus of this attention. Parliamentarians
are now more likely to refer to prostitutes as sex workers and as
employees of the sex industry. However, they still talk about prostitutes
in a contradictory fashion – as being worthy of both punishment and

protection. Clients are now less likely to be discussed as dangerous individuals with pathological sexual proclivities. This trend is particularly obvious in those jurisdictions where some form of decriminalisation is being contemplated. In all jurisdictions, however, there is now more concern than ever before to address the role of clients in prostitution transactions and to ensure that clients – like sex workers – come within the ambit of the criminal law. Political debates about the nature of prostitution transactions have certainly diversified and intensified over the last decade. Prostitution is increasingly seen as an issue of sexual 'inappropriateness' connected to important questions of social justice and gender fairness.

In the 1990s decriminalisation is still the driving force of law reform proposals. Indeed, the call for decriminalisation has now become dominant in the realm of prostitution law. Individual jurisdictions either seek to enact some form of decriminalisation or, like the Queensland government, must battle to explain why decriminalisation is not being sought. In all jurisdictions, however, there is increasing controversy about the form and content of an appropriate decriminalisation strategy. Significant legal variations have consequently emerged between the states and territories. Moreover, in the 1990s, we have also seen the appearance of significant disagreements among feminist parliamentarians about the strategy of decriminalisation. Some now explicitly reject both decriminalisation and the formulation of prostitution as sex work.

At the same time as these divisions about decriminalisation have been appearing, increasing agreement is occurring among Australian politicians about the problems to be addressed. There is widespread acceptance of the need for tougher laws to combat child prostitution and for tougher, but also more strategic, laws to prevent the transmission of HIV/AIDS in commercial sex transactions. There is also widespread acceptance among parliamentarians of the need to ensure that prostitutes have the same civil and legal rights as other citizens, particularly to combat rape and other violence against women. The widespread adoption of tougher criminal penalties for street prostitution (even in those jurisdictions where decriminalisation is being introduced) also signals the emergence of a new consensus on this practice. It appears that even parliamentarians who are supportive of decriminalisation and sex workers are now unambivalent about also supporting tough criminal laws against street prostitution. The feminist and civil libertarian voices raised in New South Wales in the 1970s (and, to a lesser extent, in Victoria in the 1980s) for the rights of street workers seem to have disappeared. I have more to say about this specific trend in the concluding chapter.

Developments in relation to pornography have been both less dramatic and less controversial. As shown in Chapter 6, pornography was the subject of intense political debate in the 1980s. In the 1990s, however, new areas of unanimity appear to have emerged as parliamentarians generally avoided sexual libertarianism and concurred on the need to prohibit the distribution of material which depicted non-consensual sexual violence. An examination of the debate which occurred on the 1995 *Classification (Publications, Films and Computer Games) Act* in the federal parliament suggests that many MPs now agree on forms of 'appropriate' regulation. The Act included measures designed to generally extend censorship powers over publications, films and videos; it is notable that these measures were relatively uncontroversial in parliament (especially in comparison to the situation in 1971, when the R classification for films was introduced, and 1983–84, when video regulation was debated). New measures to classify and restrict the distribution of computer games were also widely supported by parliamentarians from all political parties. The concern here was that children were being exposed to inappropriate violence, and sexual violence, via computer games. Consequently, few voices were raised in opposition to the imposition of tougher controls on computer games than on publications, films and videos.

New concerns about the transmission of child pornography and other obscene material via the Internet have also emerged in the 1990s. It appears that the demands of this new technology have forced a rejection of the system of classification and control. The present indications are that techniques of self-regulation – combined with the elaboration of codes of conduct and new criminal penalties – will be applied in this area.

Conclusion

There are several general conclusions which can be drawn from this investigation. First, the sexual practices that law-makers call pornography and prostitution – and the problems they see associated with these practices – have changed considerably during the period since World War II. Some of these changes have been highly visible; for example, the diversification of prostitution into massage parlours, phone sex and overseas sex tourism, and the significantly increased availability of sexually explicit material as technological change has occurred in publishing, film and computers. Law-makers have reacted in a variety of often contradictory ways to these developments.

My investigation shows that there have also been significant, if somewhat less visible, discursive changes in law-makers' understandings of prostitution and pornography. Many of these changes can be accounted for in terms of shifts in the sexual culture and, therefore, in dominant understandings of what constitutes 'normal' sexuality. Post-war culture has increasingly emphasised sexuality as the basis of individual identity. At the same time, a particular mode of sexual relation – emphasising companionate ideals of equality and mutuality – has become entrenched as the dominant discourse in our sexual culture. It is not that this ideal matches the lived experience of most people but that sexual relations are increasingly measured against this ideal (and, therefore, the ideal becomes a constitutive feature of our lived experience of relationships).

In the present day, pornography and prostitution are usually discussed as taken-for-granted, unchanging, entities. But throughout the twentieth century notions of normal sexuality have always been in play in the identification of prostitution and pornography and in the determination of an appropriate legal response to these practices. In the decades before and immediately after the war prostitution was

237

always talked about by law-makers as heterosexual, involving a (problematic) female prostitute and an (unproblematic) male client. The sexual transaction itself was seen as 'normal' – the natural outcome of male sexual drives – if also often immoral. From the late 1950s onwards, however, clients came to be regarded as increasingly problematic and as the bearers of a pathological sexuality; significantly, prostitution also came to be represented by law-makers as less uniformly heterosexual.

Since the late 1950s, prostitution transactions have increasingly and consistently been marked out by law-makers as abnormal and undesirable. Prostitution transactions are now usually seen as the dark underside of normal and appropriate sexual relations, largely because of a perceived lack of equality and mutuality. (Of course, this approach is premised on narrow definitions of both equality and mutuality. It also implies that prostitution should always be measured in terms of sexual norms and not in terms of employment norms, which are often quite different.)

One consequence of this process has been the development of more expansive prostitution laws in the post-war period as prostitution has come to be regarded as more worthy of official surveillance. During the last thirty years, legal definitions of prostitution have expanded in most Australian jurisdictions. A wide range of new laws has been applied to the prostitution industry, with street soliciting attracting the most consistent attention from law-makers and dramatically higher penalties. To be sure, a significant degree of decriminalisation has also been introduced in some states and territories. This has created new zones of legality but has usually accompanied the creation of new law (for example, law which specifies the registration requirements for workers and/or operators of prostitution businesses) and tougher penalties for illegal prostitution. The shift to decriminalisation shows, in part, a desire to introduce more enlightened prostitution laws. It is, however, also completely consistent with the desire of law-makers for more official surveillance – and the encouragement of more self-surveillance – in the prostitution industry.

The legal regulation of pornography has a similarly diverse history, one which is firmly attached to shifts in the sexual culture. In the 1950s parliamentarians became concerned about comics and pulp novels; they argued that children exposed to sexualised and other corrupting material would fail to develop normal and appropriate relations with the opposite sex. In the 1970s, however, pornography came to be vaunted as a sign of personal and cultural freedom; for many, the use of pornography by adults was now perfectly consistent with the practice of normal sexuality. Consequently, a shift occurred in the law addressed to pornography, with the introduction of a system of classification and controls which significantly extended the right of adults to use pornography. In the 1980s and 1990s libertarian approaches to pornography came into significant conflict with both anti-pornography feminism and a renewed conservatism. Specific concerns arose in relation to child pornography and material which depicted sexual violence. This was clearly material which fell outside social and sexual norms. Consequently, new legal limitations were placed on the rights of adults to use pornography.

It is clear from the design of the investigation reported in this book that it provides little ground for arguments in favour of more or less or different types of regulation of the sex industries. This project has not been designed to investigate the *impact* of various laws and policies – for example, on workers in the sex industries, on clients and consumers, or on various problems often said to be associated with the sex industries such as worker exploitation, organised crime, police corruption, drugs and HIV/AIDS. Instead, this project has traced the problematisation of prostitution and pornography in Australian political institutions. I have been concerned to look at when and under what conditions the sexual practices described as prostitution and pornography have assumed political importance, and at the legal strategies introduced to deal with perceived problems. My investigation has, therefore, focused on the arguments deployed in the public arena to support various legal initiatives rather than on the evaluation of those initiatives.

In the course of the investigation I have, however, developed views about these legal strategies and about the form of a fruitful feminist engagement with law reform processes addressed to both prostitution and pornography. In the final section of this conclusion, therefore, I propose to make explicit some of these views.

As indicated in the introduction, my initial interest in the regulation of the sex industry came from an engagement with the work of the feminist political theorist Carole Pateman. I was interested to see how the notion of a 'sexual contract' – one which produced women's sexual and (therefore) political subordination to men – would be played out in the context of parliamentary deliberations about the sex industries. In Pateman's analysis, the sex industries play a central role in the formulation and reformulation of women's oppression. She is opposed to describing prostitution as sex work because, in her view, it is not work but sexual slavery. In this study I found some evidence in support of Pateman's arguments, but came to the conclusion that her approach was mostly unconvincing and unhelpful. The link between prostitution and men's political power is probably a lot more tenuous and contingent than Pateman's approach allows (see Sullivan 1995). Male (and female) parliamentarians have enacted laws which seriously disadvantage – and criminalise – women working in the sex industries. Moreover, some of the arguments used by parliamentarians to justify these laws could be represented as a defence of male sexual interests and as the manifestation of a desire to subjugate all women. Until recently, parliametarians often made arguments about the inevitability and inescapability of male sexual needs; they assumed that women and prostitutes should service these needs and that it would be dangerous for the law to obstruct prostitution transactions. But parliamentarians have always advanced a wide range of arguments in their deliberations on the sex industries. Most appear to have little to do with the oppression of women. Since the turn of the century, for example, parliamentarians have consistently talked about prostitution laws in terms of the need to defend public health and to create amenable public space. Many have also argued that prostitution laws are necessary to discourage inappropriate sexual practices and gender relations.

Arguments about men's sexual need for prostitution are also rarely advanced in the present day. Indeed, there is ample evidence to support the view that Australian parliamentarians have become concerned over the last decade to enact laws which are less oppressive to women working in the sex industries and/or which provide equal treatment for males and females, workers and clients. As stated in Chapter 7, the Victorian government has gone so far as to enact higher penalties for clients (usually men) than for workers in street prostitution. So it appears that there is only mixed evidence in support of the view that prostitution should be regarded as part of a sexual contract whereby men maintain political power over women.

The clearest feature of parliamentary debates about the sex industries is their complexity and propensity to change. As suggested above, the category of sexual practices designated as prostitution and pornography has changed profoundly in this century, as have the problems seen to be associated with these practices and the legal strategies proposed for their solution. Prostitution and pornography cannot, therefore, be regarded as stable referents or consistent and comparable objects of law reform. This makes problematic the erection of a theory of women's oppression premised on essentialist notions of a sexual contract or, indeed, essentialist accounts of what various sexual practices mean (although Pateman is not a consistent essentialist – see Sullivan 1995).

For a feminist attempting to come to terms with arguments about what sort of laws should be applied to the sex industries, Pateman's approach has two significant disadvantages. First, it is not descriptively accurate; clearly a range of different transactions can occur under the rubric of 'prostitution' or 'pornography'. Some of these transactions are more lucrative for workers than others, some more dangerous than others, and most (like nearly all employment relations) involve a mix of individual agency and exploitation. 'Big' arguments, systematic accounts of women's oppression via prostitution and pornography, cannot address this diversity of sex work.

Second, systematic accounts of women's oppression via prostitution and pornography are not helpful in the identification of specific problems or in working out a good feminist strategy to deal with these problems. An example here is the legal harassment faced by street prostitutes in most Australian capital cities. There seems to be little feminist or other recognition that women arrested for soliciting are not doing anything more than many normal men frequently do on the street to women in their pursuit of sexual transactions. It is not clear why soliciting for the purposes of prostitution – particularly where this does not involve harassment – should be regarded as innately offensive. In most jurisdictions, however (New South Wales is an important exception), tough new soliciting penalties have been introduced in the post-war period.

If we accept the premise that prostitution always involves sexual slavery, then we have no way of identifying issues like these except in terms of the consequences of sexual slavery (hardly a flexible and nuanced term). We also have no way of distinguishing between better and worse prostitution practices, and no way to account for the professed choices of women who say they have freely chosen the work of prostitution. If prostitution is sexual slavery, we must be committed to outlawing it in all its manifestations.[1] In my view, this approach is deeply problematic. The consequences of more expansive laws are likely to be borne by prostitutes – rather than clients or the owners of sex businesses – and be evident in higher arrest and imprisonment rates for women.

With the recent shift to gender-neutral prostitution laws, and the growing public concern with gender fairness, more clients would be arrested and imprisoned than in the past. This might represent some sort of sex equality, but is hardly a desirable outcome. The investigation undertaken in this book suggests that legal definitions of prostitution are extrapolated from deliberations which seek to fix the meaning of normal sexuality and gender relations. Debates about what should count as normal and appropriate sexual practice have often been advantageous for women. For example, arguments about the superiority of sexual relations that are equal and mutual have been used over the last decade to problematise both domestic violence and rape in marriage. This is clearly a good thing. However, it is also clear that narrow definitions of equality and mutuality are often brought to bear in deliberations about normal and appropriate sexuality. Not surprisingly, the results of these deliberations usually favour companionate and (hetero)sexual relations. There are many who, because of their sexual practice – or, in the case of sex workers, their employment – fall outside these norms. My examination of parliamentary debates over the last century indicates that prostitutes and, increasingly, their clients are deeply affected in this process of sexual pathologisation.

In my view, there can be little feminist ground for condemning all prostitution transactions just because they involve prostitution, that is, some form of financial benefit in exchange for some sort of sex. There are, of course, occasions when feminists will want to be critical of certain practices in the prostitution industry – for example the hiring criteria applied to workers in Melbourne's legal brothels or the medical examination laws applied to workers in legal brothels in the Australian Capital Territory. But this is not the same as adopting a principled opposition to prostitution. Feminists need to be careful that their arguments do not slide into heteronormative accounts of sexuality which pathologise some women (sex workers), some men (clients), and sexual transactions which, in practice, can be distinguished from normal sexual relations only by the presence of an explicit economic exchange.

In most cases, a principled feminist opposition to prostitution, including its formulation as sexual slavery, is also not conducive to the development of practical feminist strategies for dealing with some of the urgent and particular problems presently facing prostitute women (and men). A feminist focus on prostitution as sex work (rather than sexual slavery), however, has some distinct strategic advantages. In general, it allows for the development of a greater range of feminist activities, ones which focus on improving the situation of prostitutes. These activities need to be engaged with the details of local legal and political contexts and to be capable of supporting a broadly based feminist mobilisation in support of decriminalisation.

In my view, there are clear arguments in favour of decriminalisation. Some legal regimes *are* better for workers than others. Decriminalisation can advantage workers because it allows them to avoid criminal proceedings, to organise openly, to claim rights as workers, and to pursue avenues of legal redress against violent clients or oppressive employers. However, several different approaches to decriminalisation have been implemented in Australia over the last decade and it is not at all clear which – if any – of the present arrangements are better for workers. Moreover, as I have already stated, decriminalisation has often been accompanied by tougher penalties against street prostitution (and other illegal prostitution practices); expanded legal definitions of prostitution; new registration requirements for workers (for instance in the Northern Territory and for solo workers in the Australian Capital Territory); and oppressive health regulations for workers (in the Australian Capital Territory). A comparative research project, one which canvassed the situation in each jurisdiction and focused on the needs and concerns of workers (rather than political concerns about public health or law and order), would certainly be advantageous at this stage to establish what sort of decriminalisation feminists might want to support.

Several feminists have argued that the focus on prostitution as sex work tends to distract attention from the pivotal role of clients – and male desire – in prostitution transactions. This is clearly an important issue. However, I emphasise that the focus on prostitution as sex work is *strategic* and designed principally to support the formation of politico-legal regimes which are conducive to better lives for prostitute women (and men). The strategic focus on prostitution as sex work need not displace the question of what clients think they are buying in prostitution transactions. My investigation suggests that questions about masculine sexual ethics are increasingly being raised in mainstream political institutions and in the public sphere more generally. There is every reason to believe these debates will continue, and that feminist institutional and cultural politics will continue to problematise both male sexual desire and men's public and private behaviour. If this process is nuanced and aware of the heteronormative tendencies discussed above, then it can broadly operate to benefit women both socially and politically.

Is a similar approach possible for pornography? I certainly favour strategic feminist approaches that support and encourage an extension of the rights of workers in the pornography industry (although most workers are located outside the ambit of Australian laws) and which enable public debate about sexual ethics. The present arrangement of laws for the classification and control of pornography is not inconsistent with this approach.

As my research indicates, pornography has no universal or fixed meaning and becomes meaningful only in particular political contexts. Over the last fifteen years, public debates about pornography and censorship in Australia have been centrally implicated in broader debates about sexual ethics and gender relations. Deliberations in the 1980s about how to censor representations of sexual violence were accompanied by new public and political concerns to address rape, sexual harassment and domestic violence. This suggests that debates about pornography (and censorship) can be productive and that female citizens might sometimes benefit from this process.

The present arrangement of censorship laws is primarily designed to protect children and to minimise the public display of potentially offensive material. More recently, there have also been attempts to take into account feminist concerns about the representation of sexual violence. This latter development is probably a good thing, although I remain concerned about the potential of this strategy to constrain the use of particular material by sexual minorities (for example, lesbian sado-masochists) who aim to construct a cultural (and sometimes feminist) politics of resistance to norms of sex and gender.

This latter issue points to the impossibility of using censorship laws to address feminist concerns about pornography. Clearly, it is not simply the representation of sexual violence or sexual explicitness which is the problem for most feminists. Scenes of sexual violence in a film can be used to critique or defend sexually violent *practices*. And many depictions of loving, non-violent, relationships (for example, in Walt Disney films, TV sitcoms and many X-rated videos) are deeply conventional and heteronormative. It is hard to see how censorship laws and regulations – with their focus on protecting children and guarding against public offence – might change in order to deal with the broad feminist concern to critique and change 'normal' relations of sex and gender.

For this reason I would not want to campaign for less or more censorship in Australia. To do so would be to imply that the present system of censorship practices is able to further a feminist politics focused on representation (although, as I have already suggested, public *debates* about censorship – as distinct from the practices of censorship – can be productive in other ways). A feminist cultural politics that engages with a variety of representation (including pornography, advertising and mainstream entertainment) is more likely to advance the position of women than more or 'better' censorship practices. Clearly, this also means I do not support the federal coalition government's plans to prohibit the distribution of X-rated videos in Australia. As I have already suggested, a proposal like this will not, cannot, advance feminist agendas. But it would inhibit a feminist cultural politics broadly aimed at representations of gender and sexuality. It would, for example, inhibit the production and distribution of feminist material which is sexually explicit ('pornography' if you like to call it that), but which also calls into question the assumptions of 'normal' and mainstream representations of gender and sexuality.

Notes

Introduction

1. In Australia there is a mostly clear federal/state delineation of responsibility for prostitution and pornography. The federal government is responsible for customs and excise and, therefore, for regulations addressed to the importation of pornography. By agreement, federal authorities – the Classification Board and Classification Review Board – are responsible for the initial classification of publications, films, videos and computer games (including those produced within Australia). State laws prescribe how classified material can be distributed within their jurisdiction. The states are also responsible for laws addressed to prostitution.
2. Terms like *decriminalisation* and *legalisation* appear from the late 1970s onwards in debates about prostitution law reform. As the Queensland Criminal Justice Commisssion (1991: 34) has commented, these terms are used widely but with little consistency. I use the term *decriminalisation* to denote any law reform which creates legally permissible areas of sex work, whether that does or does not also create new regulations for controlling prostitution.

1 Marking Danger

1. The only other explicit acknowledgement I have located in parliamentary debates, that parliamentarians are (sometimes) also clients of prostitutes, is to be found in New South Wales in 1995. During debate on the Disorderly Houses Amendment Bill, one member of the Legislative Council confessed that he 'went with two prostitutes' when he was much younger. This confession was marked by none of the jocularity of the 1916 Queensland debate. The Legislative Councillor said that it was 'the least satisfying sexual experience of my life' and he 'got an illness ... which served me right'. Also, his view of the prostitution transaction was that it involved 'exploitation'. Clearly, the terms in which male parliamentarians

conceptualise prostitution has undergone a significant transformation since 1916 (see Chapter 7).

2. This case involved Jean Barrin's translated version of *Venus in the Cloister, or the Nun in Her Smock*, printed and sold by Edmund Curll – see *R v. Curll* (1727) 93 ER 849. For a good discussion of this case see Hunter *et al.* 1993: 49–52.

3. In the United States the power of both federal and state governments to make laws in relation to obscene and indecent materials has often been constrained by the right to free speech inherent in the Bill of Rights. Since the late 1950s in the United States, censorship regulations and laws against obscene and indecent material have frequently been declared unconstitutional and therefore illegal. In Australia no general and constitutional right to free speech exists, although the High Court recently found there is an implied right to free 'political' speech in the Australian constitution: *Nationwide News v. Wills* (1992) CLR 106.

2   A New Moral Economy?

1. In the whole of the pre-war period only three women were elected to Australian parliaments; three more were elected during World War II, while six took up seats in the decade 1945–55 (Sawer and Simms 1984: 41–2).

2. A baby boom due to the increased popularity of marriage was already evident during World War II. In Victoria, for example, the birth rate per 1000 of population declined from 228.9 in 1929 to 158.5 in 1939; this had already climbed back to 204.6 by 1945 (VPD 222: 2620).

3. Soft-core pornography was again used by the military in the early years of the Cold War when pictures of American 'bathing beauties' were used as a weapon in the propaganda war with Moscow (*SMH*, 11 February 1951).

4. With the lifting of wartime National Security Regulations in 1945, South Australia was the only state that did not have legislation already in place (from before the war) to provide for the compulsory examination and treatment of those suspected to be suffering from a venereal disease.

5. Female inmates of the Brisbane Prison, many of whom would be serving sentences for prostitution-related activities, as well as delinquent girls at the St Mary's Home, Toowong, were also subject to routine examinations for venereal disease at this time. No such examinations were performed on male prison inmates or on delinquent boys.

6. The relevant table does say that 'Females Detained' shows the number of women against whom a detention order was issued during the respective month and not the total number actually in detention in that month.

7. Florence Cardell-Oliver (1876–1965) was the member for Subiaco in the Western Australian Assembly between 1936 and 1956. She was the first woman to enter an Australian cabinet (Minister without portfolio 1947–48; Minister for Supply and Shipping 1948–49; Minister for Health, Minister for Supply and Shipping 1949–53) (Sawer and Simms 1984: 209; Greenwood 1975). In 1955 Cardell-Oliver told the Assembly that one of the main reasons she had entered parliament was to address the social problems posed by SP betting and prostitution (WAPD 142: 301).

8. Section 4(2) of the *Vagrancy Act* prescribed a gaol term not exceeding six

months with hard labour for a male person who (i) knowingly lives wholly or in part on the earnings of prostitution or (ii) in any public place solicits or importunes for immoral purposes. In *Ex parte Langley* (1953) 53 SR (NSW) 324, Clancy J. found that this section of the Act referred to female prostitution only. It could be applied to cases where a male solicits another male to have intercourse with a female, but did not apply to 'unnatural offences'.

9. This amendment also ended the death penalty in New South Wales.

10. Rosaleen Norton, a Sydney-based artist, was charged in 1949 under Victorian state obscenity laws for exhibiting obscene pictures (*SMH*, 20 August 1949). The pictures concerned had an explicit sex and witchcraft theme. While this case was dismissed, police in New South Wales later charged the publisher and printer of a collection of Rosaleen Norton's art (*SMH*, 6 February, 7 March 1953). In 1955 Norton was charged with having committed an 'unnatural offence' (sodomy) and, under state obscenity laws, for having made an obscene film (*SMH*, 5 October 1955). It appears that the film concerned was made privately by Norton and her lover and was subsequently stolen from her home.

11. New South Wales, *Obscene and Indecent Publications Act (Amendment) Act*, 1955; South Australia, *Police Offences (Amendment) Act*, 1954; Victoria, *Police Offences Act (Amendment) Act*, 1955; Queensland, *Objectionable Literature Act*, 1955.

12. This category contained comics as well as pulp novels including, most notably, those by the Australian author Carter Brown (*Honky-Tonk Homicide* and *The Lady's Alive*).

13. Although several speakers argued that the consumption of American comics and magazines caused juvenile delinquency (for example, NSWPD 12: 2773), others argued that the literature problem was an effect rather than a cause of declining community standards and juvenile delinquency; poor housing, poor family conditions and working mothers were said to be responsible for the post-war phenomenon of juvenile delinquency (NSWPD 12: 2782).

14. Melville was a Labor member of the Legislative Council, 1952–59 (Sawer and Simms 1984: 202), and the only female parliamentarian to comment in this debate.

3   The Sexual Revolution and Pornography

1. Weeks (1981: 256–67) has demonstrated this trend dramatically. He says that in Britain 552 women per 1000 were married in 1911. By 1931, this had become 572 per 1000; and by 1960, 808 per 1000. By the mid-1960s in Britain 95 per cent of men and 96 per cent of women were married by the age of forty-five. Mathews (1984: 35) has suggested a similar trend in Australia.

2. They also emphasised the 'definitive role of the clitoris' in female sexual response, in opposition to existing sexological and psychoanalytic literature which emphasised the importance of a separate (and superior) 'vaginal orgasm'. However, Masters and Johnson went on to argue that the vagina provided 'the primary physical means of heterosexual expression for the human female' (1966: 56–68). It appears, therefore, that they were

unaware of an inconsistency in their position – identifying the clitoris as the main site of female sexual response but penis–vagina sex as the primary physical means of heterosexual expression.

3. This point has also been noted recently by Sheila Jeffreys (1990: 135–6). Jeffreys argues that the sex 'therapy' advocated by Masters and Johnson was (and is) deeply implicated in the oppression of women because their treatment for male impotence clearly links the 'efficient and frequent wielding of the penis' with the maintenance of men's power over women.

4. In 1956 several publishers of romance comics won a High Court appeal against prohibition orders issued by the board – see *Transport Publishing Co. Pty Ltd v. Literature Board of Review* (1957) 99 CLR 111. The eight periodicals which had been subject to prohibition orders contained pictures and stories of love, courtship and marriage. The High Court found that 'In most of the stories courtship was followed by marriage and in none of the pictures was there any suggestion of improper attire' although there were 'passionate embraces'. In commenting on this decision, the board said that it would continue to act 'as wise and prudent parents would act in relation to their children to ensure that the literature at large on the bookstalls of this State should be such as the normal parent would be willing to have available for his [*sic*] children' (QLBR 1956–57: 2). Romance comics were not a major target for prohibition orders after 1955.

5. See, for example, QPD 219: 1269; QPD 229: 2677; QPD 233: 898; QPD 243: 778.

6. Scientific texts such as these were available only to *bona fide* students.

7. While the reasons for the cross-party opposition to this measure are not completely evident from the recorded debate in parliament, it is likely that the government at this time was opposed to any liberalisation of the laws against obscene and indecent material. The Labor Party would have been opposed to the establishment of a statutory authority for censorship decisions.

8. See *R v. Neville et al.* (1966) 83 WN (Pt 1) (NSW) 501; *R v. Sharp* (1964) 82 WN (Pt 1) (NSW) 129.

9. Judge Levine eventually decided the appeals in both the *Tharunka* and *Oz* cases. He was later to assume some prominence in relation to abortion law reform. In 1971 the 'Levine ruling' substantially liberalised the conditions under which women could obtain lawful abortions in New South Wales.

10. This brief review of the contents of the *Kings Cross Whisper* is based on an examination of No. 1 (January 1965) through to No. 40 (1967).

11. *Crowe v. Graham* (1969) 121 CLR 395.

4 Revolutionary Limits

1. Many of the Wolfenden Report recommendations on street prostitution were enacted in Britain in the 1959 *Street Offences Act*. Weeks (1981: 244) says that this legislation drove prostitutes off the streets and produced 'a vast expansion of commercial prostitution agencies and call-girl rackets'.

2. However, the Sydney City Council had already declared its intentions in regard to the prostitution industry. In August 1966 it announced that it intended to make full use of its powers in order to curb the proliferation

of prostitution outlets, particularly sauna baths, massage studios and boarding houses in the city and Kings Cross area. The council said that it would use town planning laws to close down premises being used for unauthorised purpose in areas zoned residential (*SMH*, 2 August 1966).

3. See *Ex parte Fergusson* (1966) 84 WN (Pt 1) (NSW) 446.

4. See *Fergusson v. Gee* (1967) 86 WN (Pt 1) (NSW) 149.

5. From the mid-1950s onwards there was an increasing incidence of venereal disease throughout the Western world as penicillin-resistant strains of syphilis and gonorrhea began to appear (QHAR 1961–62).

6. Similar concerns about teenage prostitutes emerged in the Sydney press during 1966. In response to the suggestion that prostitution was declining, Kings Cross businessmen and social workers argued that there were now more and younger prostitutes working the streets than ever before: 'they are younger, better dressed, more attractive and more intelligent than was the case a few years ago. These young women appear to have gone into this with their eyes open. They know what they are doing. And that is the saddest thing about it' (*SMH*, 29 November 1966).

7. The only exception here was Petersen, who argued in the New South Wales parliament that amendments to the *Vagrancy, Disorderly Houses and Other Acts* in 1968 were 'an invasion of civil liberties' (NSWPD 75: 1502).

8. Phrased in the masculine person like this, and with due regard to the way in which the 1968 legislation in New South Wales focused on the largely female workforce of the sex industry, it seems that this really was an argument for a sexually differentiated set of rights.

5   Libertarian Moments

1. However, Liberal and Liberal–National coalition parties continued to govern throughout the 1970s in Victoria and Queensland. In New South Wales the long-serving Liberal–Country Party government lost office in 1976; the Labor Party, initially under the leadership of Neville Wran, was to govern for the next decade. In South Australia a Labor government – mostly under the leadership of Don Dunstan – held office between 1970 and 1979. In Western Australia the Labor Party held office between 1971 and 1974; a Liberal–National coalition then governed until 1982. In Tasmania a Liberal–Centre Party held office between 1969 and 1971, after which Labor remained in government until 1982 (Galligan 1986: 270).

2. Hugo (1986: 45) documents a dramatic decline in Australia's total fertility rate during the 1970s; it fell by nearly one-third, from 2.88 in 1966 to 1.94 in 1978. The decline in fertility in Australia over this period was faster than in any other Western country.

3. In 1961 there were 2.8 divorces for every 1000 married women in Australia; by 1971 this had increased to 4.3 and was to rise to 12.7 by 1981. The divorce rate peaked at 19.2 in 1976 following the promulgation of the *Family Law Act* (Hugo 1986: 203–4).

4. The 'Menhennitt ruling' in Victoria – see *R v. Davidson* [1969] VR 667; and the 'Levine ruling' in New South Wales – see *R v. Wald* (1972) 3DCR 25.

5. The lower age limit was later reduced to two years of age in all states.

6. Queensland, *Censorship of Films Act Amendment Act*; Victoria, *Films Act*; New

South Wales, *Theatres and Public Halls and Cinematographic Films Amendment Act*; South Australia, *Film Classification Act*; Western Australia, *Censorship of Films Act*; Tasmania, *Films Act.*

7. In the 1990s, similar attention has been focused on Brett Easton Ellis's *American Psycho.*

8. Libertarianism was, however, a more important feature of the debate in New South Wales than in Victoria.

9. The film *Julia* was prohibited because the distributors indicated that it would be shown at a drive-in theatre. The board did not regard R films as suitable for exhibition at drive-in theatres because of their visibility from outside the theatre confines (QFBR 1975–76: 2).

10. Male homosexuality was said to have 'very little commercial appeal'. On the other hand lesbianism was said to be 'an essential prerequisite to commercial success' (QFBR 1974–75: 2). This was probably because representations of lesbian sexual activity have been purchased for their interest to male heterosexuals.

11. The 1975 amendments tightened up the legal definition of a brothel and of 'premises' (these were expanded to included cars, caravans, parts of premises, etc.); the law was also strengthened in relation to soliciting and loitering, organising, assisting and protecting prostitution, and in relation to women working alone from their own premises.

12. In the 1970s such 'possessive individualism' (Macpherson 1962) was an important feature of other feminist campaigns, for example for the right to abortion and against rape.

13. As theorists of governmentality have recently argued, modern political subjects have become attached to the project of 'freedom', 'have come to live it in terms of identity' (Rose 1989). But this does not represent a liberation from power, for 'individuals can be governed through their freedom to choose'; in modern Western societies, self-regulatory techniques are installed in citizens 'that will align their personal choices with the ends of government'. In this way, the 'freedom and subjectivity of citizens ... become an ally, and not a threat, to the orderly government of a polity and a society' (Rose and Miller 1992: 201, 188–9).

6 New Sexual Politics

1. See South Australia, 1980, *Report of the Select Committee of Inquiry into Prostitution*; New South Wales, 1986, *Report of the Select Committee of the Legislative Assembly upon Prostitution*; Victoria, 1985, *Inquiry Into Prostitution* (the Neave Report); Queensland, 1989, *Report of a Commission of Inquiry Pursuant to Orders in Council ...* (Chairperson G. E. Fitzgerald QC); Criminal Justice Commission (Queensland), 1991, *Regulating Morality? An Inquiry Into Prostitution in Queensland*; Western Australia, 1990, *Final Report of the Community Panel on Prostitution*; Australian Capital Territory Legislative Assembly, 1991, *Interim Report of the Select Committee on HIV, Illegal Drugs and Prostitution.*

2. See Commonwealth of Australia, 1988, *Report of the Joint Select Committee on Video Material.*

3. Unlike the other states, Queensland had not adopted a system of classifying and regulating the distribution of pornographic publications. The

Literature Board of Review claimed that its vigilance meant that Queensland, alone among the states, was organised to annihilate the menace of
child pornography (QLBR 1976–77: 1).

4. New South Wales, *Indecent Articles and Classified Publications (Amendment)
   Act*; Victoria, *Police Offences (Child Pornography) Act*; South Australia, *Classification of Publications (Amendment) Act*.

5. The package included amendments to the Customs (Prohibited Imports)
   Regulations, and the Customs (Cinematographic Films) Regulations, as
   well as the Classification of Publications Ordinance 1983, as contained in
   ACT Ordinance No. 59 of 1983.

6. See, for example, Senate 102: 1173, 1243, and 103: 1934; QPD 296: 2466.

7. This sort of argument was also deployed in the immediate post-war period
   (see Chapter 2).

8. The committee described pornography as 'a form of prostitution advertising' and recommended that 'any policies pursued by the government in
   the control and regulation of prostitution should take account of the need
   to break the nexus between violent pornography and prostitution'
   (NSWSCP: 91).

9. See for example VPD 308: 307; 315: 3196; 319: 1323–34, 2281; 327: 1329;
   336: 83, 166; 349: 8402.

10. Originally, the government also intended to decriminalise homosexual
    soliciting (soliciting for 'immoral purposes') although not where this was
    for the purposes of prostitution. As a result of political pressure, the
    government amended its own bill once again to include sanctions against
    soliciting for 'immoral purposes' (VPD 355: 4459).

7   Current Issues

1. However, a survey by a researcher from the University of New England, Dr
   Hugh Potter, suggests that only 10 per cent of those who watch pornographic videos are women. The majority of viewers are male, married,
   university graduates and most likely to vote Labor (*Weekend Australian*,
   20–21 January 1996).

2. With mixed success. Although sex worker rights groups attended the
   forum of non-government organisations, the Final Draft Platform for
   Action drawn up at the Beijing Conference focused on 'forced prostitution' and trafficking in women.

3. There are, for example, important differences between child and adult
   prostitution, as well as varying degrees of consent and coercion in most
   adult prostitution. Whether in Australia or Thailand, women and men
   'choose' to work in prostitution (as they might 'choose' to work in other
   jobs) out of economic necessity. Clearly, however, the impetus of this
   economic necessity varies between cultures (and is greater in countries
   where poverty is more widespread and where unemployment and welfare
   assistance are unavailable). My point here is that there is a need (politically and legally) to distinguish between different prostitution practices
   and to use the term *sexual slavery* a lot more carefully. However, *sexual
   slavery* is entirely appropriate (and preferable to *forced prostitution*) where
   children are involved or where adults have been imprisoned and subject
   to sexual assault.

4. However, the Australian branch of the Global Alliance Against Trafficking in Women has recently stated that it is not abolitionist.

5. There are, however, significant disparities in the ways that the law is applied within these jurisdictions. While South Australian police have been blitzing the prostitution industry in Adelaide (a campaign code-named Operation Patriot), Western Australia has recently formalised a long-term policy of 'containment and control' of certain police-approved brothels in Perth and Kalgoorlie.

6. During debate in the House, however, this measure was referred to as 'the Charlene provision'. Charlene was an HIV-positive woman, an intravenous drug user, who worked as a prostitute in the streets of Sydney's Kings Cross. Her activities achieved some media notoriety during 1992 and brought to public attention the fact that the law might be powerless to prevent HIV-positive prostitutes from working. The Act aims to ensure that a similar situation in the Australian Capital Territory can be dealt with by the law.

7. This measure was controversial because it tended to target those who were involved in providing security for sex workers. Previously, workers employed by escort agencies were often driven and accompanied to 'out' calls. The murder of a young escort worker (who prior to the new Act had been working in a brothel) on the Gold Coast in 1994 drew public attention to the ways in which the new laws made the practice of prostitution more dangerous.

8. Previously police had to act as clients in order to gather evidence. Anecdotal evidence suggests that certificates of discharge are now most likely to be offered to clients for evidence against workers and those 'knowingly' participating in the provision of prostitution.

9. As in other Australian jurisdictions, eighteen is the age of consent for prostitution, that is, the age at which an escort agency may legally employ a worker.

10. One of these brothels, the Daily Planet, announced plans to publicly list shares – to the value of $4 million – on the Australian Stock Exchange (Reuters, 6 October 1994).

11. In 1990 the ACT government passed the *Business Franchise ('X' Videos) Act* which established a licensing scheme to cover distributors of X-rated videos. In 1993 the High Court found that significant sections of the Act were invalid. The various licensing fees were found to be duties of excise and thus to contravene Section 90 of the Commonwealth Constitution which provides that duties of excise are the exclusive power of the Commonwealth. See *Capital Duplicators Pty Ltd v. Australian Capital Territory* [No. 1] (1992), 177, CLR 248; *Capital Duplicators Pty Ltd v. Australian Capital Territory* [No. 2] (1993), 178, CLR 561.

12. In 1995 distributors claimed that 50 per cent of customers for computer games were adults. They also contested the banning of some computer games. In the most recent case, involving a game called 'Phantasmagoria', there is a short – apparently non-consensual – sex scene between a husband and wife. This scene was the reason the game was 'refused classi-fication' although, as the distributors argued, it was nothing compared to the longer rape scene in the Jodie Foster film *The Accused*, which attracted only an M rating (*SMH*, 19 August 1995).

13. This approach is, however, based on a specific misunderstanding of the way in which all media is interactive. Reading and viewing are not passive

processes; a reader or viewer is always actively participating in the creation of the meaning of a text. Perhaps all that can be said about computer games is that the interactive activity is both more visible and more explicit.

14. Although, clearly, the system of classification and controls involves a measure of self-regulation as (within some pre-defined limitations) adults determine for themselves what material they will read and view.

Conclusion

1. Pateman does not, however, draw this logical conclusion. Barry (1995) also uses the argument that prostitution should be understood as sexual slavery, but she recommends legal measures addressed only to the 'perpetrators' of prostitution – clients and the owners and operators of sex businesses – and not to the 'victims', that is, prostitutes.

Bibliography

Primary Sources

Australian Capital Territory. Legislative Assembly. *Debates*.

Australian Capital Territory. 1991. *Interim Report of the Select Committee on HIV, Illegal Drugs and Prostitution*. Canberra: ACT Legislative Assembly.

Commonwealth of Australia. Senate. *Debates*. 1945–90.

Commonwealth of Australia. House of Representatives. *Debates*. 1945–90.

Commonwealth of Australia. 1977. *Royal Commission on Human Relationships, Final Report*. Canberra: AGPS.

Commonwealth of Australia. 1988. *Report of the Joint Select Committee on Video Material*. Canberra: AGPS.

Commonwealth of Australia. 1992. House of Representatives Standing Committee on Legal and Constitutional Affairs. *Half Way to Equal: Report of the Inquiry Into Equal Opportunity and Equal Status for Women in Australia*. Canberra: AGPS.

Commonwealth of Australia. 1995. *Regulation of Computer Bulletin Board Systems*. Canberra: AGPS.

Commonwealth of Australia. Attorney-General's Department and Department of Communications and the Arts. 1995. *Consultation Paper on the Regulation of On-line Information Services*.

Commonwealth Law Reports. 1955. Transport Publishing Company, Action Comics Pty Ltd, Popular Publications Pty Ltd and the Literature Board of Review, On Appeal from the Supreme Court of Queensland. (pp. 111–31).

Criminal Justice Commission (Queensland). 1991. Regulating Morality? *An Inquiry Into Prostitution in Queensland*.

Great Britain. 1957. *Report of the Committee on Homosexual Offences and Prostitution* (Wolfenden Report). UK Cmnd 247, HMSO.

Kings Cross Whisper. Sydney. 1–40, 1965–67.

Male. Sydney. 1955–58. 1(8)–3(8)

Man: The Australian Magazine for Men. 1936–57.

New South Wales. 1986. *Select Committee of the Legislative Assembly upon Prostitution: Final Report*.

New South Wales. Parliament. *Debates*.

Northern Territory. Legislative Assembly. *Parliamentary Record*.

Queensland. 1987–88. Unpublished Transcript of Proceedings. Commission of Inquiry Pursuant to Orders in Council (Chairperson G. E. Fitzgerald QC).

Queensland. 1989. *Report of a Commission of Inquiry Pursuant to Orders in Council.* ... (Chairperson G. E. Fitzgerald QC). Brisbane: Government Printer.

Queensland. Department of Health. *Annual Reports* 1945–70.

Queensland. Films Board of Review. *Annual Reports* 1974–88.

Queensland. 1991. Legislative Assembly of Queensland. Parliamentary Criminal Justice Committee. *Report on Prostitution.*

Queensland. Literature Board of Review. *Annual Reports* 1955–88.

Queensland. Parliament. *Debates.*

Queensland Police Department. *Annual Reports* 1946–90.

South Australia. 1979–80. Legislative Assembly. Report of the Select Committee of Inquiry into Prostitution. *Parliamentary Papers,* 4: 152.

South Australia Parliament. *Debates.*

Sturgess, D. 1985. *An Inquiry into Sexual Offences Involving Children and Related Matters* (Sturgess Report). Brisbane.

United Kingdom. 1982. *Working Paper on Offences Relating to Prostitution and Allied Offences.* London.

Victoria. 1985. *Inquiry into Prostitution: Final Report* (Neave Report). Melbourne.

Victoria. Parliament. *Debates.*

Victorian Law Reports. 1948. *R v. Close.* (pp. 446–7).

Western Australia. 1975–6. Royal Commission into Matters Surrounding the Administration of the Law Relating to Prostitution. *Parliamentary Papers,* 8.

Western Australia. 1990. *Final Report of the Community Panel on Prostitution.* Government of WA.

Western Australia. Parliament. *Debates.*

Women's Electoral Lobby (NSW). *WEL-Informed.* June 1976–August 1979.

Secondary Sources

Aitken, J. 1977. 'Prostitutes in NSW', Paper presented to seminar on Victimless Crimes, Macquarie University, 24–27 February.

Aitkin, J. 1978. 'The Prostitute as Worker', in *Women and Labour Conference Papers,* pp. 240–8. Sydney.

Allen, J. A. 1984. 'The Making of a Prostitute Proletariat in Early Twentieth-century New South Wales', in Daniels 1984b.

Allen, J. A. 1989. 'From Women's History to a History of the Sexes', in J. Walter, ed., *Australian Studies: A Survey.* Melbourne: Oxford University Press.

Allen, J. A. 1990. *Sex and Secrets: Crimes Involving Australian Women Since 1880.* Melbourne: Oxford University Press.

Allen, J. A. 1995. *Rose Scott. Vision and Revision in Feminism.* Melbourne: Oxford University Press.

Allen, W. K. A. 1971. *Allen's Police Offences of Queensland.* 3rd edn. Sydney: Law Book Co.

Altman, D. 1970. 'Students in the Electric Age'255254, in R. Gordon, ed., *The Australian New Left: Critical Essays and Strategy,* pp. 126–47. Melbourne: Heinemann.

Altman, D. 1971. *Homosexual: Oppression and Liberation.* Sydney: Angus and Robertson.

Anderson, K. 1992. 'The Process of Change in Queensland: A Worker's

Perspective', in Gerull and Halstead, 1992.

Aries, P., and A. Bejin, eds. 1985. *Western Sexuality: Practice and Precept in Past and Present Times*. Oxford: Basil Blackwell.

Arnot, M. 1986. 'Prostitution and the State in Victoria 1890–1914', MA Dissertation, Department of History, University of Melbourne.

Assiter, A. 1989. *Pornography, Feminism and the Individual*. London: Pluto.

Bacon, J. 1976–77. 'The Real Estate Industry in Women', *Vashti: A Women's Liberation Magazine* (Melb.), 17: 5–6.

Bacon, W. 1972. *Uni Sex: A Study of Sexual Attitudes and Behaviour at Australian Universities*. Netley: Eclipse Paperbacks.

Ballard, J. 1992. 'Australia: Participation and Innovation in a Federal System', in D. Kirp and R. Bayer, eds, *AIDS in the Industrialized Democracies: Passions, Politics and Policies*, pp. 134–67. New Brunswick: Rutgers University Press.

Barber, R. N. 1969. 'Prostitution and the Increasing Number of Convictions for Rape in Queensland', *Australian and New Zealand Journal of Criminology*, 2(3): 169–74.

Barclay, E. 1974. 'Queensland's Contagious Diseases Act, 1868 – "The Act for the Encouragement of Vice" and some Nineteenth-Century attempts to Repeal It', *Queensland Heritage*, Part 1, 2(10): 27–34; Part 2, 3(1): 21–9.

Barry, K. 1979. *Female Sexual Slavery*. Englewood Cliffs, NJ: Prentice-Hall.

Barry, K. 1995. *The Prostitution of Sexuality*. New York: NYU Press.

Barton, L., and M. A. Straus, 1987. 'Four Theories of Rape: A Macrosociological Analysis', *Social Problems*, 34(5): 467–89.

Bell, L., ed. 1987. *Good Girls—Bad Girls: Feminists and Sex Trade Workers Face to Face*. Toronto: Seal Press.

Bell, R. R. 1974. *The Sex Survey of Australian Women*. Melbourne: Sun Books.

Bell, S. 1994. *Reading, Writing and Rewriting the Prostitute Body*. Bloomington: Indianapolis University Press.

Bertrand, I. 1978. *Film Censorship in Australia*. St Lucia, Qld: University of Queensland Press.

Bitzer, L. F. 1981. 'Political Rhetoric', in D. D. Nimmo and K. R. Saunders, eds, *Handbook of Political Communication*, pp. 225–48. Beverley Hills and London: Sage.

Blackshield, A. 1970. 'Censorship and the Law', in Dutton and Harris, 1970, pp. 9–26.

Borchardt, D. H. 1986. *Checklist of Royal Commissions, Select Committees of Parliament and Boards of Inquiry*, pp. 239–40. Melbourne: La Trobe Library Publications.

Brants, C., and E. Kok. 1986. 'Penal Sanctions as a Feminist Stategy: A Contradiction in Terms? Pornography and Criminal Law in the Netherlands', *International Journal of the Sociology of Law*, 14: 269–86.

Brindal, M. 1995. Discussion Papers I and II. Issues and Options in the Regulation of Prostitution in South Australia. Paper by the Member for Unley, SA.

Brod, H. 1990. 'Pornography and the Alienation of Male Sexuality', in J. Hearn and D. Morgan, eds, *Men, Masculinities and Social Theory*, pp. 124–39. London: Unwin Hyman.

Brown, B. 1980. 'Private Faces in Public Places', *Ideology and Consciousness*, 7: 3–16.

Brown, B. 1981. 'A Feminist Interest in Pornography – Some Modest Proposals', *M/F*, 5–6: 5–18.

Brown, B. 1982. 'A Curious Arrangement', *Screen*, 23(5): 2–25.

Brown, W. 1995. 'The Mirror of Pornography' in her *States of Injury: Power and Freedom in Late Modernity*, pp. 77–95. Princeton University Press.

Brunt, R. 1982. '"An Immense Verbosity": Permissive Sexual Advice in the 1970s', in R. Brunt and C. Rowan, eds, *Feminism, Culture and Politics*, pp. 143–70. London: Lawrence and Wishart.

Bryant, T. L. 1987. 'Planning and Social Issues of the Prostitution Regulation Act 1986', *Law Institute Journal* (Victoria), 61(9): 902–3.

Buckley, K. 1968. 'Vagrancy and Prostitution', paper presented to the First Convention of Councils for Civil Liberties, Sydney.

Buckley, K. 1970. *Offensive and Obscene: A Civil Liberties Case Book*. Sydney: Ure Smith.

Bullough, V. L. 1964. *The History of Prostitution*. New York: University Books.

Burgmann, V. 1993. *Power and Protest: Movements for Change in Australian Society*. Sydney: Allen and Unwin.

Burton, F., and P. Carlen. 1979. *Official Discourse: On Discourse Analysis, Government Publications, Ideology and the State*. London: Routledge and Kegan Paul.

Butler, J. 1993. *Bodies That Matter: On the Discursive Limits of 'Sex'*. New York and London: Routledge.

Cameron, D. 1985. *Feminism and Linguistic Theory*. London: Macmillan.

Campbell, R. 1989. *Heroes and Lovers: A Question of National Identity*. Sydney: Allen and Unwin.

Carpenter, B. 1994. 'The Dilemma of Prostitution for Feminists', *Social Alternatives*, 12(4): 25–8.

Carter, A. 1979. *The Sadeian Woman: An Exercise in Cutural History*. London: Virago.

Carter, R. F. 1982. *Carter's Criminal Law of Queensland*. 6th edn. Brisbane: Butterworths.

Caught Looking Inc. 1988. *Caught Looking: Feminism, Pornography and Censorship*. Seattle, WA: Real Comet Press.

Chesser, E. 1962. *Live and Let Live: The Moral of the Wolfenden Report*. London: Mayfair Books.

Chester, G., and J. Dickey. 1988. *Feminism and Censorship: The Current Debate*. Bridport, Dorset: Prism.

Clark, L. M. G. 1983. 'Liberalism and Pornography', in Copp and Wendell, 1983, pp. 45–60.

Clarke, J., and K. White. 1983. *Women in Australian Politics*. Sydney: Fontana.

Close, R. 1945. *Love Me Sailor*. Melbourne: Georgian House.

Coates, J. 1986. *Women, Men and Language: A Sociolinguistic Account of Sex Differences in Language*. London and New York: Longman.

Coleman, P. 1974. *Obscenity, Blasphemy, Sedition: Censorship in Australia*. Brisbane: Jacaranda.

Connell, R. W. 1983. *Which Way Is Up? Essays on Sex, Class and Culture*. Sydney: Allen and Unwin.

Connell, R. W. 1986. 'Men, Masculinity and War', in P. Patton and R. Poole, eds, *War/Masculinity*. Sydney: Intervention Publications.

Connell, R. W. 1987. *Gender and Power*. Sydney: Allen and Unwin.

Counell, R. W., and T. H. Irving. 1980. *Class Structure in Australian History: Poverty and Progress*. Melbourne: Longman Cheshire.

Copp, D., and S. Wendell, eds. 1983. *Pornography and Censorship*. Buffalo, NY: Prometheus.

Corbin, A. 1990. *Women for Hire: Prostitution and Sexuality in France after 1850.* Trans. A. Sheridan. Cambridge, Mass. Harvard University Press.

Cornell, D. 1995. *The Imaginary Domain: Abortion, Pornography and Sexual Harassment.* New York: Routledge.

Costain, A. N. 1981. 'Representing Women: The Transition from Social Movement to Interest Group', *Western Political Quarterly*, 34: 100–13.

Coveney, L., L. Kay and P. Mahoney. 1984. 'Theory into Practice: Sexual Liberation or Social Control? (*Forum* magazine 1968–81)', in L. Coveney *et al.*, eds, *The Sexuality Papers: Male Sexuality and the Social Control of Women*, pp. 85–103. London: Hutchinson.

Coward, R. 1987. 'Sexual Violence and Sexuality', in Feminist Review, ed., *Sexuality: A Reader*, pp. 307–25. London: Virago.

Crowe, P. H. 1976. 'A Study of a Social Movement: the Dynamics of an Anti-pornography Campaign in Queensland, Australia', PhD dissertation, State University of New York at Albany.

Crowley, F. 1986. *Tough Times: Australia in the Seventies.* Richmond, Vic.: Heinemann.

Cusack, D., and F. James. [1951] 1990. *Come In Spinner.* North Ryde: Collins/Angus and Robertson.

Daniels, K. 1984a. 'Prostitution in Tasmania during the Transition from Penal Settlement to "Civilised" Society, in Daniels, 1984b, pp. 15–86.

Daniels, K., ed. 1984b. *So Much Hard Work: Women and Prostitution in Australian History.* Sydney: Fontana/Collins.

Davidson, R. 1984. 'Dealing with the "Social Evil": Prostitution and the Police in Perth and on the Eastern Goldfields, 1895–1925', in Daniels, 1984b, pp. 162–91.

Davis, K. 1937. 'The Sociology of Prostitution', *American Journal of Sociology.* pp. 746–55.

Day, G., and C. Bloom. 1988. *Perspectives on Pornography: Sexuality in Film and Literature.* New York: St Martins Press.

Delacoste, F., and P. Alexander. 1988. *Sex Work: Writings by Women in the Sex Industry.* London: Virago.

D'Emilio, J., and E. B. Freedman, 1988. *Intimate Matters: A History of Sexuality in America.* New York: Harper and Row.

Devlin, P. 1965. *The Enforcement of Morals.* London: Oxford University Press.

Diamond, I., and L. Quinby, eds. 1988. *Feminism and Foucault: Reflections on Resistance.* Boston: Northeastern University Press.

Diana, L. 1985. *The Prostitute and Her Clients: Your Pleasure Is Her Business.* Springfield, Ill.: Charles C. Thomas.

Dickie, P. 1988. *The Road to Fitzgerald: Revelations of Corruption Spanning Four Decades.* St Lucia, Qld: University of Queensland Press.

Dixson, M. 1976. *The Real Matilda.* Ringwood, Vic.: Penguin.

Dobinson, S. 1992. 'Victorian Situation with Legislation', in Gerull and Halstead, 1992.

Donnerstein, E., D. Linz and S. Penrod. 1987. *The Question of Pornography: Research Findings and Policy Implications.* New York: Free Press/Macmillan.

Dowse, S. 1983. 'The Women's Movement's Fandango with the State: the Movement's Role in Public Policy since 1972', in C. Baldock and B. Cass, eds, *Women, Social Welfare and the State in Australia*, pp. 201–22. Sydney: George Allen and Unwin.

Duggan, L., N. Hunter and C. S. Vance. 1985. 'False Promises: Feminist Antipornography Legislation in the U.S.', in V. Burstyn, ed., *Women Against Censorship*, pp. 130–51. Toronto: Douglas and McIntyre.

Dunstan, K. 1968. *Wowsers: Being an Account of the Prudery Exhibited by Certain Outstanding Men and Women in Such Matters as Drinking, Smoking, Prostitution, Censorship and Gambling.* Melbourne: Cassell.

Dutton, G., and M. Harris, 1970. *Australia's Censorship Crisis: The Uncensored Examination of Australian Censorship.* Melbourne: Sun Books.

Dworkin, A. [1979] 1981. *Pornography: Men Possessing Women.* London: Women's Press.

Dworkin, R. 1978. *Taking Rights Seriously.* Cambridge, Mass.: Harvard University Press.

Dyer, R. 1982. 'Don't Look Now – The Male Pin-up', *Screen*, 23(3–4): 61–73.

Eckersley, R. 1987. 'Whither the Feminist Campaign? An Evaluation of Feminist Critiques of Pornography', *International Journal of the Sociology of Law*, 15: 149–78.

Edwards, A. 1987. 'Male Violence in Feminist Theory: An Analysis of the Changing Conceptions of Sex/Gender Violence and Male Domination', in Hanmer and Maynard, 1987, pp. 13–29.

Edwards, J. 1986. *Prostitution and Human Rights: A Western Australian Case Study.* Perth: Human Rights Commission.

Edwards, S. 1989. 'Protecting the Honour of Innocent Men', in C. Dunhill, ed., *The Boys in Blue: Women's Challenge to the Police*, pp. 193–204. London: Virago.

Edwards, S. M. 1984. *Women on Trial: A Study of the Female Offender in the Criminal Law and Criminal Justice System.* Manchester: Manchester University Press.

Edwards, S. M. 1987. 'Prostitutes: Victims of Law, Social Policy and Organised Crime', in P. Carlen and A. Worrall, eds, *Gender, Crime and Justice*, pp. 43–56. Milton Keynes: Open University Press.

Egger, S., and M. Findlay. 1988. 'The Politics of Police Discretion', in M. Findlay and R. Hogg, *Understanding Crime and Criminal Justice*, pp. 209–23. North Ryde, NSW: Law Book Co.

Ehrenreich, B. 1983. *The Hearts of Men: American Dreams and the Flight from Commitment.* Garden City, NY: Anchor/Doubleday.

Ehrenreich, B., E. Hess and G. Jacobs. 1986. *Re-making Love: The Feminization of Sex.* London: Fontana/Collins.

Eisenstein, H. 1984. *Contemporary Feminist Thought.* Sydney: Allen and Unwin.

Eisenstein, H. 1985. 'The Gender of Bureaucracy: Reflections on Feminism and the State', in J. Goodnow and C. Pateman, eds, *Women, Social Science and Public Policy.* Sydney: Allen and Unwin.

Eisenstein, Z. 1981. *The Radical Future of Liberal Feminism.* New York: Longman.

Eisenstein, Z. 1984. *Feminism and Sexual Equality: Crisis in Liberal America.* New York: Monthly Review Press.

Elkin, A. P., ed. 1957. *Marriage and the Family in Australia.* Sydney: Angus and Robertson.

Elshtain, J. B. 1981. *Public Man, Private Woman: Women in Social and Political Thought.* Princeton, Princeton University Press.

Elshtain, J. B. 1990. 'Pornography Politics', in her *Power Trips and Other Journeys: Essays in Feminism as Civic Discourse*, pp. 119–33. Madison: University of Wisconsin Press.

Enloe, C. 1989. *Bananas, Beaches and Bases: Making Feminist Sense of International Politics.* University of California Press.

Ericsson, L. O. 1980. 'Charges Against Prostitution: An Attempt at a Philosophical Assessment', *Ethics*, 90: 335–66.

Eros Foundation. 1992. *Sex Fights Back: A Rational Approach to the Reform of Australia's Censorship Laws.* Canberra: Eros Foundation.

Evans, R. 1984. '"Soiled Doves": Prostitution in Colonial Queensland' in Daniels, 1984b, pp. 127–61.

Falk, P. 1994. *The Consuming Body.* London: Sage.

Faust, B. 1980. *Women, Sex and Pornography.* Harmondsworth: Penguin.

Filla, R. 1975. 'Towards an Understanding of Prostitution', in A. R. Edwards and P. Wilson, eds, *Social Deviance in Australia.* Melbourne: Longman Cheshire.

Finnane, M. 1988. 'The Fitzgerald Commission: Law, Politics and State Corruption in Queensland'. Paper presented to ANZAAS Congress, Sydney.

Foucault, M. 1975. *The Order of Things: An Archaeology of the Human Sciences.* New York: Vintage.

Foucault, M. [1975] 1986. *Discipline and Punish.* Harmondsworth: Penguin.

Foucault, M. [1976] 1981. *The History of Sexuality,* Vol. 1: *An Introduction.* Trans. R. Harley. Harmondsworth: Penguin.

Foucault, M. 1978. 'Politics and the Study of Discourse', *Ideology and Consciousness,* 3: 1–9.

Foucault, M. 1979. 'Governmentality', *Ideology and Consciousness,* 6: 5–21.

Foucault, M. 1980. 'Body/Power', 'Two Lectures' and 'Truth and Power' in C. Gordon, ed., *Power/Knowledge: Selected Interviews and Other Writings, 1972–1977, by Michel Foucault,* Brighton: Harvester.

Foucault, M. 1986. *The History of Sexuality,* vol. 3. New York: Pantheon.

Foucault, M. 1991. 'Questions of Method', in G. Burchell, C. Gordon and P. Miller, eds, *The Foucault Effect: Studies in Governmentality.* London: Harvester.

Franzway, S., D. Court and R. W. Connell. 1989. *Staking a Claim: Feminism, Bureaucracy and the State.* Sydney: Allen and Unwin.

Gagnon, J. H. and W. Simon. 1967. *Sexual Deviance.* New York: Harper and Row.

Gagnon, J. H. and W. Simon, eds. [1970] 1973. *The Sexual Scene.* New Brunswick, NJ: Transaction.

Galligan, B., ed. 1986. *Australian State Politics.* Melbourne: Longman Cheshire.

Game, A., and R. Pringle. 1978. 'Women and Class in Australia: Feminism and the Labor Government', in G. Duncan, ed., *Critical Essays in Australian Politics,* pp. 114–34. Melbourne: Edward Arnold.

Game, A., and R. Pringle. 1983a. 'The Making of the Australian Family', in A. Burns, G. Bottomley and P. Jools, eds, *The Family in the Modern World.* Sydney: Allen and Unwin.

Game, A., and R. Pringle. 1983b. 'From Here to Fraternity: Women and the Hawke Government', *Scarlet Woman,* 17: 5–11.

Garry, A. 1983. 'Pornography and Respect for Women', in Copp and Wendell, 1983, pp. 61–82.

Gerull, S., and B. Halstead, eds. 1992. *Sex Industry and Public Policy: Conference Proceedings.* Canberra: Australian Institute of Criminology.

Giddens, A. 1993. *The Transformation of Intimacy: Love, Sexuality and Eroticism in Modern Societies.* London: Polity.

Giglio, P. P. 1972. *Language and Social Context.* Harmondsworth: Penguin.

Gilding, M. 1991. *The Making and Breaking of the Australian Family.* Sydney: Allen and Unwin.

Glassop, L. 1945. *We Were The Rats.* Sydney: Angus and Robertson.

Glezer, H. 1984. 'Changes in Marriage and Sex-role Attitudes among Young, Married Women: 1971–1982', in Australian Institute of Family Studies, *Australian Family Research Conference,* vol. 1, Melbourne: AIFS.

Golder, H., and J. Allen. 1980. 'Prostitution in NSW 1870–1932: Restructuring an Industry', *Refractory Girl,* 18–19: 17–25.

Goldman, E. [1917] 1970. 'The Traffic in Women', in A. K. Shulman, ed., *The Traffic in Women and other Essays*, pp. 19–32. Albion, Calif.: Times Change Press.

Goldstein, M. J. and H. S. Kant. 1973. *Pornography and Sexual Deviance*. Berkeley: University of California Press.

Gordon, R., ed. 1970. *The Australian New Left: Critical Essays and Strategy*. Melbourne: Heinemann.

Graber, D. 1981. 'Political Languages', in D. Nimmo and K. Sanders, eds, *Handbook of Political Communication*, pp. 189–202. Beverley Hills: Sage.

Graham, J. 1958. 'If Roe Street Could Talk', *Observer*, 6 September, p. 455.

Greenwood, I. 1975. 'A Lifetime of Political Activity', in *Women and Politics Conference 1975*, Vol. 1, pp. 57–64. Canberra: AGPS.

Gregg, P. M. 1976. *Problems of Theory in Policy Analysis*. Lexington: Lexington Books.

Griffin, S. 1981. *Pornography and Silence: Culture's Revenge Against Nature*. New York: Harper and Row.

Gross, E. 1981. 'On Speaking About Pornography', *Scarlet Woman*, 13: 6–21.

Gubar, S., and J. Hoff. 1989. *For Adult Users Only: The Dilemma of Violent Pornography*. Bloomington: Indiana University Press.

Hall, J., and S. Hall. 1970. *Australian Censorship: The XYZ of Love*. Sydney: Jack de Lissa.

Halperin, D. M. 1989. 'The Democratic Body: Prostitution and Citizenship in Classical Athens', *South Atlantic Quarterly*, 88(1): 149–60.

Hancock, L. 1992. 'Legal Regulation of Prostitution: Who or What is Being Controlled?', in Gerull and Halstead, 1992.

Hanmer, J., and M. Maynard. 1987. *Women, Violence and Social Control*. London: Macmillan.

Harcourt, C. 1994. 'Prostitution and Public Health in the Era of AIDS', in Perkins *et al*, 1994.

Hart, H. L. A. 1963. *Law, Liberty and Morality*. London: Oxford University Press.

Harwood, V., D. Oswell and K. Parkinson, eds. 1993. *Pleasure Principles: Politics, Sexuality and Ethics*. London: Lawrence and Wishart.

Hatty, S. 1989. 'Violence Against Prostitute Women: Social and Legal Dilemmas', *Australian Journal of Social Issues*, 24(4): 235, 239–40.

Hatty, S. 1991. 'The Desired Object: Prostitution in Canada, United States and Australia'. Paper presented at the Sex Industry and Public Policy Conference, Australian Institute of Criminology, Canberra.

Hawkins, G., and F. E. Zimring. 1988. *Pornography in a Free Society*. Cambridge: Cambridge University Press.

Hebditch, D., and N. Anning. 1988. *Porn Gold: Inside the Pornography Business*. London and Boston: Faber and Faber.

Heney, H. 1978. *Australia's Founding Mothers*. West Melbourne: Thomas Nelson.

Henriques, F. 1965. *The Pretence of Love*. London: Panther.

Herbert, X. 1972. *Soldiers' Women*. Melbourne: Fontana.

Hewlett, S. A. 1987. *A Lesser Life: The Myth of Women's Liberation*. London: Michael Joseph.

Hindess, B. 1988. *Choice, Rationality and Social Theory*. London: Unwin Hyman.

Hindess, B. 1989. *Political Choice and Social Structure: An Analysis of Actors, Interests and Rationality*. Aldershot, Hants: Edward Elgar.

Hite, S. 1977. *The Hite Report*. Dee Why, NSW: Summit (Paul Hamlyn).

Hite, S. 1981. *The Hite Report on Male Sexuality*. New York: Alfred Knopf.

Hobson, B. M. 1987. *Uneasy Virtue: The Politics of Prostitution and the American Reform Tradition*. New York: Basic Books.

Hoigard, C., and L. Finstad. 1992. *Backstreets: Prostitution, Money and Love.* London: Polity.

Holmes, J. 1976. *The Government of Victoria.* St Lucia, Qld: University of Queensland Press.

Horan, S. 1984. '"More Sinned Against than Sinning"? Prostitution in South Australia 1836–1914', in Daniels, 1984b, pp. 87–126.

Horn, P. L., and M. B. Pringle. 1984. *The Image of the Prostitute in Modern Literature.* New York: Frederick Ungar.

Horowitz, G. 1987. 'The Foucauldian Impasse: No Sex, No Self, No Revolution', *Political Theory*, 15(1): 61–80.

Huer, J. 1987. *Art, Beauty and Pornography: A Journey Through American Culture.* Buffalo, NY: Prometheus.

Hugo, G. 1986. *Australia's Changing Population: Trends and Implications.* Melbourne: Oxford University Press.

Hunnings, N. M. 1967. *Film Censors and the Law.* London: George Allen and Unwin.

Hunt, L., ed. 1991. *Eroticism and the Body Politic.* Baltimore: Johns Hopkins University Press.

Hunter, A. 1991. 'The Development of Theoretical Approaches to Sex Work in Australian Sex Worker Rights Groups', in Gerull and Halstead, 1992.

Hunter, I., D. Saunders and D. Williamson. 1987. 'Obscenity, Literature and the Law', in G. Wickham, *Social Theory and Legal Politics.* Sydney: Local Consumption.

Hunter, I., D. Saunders and D. Williamson. 1993. *On Pornography: Literature, Sexuality and the Law.* London: Macmillan.

Hyde, H. M. 1964. *A History of Pornography.* London: Heinemann.

Imray, L., and A. Middleton. 1983. 'Public and Private: Marking the Boundaries', in E. Garmanikow *et al.*, eds, *The Public and the Private.* London: Heinemann.

Inglis, J. 1983. 'Working Towards a Collective of Prostitutes', *Scarlet Woman*, 18: 16–19.

Irvine, J. M. 1990. 'From Difference to Sameness: Gender Ideology in Sexual Science', *Journal of Sex Research*, 27(1): 7–24.

Jackson, M. 1984. 'Sexology and the Universalization of Male Sexuality (from Ellis to Kinsey, and Masters and Johnson)', in L. Coveney *et al.*, eds, *The Sexuality Papers: Male Sexuality and the Social Control of Women*, pp. 69–84. London: Hutchinson.

Jackson, S., and D. Otto. [1976] 1984. 'From Delicacy to Dilemma: A Feminist Perspective', in Daniels, 1984b, pp. 366–82.

Jaggar, A. 1980. 'Prostitution', in A. Soble, ed., *The Philosophy of Sex.* pp. 348–68. Totowa, NJ: Rowman and Littlefield.

Jansen, S. C. 1988. *Censorship: The Knot That Binds Power and Knowledge.* New York and Oxford: Oxford University Press.

Jeffreys, S. 1984. '"Free from All Uninvited Touch of Man": Women's Campaigns around Sexuality 1880–1914', in L. Coveney *et al.* eds., *The Sexuality Papers: Male Sexuality and the Social Control of Women*, pp. 22–44. London: Hutchinson.

Jeffreys, S. 1985. 'Prostitution', in D. Rhodes and S. McNeil, eds, *Women Against Violence Against Women.* London: Onlywomen Press.

Jeffreys, S. 1990. *Anticlimax: A Feminist Perspective on the Sexual Revolution.* London: Women's Press.

Jenness, V. 1990. 'From Sex as Sin to Sex as Work: COYOTE and the Reorganization of Prostitution as a Social Problem', *Social Problems*, 37(3): 403–20.

Johnson, L. 1993. *The Modern Girl: Girlhood and Growing Up*. St Leonards, NSW: Allen and Unwin.

Jones, L. 1984. 'Some Thoughts on Pornography with Particular Reference to Video Pornography and Its Effects on Women in Australia', *Fourth Women and Labour Conference Papers*, pp. 245–56. Brisbane.

Kaite, B. 1989. 'The Pornographic Body Double: Transgression is the Law', in A. and M. Kotke, eds, *Body Invaders: Panic Sex in America*, pp. 150–68. New York: St Martins Press.

Kaplan, E. A. 1983. 'Is the Gaze Male?', in A. Snitow, C. Stansell and S. Thompson, eds, *Powers of Desire: The Politics of Sexuality*, pp. 309–27. New York: Monthly Review Press.

Kappeler, S. 1986. *The Pornography of Representation*. Cambridge: Polity.

Kedar, L., ed. 1987. *Power Through Discourse*. Norwood, NJ: Ablex.

Kendall, C. 1995. 'Gay Male Pornography: An Issue of Sex Discrimination', *Australian Feminist Law Journal*, 5: 81–90.

Kendrick, W. 1987. *The Secret Museum: Pornography in Modern Culture*. New York: Viking.

Kimmel, M., ed. 1987. *Changing Men: New Directions in Research on Men and Masculinity*. Newbury Park, Calif: Sage.

Kimmel, M., ed. 1990. *Men on Pornography*. New York: Crown.

King, L., and A. Gronau. 1985. 'Censorship and Law Reform: Will Changing the Laws Mean a Change for the Better?', in V. Burstyn, ed., *Women Against Censorship*. Toronto: Douglas and McIntyre.

Kinsey, A. C., W. B. Pomeroy and C. E. Martin. 1948. *Sexual Behaviour in the Human Male*. Philadelphia: W. B. Saunders.

Kinsey, A. C., W. B. Pomeroy and C. E. Martin. 1953. *Sexual Behaviour in the Human Female*. Philadelphia: W. B. Saunders.

Kuhn, A. 1982. *Women's Pictures: Feminism and Cinema*. London: Routledge and Kegan Paul.

Kuhn, A. 1985. *The Power of the Image: Essays on Representation and Sexuality*. London: Routledge and Kegan Paul.

Kuhn, A. 1986. 'The "Married Love" Affair', *Screen*, 27(2): 5–21.

Kuhn, A. 1988. *Cinema, Censorship and Sexuality, 1909–1925*. London: Routledge.

LaCapra, D. 1983. *Rethinking Intellectual History: Texts, Contexts, Language*. Ithaca: Cornell University Press.

Lacombe, D. 1988. *Ideology and Public Policy: The Case Against Pornography*. Toronto: Garamond.

Lake, M. 1990. 'Female Desires: The Meaning of World War II', *Australian Historical Studies*, 24(95): 267–84.

Lederer, L., ed. 1980. *Take Back the Night: Women on Pornography*. New York: Bantam Books.

Lees, S., and J. Senyard. 1987. *The 1950s … How Australia Became a Modern Society, and Everyone Got a House and a Car*. South Yarra, Vic.: Hyland House.

Lerner, G. 1986. 'The Origin of Prostitution in Ancient Mesopotamia', *Signs: Journal of Women in Culture and Society*, 11: 236–54.

Lockhart, W. B. 1970. *United States Commission on Obscenity and Pornography*. NY: Random House.

Lowman, J., M. A. Jackson, T. S. Palys and S. Gavigan. 1986. *Regulating Sex: An Anthology of Commentaries on the Findings and Recommendations of the Badgley and Fraser Reports*. Burnaby: School of Criminology, Simon Fraser University.

MacDonell, D. 1986. *Theories of Discourse: An Introduction.* Oxford: Basil Black-well.

MacKinnon, C. A. 1983. 'Feminism, Marxism, Method and the State: Towards a Feminist Jurisprudence', *Signs: Journal of Women in Culture and Society,* 8(4): 621–43.

MacKinnon, C. A. 1987. *Feminism Unmodified: Discourses on Life and Law.* Cambridge, Mass.: Harvard University Press.

MacKinnon, C. A. 1989a. *Toward a Feminist Theory of the State.* Cambridge, Mass.: Harvard University Press.

MacKinnon, C. A. 1989b. 'Sexuality, Pornography and Method: Pleasure Under Patriarchy', *Ethics,* 99(2): 314–46.

Macpherson, C. B. 1962. *The Political Theory of Possessive Individualism.* Oxford: Clarendon.

Malamuth, N. M., and B. Spinner. 1980. 'A Longitudinal Content Analysis of Sexual Violence in the Best-Sellling Erotic Magazines', *Journal of Sex Research,* 16(3): 226–37.

Marcus, S. 1966. *The Other Victorians: A Study of Sexuality and Pornography in Mid-Nineteenth Century England.* New York: Basic Books.

Masters, W., and V. Johnson 1966. *Human Sexual Response.* Boston: Little, Brown and Co.

Masters, W., and V. Johnson. 1970. *Human Sexual Inadequacy.* Boston: Little, Brown and Co.

Masters, W., and V. Johnson. 1975. *The Pleasure Bond.* Boston: Little, Brown and Co.

Mathews, J. J. 1984. *Good and Mad Women: The Historical Construction of Femininity in Twentieth-century Australia.* Sydney: George Allen and Unwin.

McConville, C. 1980. 'The Location of Melbourne's Prostitutes, 1870–1920', *Historical Studies,* 19: 8–89.

McCoy, A. 1980. *Drug Traffic, Narcotics and Organized Crime in Australia.* Sydney: Harper and Row.

McDonald, P. F. 1975. *Marriage in Australia.* Canberra: ANU Press.

McGrath, A. 1984. '"Black Velvet". Aboriginal Women and Their Relations with White Men in the Northern Territory 1910–40', in Daniels, 1984b, pp. 233–97.

McIntosh, M. 1973. 'The Growth of Racketeering', *Economy and Society,* 2: 35–69.

McIntosh, M. 1975. *The Organisation of Crime.* London: Macmillan.

McIntosh, M. 1978. 'Who Needs Prostitutes? The Ideology of Male Sexual Needs', in C. Smart and B. Smart, eds, *Women, Sexuality and Social Control.* London: Routledge and Kegan Paul.

McLeod, E. 1982. *Women Working: Prostitution Now.* London: Croom Helm.

Metcalf, A., and M. Humphries, eds. 1985. *The Sexuality of Men.* London: Pluto.

Mill, J. S. [1859] 1972. *On Liberty.* London: Dent/Dutton.

Millbank, J., and W. Fong. 1988. 'Are You a Prostitute', *Union Recorder,* 68(3): 7.

Millett, K. 1971. *The Prostitution Papers: A Quartet for Female Voice.* New York: Ballantine Books.

Mills, H. 1984. 'Prostitution and the Law: The Question of Decriminalization', in Daniels, 1984b, pp. 298–316.

Moore, K. 1985. 'Gains for Women in the ALP', in M. Sawer, ed., *Programme for Change: Affirmative Action in Australia.* Sydney: Allen and Unwin.

Morgan, R. 1980. 'Theory and Practice: Pornography and Rape', in Lederer, 1980, pp. 134–40.

Morris, A. 1987. *Women, Crime and Criminal Justice.* Oxford: Basil Blackwell.

Murnane, M., and K. Daniels. 1979. 'Prostitutes as "Purveyors of Disease": Venereal Disease Legislation in Tasmania, 1868–1945', *Hecate: A Women's Interdisciplinary Journal,* 5(1): 5–19.

Neave, M. 1988. 'The Failure of Prostitution Law Reform', *Australian and New Zealand Journal of Criminology,* 21: 202–11.

Neave, M. 1994. 'Prostitution Laws in Australia: Past History and Current Trends', in Perkins *et al.,* 1994, pp. 67–99.

O'Connor, K., and N. E. McGlen. 1989. 'The Effects of Government Organization on Women's Rights: An Analysis of the Status of Women in Canada, Great Britain and the United States', *International Journal of Women's Studies,* 6: 588–601.

O'Donnell, C., and P. Hall. 1988. *Getting Equal: Labour Market Regulation and Women's Work.* Sydney: Allen and Unwin.

Overall, C. 1992. 'What's Wrong With Prostitution?', *Signs: Journal of Women in Culture and Society,* 17(4): 705–24.

Overs, C. 1989. 'Prostitution: We Call it Sex Work Now (A Comment)', *Lilith: A Feminist History Journal,* 6: 64–8.

Oxley, D. 1996. *Convict Maids: The Forced Migration of Women to Australia.* Melbourne: Cambridge University Press.

Paden, R. 1984. 'On the Discourse of Pornography', *Philosophy and Social Criticism,* 10(1): 17–38.

Paine, R., ed. 1981. *Politically Speaking: Cross-Cultural Studies of Rhetoric.* Philadelphia: Institute for the Study of Human Issues.

Pateman, C. 1980. 'Women and Consent', *Political Theory,* 8: 149–68.

Pateman, C. 1983a. 'Defending Prostitution: Charges against Ericsson', *Ethics,* 93: 561–5.

Pateman, C. 1983b. 'Feminist Critiques of the Public/Private Dichotomy', in S. I. Benn and G. F. Gaus, eds, *Public and Private in Social Life,* pp. 281–303. London and Canberra: Croom Helm.

Pateman, C. 1988. *The Sexual Contract.* Cambridge: Polity.

Pateman, C. 1989. *The Disorder of Women: Democracy, Feminism and Political Theory.* Oxford: Polity.

Perkins, R. 1986. 'Push and Pull Politics: Prostitution, Prejudice and Punishment', *Arena,* 74: 90–103.

Perkins, R. 1989. 'Working Girls in "Wowserville": Prostitute Women in Sydney since 1945', in R. Kennedy, ed., *Australian Welfare: Historical Sociology,* pp. 362–89. Melbourne: Macmillan.

Perkins, R. 1991. *Working Girls.* Canberra: Australian Institute of Criminology.

Perkins, R., and G. Bennett. 1985. *Being A Prostitute: Prostitute Women and Prostitute Men.* Sydney: George Allen and Unwin.

Perkins, R., G. Prestage, R. Sharp and F. Lovejoy, eds. 1994. *Sex Work and Sex Workers in Australia.* Sydney: UNSW Press.

Perry, J. W. 1968. 'Recent Developments in the Law of Censorship of Literature'. Paper delivered at the First Convention of Councils for Civil Liberties.

Peters, D. 1989. 'The Economic and Social Status of Prostitutes in Thailand and the Philippines', *Macquarie Papers in Women's Studies,* vol. 1.

Pheterson, G., ed. 1989. *A Vindication of the Rights of Whores.* Seattle, Wash.: Seal Press.

Pinto, S., A. Scandia and P. Wilson. 1991. 'Prostitution Laws in Australia', *Trends and Issues,* No. 22, Canberra: Australian Institute of Criminology.

Plant, M., ed. 1990. *AIDS, Drugs and Prostitutes*. London: Routledge.
Polsky, N. 1967. 'On the Sociology of Pornography', in N. Polsky, *Hustlers, Beats and Others*, pp. 186–202. Chicago: Aldine.
Pomeroy, W. B. 1972. *Dr Kinsey and the Institute for Sex Research*. London: Nelson.
Potts, E. D., and A. Potts. 1985. *Yanks Down Under, 1941–45: The American Impact on Australia*. Melbourne: Oxford University Press.
Pringle, R. 1981. 'The Dialectic of Porn', *Scarlet Woman*, 12: 7–14.
Pringle, R. 1983. 'Women and Consumer Capitalism', in C. Baldock and B. Cass, eds, *Women, Social Welfare and the State in Australia*. Sydney: George Allen and Unwin.
Pringle, R. 1988. *Secretaries Talk: Sexuality, Power and Work*. Sydney: Allen and Unwin.
Ralston, C. 1988. 'Polyandry, "Pollution", "Prostitution": The Problems of Eurocentrism and Androcentrism in Polynesian Studies', in B. Caine, E. A. Grosz and M. de Lepervanche, *Crossing Boundaries: Feminisms and the Critique of Knowledges*, pp. 71–80. North Sydney: Allen and Unwin.
Randall, R. S. 1989. *Freedom and Taboo: Pornography and the Politics of a Self Divided*. Berkeley: University of California Press.
Reekie, G. 1985. 'War, Sexuality and Feminism: Perth Women's Organizations 1938–1945', *Historical Studies*, 21(85): 576, 591.
Reynolds, H. 1986. *The Economics of Prostitution*. Springfield, Ill.: C. C. Thomas.
Reynolds, P. 1991. *Political Sociology: An Australian Perspective*. Melbourne: Longman Cheshire.
Rich, B. R. 1986. 'Anti-Porn: Soft Issue, Hard World', in C. Brunsden, *Films for Women*, pp. 31–43. London: Brititsh Film Institute.
Richards, D. A. J. 1982. *Sex, Drugs, Death and the Law: An Essay on Human Rights and Decriminalization*. Totowa, NJ: Rowman and Littlefield.
Richardson, P., 1992. 'The Victorian Brothel Owners' Perspective', in Gerull and Halstead, 1992.
Robinson, P. 1979. 'The First Forty Years', in J. Mackinolty and H. Radi, eds, *In Pursuit of Justice*. Sydney: Hale and Iremonger.ß
Robinson, P. A. 1969. *The Freudian Left: Wilhelm Reich, Geza Roheim, Herbert Marcuse*. New York: Harper and Row.
Robson, L. L. 1963. 'The Origin of the Women Convicts Sent to Australia, 1787–1852', *Historical Studies*, 41: 47–8, 53.
Rock, P., and M. McIntosh. 1974. *Deviance and Social Control*. London: Tavistock.
Rose, J. 1986. *Sexuality in the Field of Vision*. London: Verso.
Rose, N. 1989. *Governing the Soul: The Shaping of the Private Self*. London: Routledge.
Rose, N., and P. Miller. 1992. 'Political Power Beyond the State: Problematics of Government', *British Journal of Sociology*, 43(2): 173–205.
Rosen, R. 1982. *The Lost Sisterhood: Prostitution in America, 1900–1918*. Baltimore: Johns Hopkins University Press.
Rowley, K. 1972. 'The Political Economy of Australia Since the War', in J. Playford and D. Kirsner, eds, *Australian Capitalism: Towards a Socialist Critique*, pp. 265–324. Harmondsworth: Penguin.
Rubin, G. 1975. 'The Traffic in Women: Notes on the "Political Economy" of Sex', in R. Reiter, ed., *Toward an Anthropology of Women*. New York: Monthly Review Press.
Rubin, G. 1984. 'Thinking Sex: Notes for a Radical Theory of the Politics of Sexuality', in Carole S. Vance, ed., *Pleasure and Danger: Exploring Female Sexuality*. London: Routledge and Kegan Paul.

Russell, D. E. H., ed. 1993. *Making Violence Sexy: Feminist Views on Pornography*. Buckingham: Open University Press.

Ryan, E., and A. Conlon. 1975. *Gentle Invaders: Australian Women at Work, 1788–1974*. Melbourne: Nelson.

Saunders, K., and H. Taylor. 1984. '"To Combat the Plague": The Construction of Moral Alarm and the Role of State Intervention in Queensland during World War II', in *Fourth Women and Labour Conference Papers*. Brisbane.

Sawer, M. 1989. 'Women: The Long March Through the Institutions', in B. W. Head and A. Patience, eds, *From Fraser to Hawke. Australian Public Policy in the 1980s*, pp. 427–62. Melbourne: Longman Cheshire.

Sawer, M. 1990. *Sisters in Suits. Women and Public Policy in Australia*. Sydney: Allen and Unwin.

Sawer, M., and M. Simms. 1984. *A Woman's Place: Women and Politics in Australia*. Sydney: George Allen and Unwin.

Schipper, H. 1980. 'Filthy Lucre: A Tour of America's Most Profitable Frontier', *Mother Jones*, 5(3): 30–3, 60–2.

Scott, J. E., and S. J. Cuvelier. 1987. 'Sexual Violence in *Playboy* Magazine: A Longitudinal Content Analysis', *Journal of Sex Research*, 23: 534–9.

Scutt, J. A. 1983. 'Legislating for the Right to be Equal: Women, the Law and Social Policy', in C. Baldock and B. Cass, eds, *Women, Social Welfare and the State in Australia*. Sydney: George Allen and Unwin.

Scutt, J. A. 1986. 'The Economic Regulation of the Brothel Industry in Victoria', *Australian Law Journal*, 60: 399–406.

Sedgewick, E. K. 1993. *Tendencies*. Durham, NC: Duke University Press.

Seidler, V. J. 1989. *Rediscovering Masculinity: Reason, Language and Sexuality*. London: Routledge.

Sellen, B., and P. A. Young. 1987. *Feminists, Pornography and the Law: An Annotated Bibliography of Conflict, 1970–1986*. Hamden, Conn.: Library Professional Publications.

Shapiro, M. J. 1981. *Language and Political Understanding: The Politics of Discursive Practices*. New Haven: Yale University Press.

Shapiro, M. J. 1984. *Language and Politics*. Oxford: Basil Blackwell.

Shilton, L. R., ed. 1971. *No No Calcutta*. Adelaide: Brolga Books.

Shoesmith, D. 1972. 'Nature's Law: The Venereal Disease Debate, Melbourne 1918–19', *ANU Historical Journal*, 9: 20–5.

Shrage, L. 1989. 'Should Feminists Oppose Prostitution?', *Ethics*, 99: 347–61.

Siedlecky, S., and D. Wyndham. 1990. *Populate and Perish: Australian Women's Fight for Birth Control*. Sydney: Allen and Unwin.

Simms, M., and D. Stone, 1990. 'Women's Policy', in C. Jennett and R. G. Stewart, eds, *Hawke and Australian Public Policy: Consensus and Restructuring*. South Melbourne: Macmillan.

Sissons, D. C. S. 1977. 'Karyuki-San: Japanese Prostitutes in Australia, 1887–1916', *Historical Studies*, Part 1, 17(68): 323–41; Part 2, 17(69): 474–88.

Snitow, A. 1988. 'Retrenchment vs. Transformation: The Politics of the Antipornography Movement', Caught Looking Inc. 1988, pp. 10–17.

Soble, A. 1980. 'Introduction', in A. Soble, ed., *The Philosophy of Sex*, pp. 1–56. Totowa, NJ: Rowman and Littlefield.

Soble, A. 1986. *Pornography: Marxism, Feminism and the Future of Sexuality*. New Haven, Yale University Press.

Stern, L. 1982. 'The Body As Evidence: A Critical Review of the Pornography Problematic', *Screen*, 23(5): 38–60.

Stevens, B., and J. Wanna, eds. 1993. *The Goss Government: Promise and Performance of Labor in Queensland.* South Melbourne: Macmillan.

Strong, R. A., and J. A. Strong, 1971. *Mr Chipp and the Porno Push.* Melbourne: Minton.

Sturma, M. 1989. 'Loving the Alien: The Underside of Relations between American Servicemen and Australian Women in Queensland, 1942–45', *Journal of Australian Studies,* 25: 31–42.

Suleiman, S. R. 1986. 'Pornography, Transgression and the Avant-Garde: Bataille's Story of the Eye', in C. G. Heilbron and N. K. Miller, eds, *The Poetics of Gender.* New York: Columbia University Press.

Sullivan, B. A. 1991. 'The Business of Sex: Australian Government and the Sex Industry', *Australian and New Zealand Journal of Sociology* , 27(1): 3–18.

Sullivan, B. A. 1993. 'Women and the Goss Government', in Stevens and Wanna, 1993.

Sullivan, B. A. 1994. 'Feminism and Female Prostitution', in Perkins *et al.* 1994, pp. 253–68.

Sullivan, B. A. 1995. 'Rethinking Prostitution', in Barbara Caine and Rosemary Pringle, eds, *Transitions: New Australian Feminisms,* pp. 184–97. Sydney: Allen and Unwin.

Summers, A. 1975. *Damned Whores and God's Police: The Colonization of Women in Australia.* Ringwood, Vic.: Penguin.

Sutherland, J. 1982. *Offensive Literature: Decensorship in Britain, 1960–1982.* London: Junction.

Swan, R. 1992. 'Censorship and Public Opinion', in Gerull and Halstead, 1992.

Tabet, P. 1989. '"I'm the Meat, I'm the Knife": Sexual Service, Migration, and Repression in Some African Societies', in Pheterson, 1989.

Talese, G. 1980. *Thy Neighbour's Wife.* New York: Dell.

Thomas, S. 1989. 'The Impact of Women on State Legislative Policies", *Journal of Politics,* 53(4): 958–76.

Thornton, N. 1986. 'Is the Old Right Now New? The State, the Family and Sexual Repression in Queensland", *Social Alternatives,* 5(4): 6–13.

Todd, A. D. and S. Fisher. 1988. 'Introduction: Theories of Gender, Theories of Discourse", in Todd and Fisher, eds, *Gender and Discourse: The Power of Talk,* pp. 1–16 (Advances in Discourse Processes, vol. 30). NJ: Ablex.

Tolson, A. *The Limits of Masculinity.* London: Tavistock.

Truong, T. 1990. *Sex, Money and Morality: Prostitution and Tourism in South-East Asia.* London: Zed Books.

Turner, A. 1975. *Censorship: Wendy Bacon versus Peter Coleman.* South Yarra, Vic.: Heinemann.

Turner, B. S. 1984. *The Body and Society: Explorations in Social Theory.* Oxford: Basil Blackwell.

Valaverde, M. 1987. *Sex, Power and Pleasure.* Toronto: Women's Press.

Vega, J. 1988. 'Coercion and Consent: Classic Liberal Concepts in Texts on Sexual Violence", *International Journal of the Sociology of Law,* 16: 75–89.

Waldby, C., S. Kippax and J. Crawford. 1991. 'Equality and Eroticism: AIDS and the Active/Passive Distinction", Paper, AIDS Research Unit, School of Behavioural Sciences, Macquarie University.

Walkowitz, J. 1980a. *Prostitution and Victorian Society: Women, Class and the State.* Cambridge: Cambridge University Press.

Walkowitz, J. 1980b. 'The Making of an Outcast Group: Prostitutes and Working Women in Nineteenth-century Plymouth and Southampton", in

M. Vicinus, ed., *A Widening Sphere: Changing Roles of Victorian Women*, pp. 72–93. Bloomington: Indiana University Press.

Walkowitz, J., and D. Walkowitz. 1974. '"We Are Not Beasts of the Field": Prostitution and the Poor in Plymouth and Southampton Under the Contagious Diseases Acts', in M. S. Hartman and L. Banner, eds, *Clio's Consciousness Raised: New Perspectives on the History of Women*, pp. 192–225. New York: Harper and Row.

Walter, I. 1985. *Secret Money*. Lexington, Mass.: Lexington Books.

Walter, J. 1988. 'Intellectuals and the Political Culture', in B. Head and J. Walter, eds, *Intellectual Movements and Australian Society*, pp. 240–67. Melbourne: Oxford University Press.

Watney, S. 1987. *Policing Desire: Pornography, AIDS and the Media*. London: Methuen.

Watson, S., ed. 1990. *Playing the State: Australian Feminist Interventions*. London: Verso.

Weedon, C. 1987. *Feminist Practice and Poststructuralist Theory*. Oxford: Basil Blackwell.

Weeks, J. 1981. *Sex, Politics and Society: The Regulation of Sexuality since 1800*. London: Longman.

Weeks, J. 1986. *Sexuality*. London: Ellis Horwood.

Weitzer, R. 1991. 'Prostitutes' Rights in the United States', *Sociological Quarterly*, 32(1): 24–30.

Wells, D. 1990. *In Defence of the Common Wealth: Reflections on Australian Politics*. Melbourne: Longman Cheshire.

Wells, J. 1982. *A Herstory of Prostitution in Western Europe*. Berkeley, Calif: Shameless Hussy Press.

Whip, R. 1991. 'Representing Women: Australian Female Parliamentarians on the Horns of a Dilemma', *Women and Politics*, 11(3): 1–22.

White, A. 1989. 'Porn King Seeks Public Export Grant', *Financial Review*, 13 October.

White, L. 1986. 'Prostitution, Identity and Class Consciousness in Nairobi during World War II', *Signs: Journal of Women in Culture and Society*, 11: 255–73.

Whitwell, G. 1989. *Making the Market: The Rise of Consumer Society*. Melbourne: McPhee Gribble.

Williams, E. 1970. 'Cultural Despotism: Film Censorship', in Dutton and Harris, 1970, pp. 52–76.

Williams, L. 1989. *Hard Core: Power, Pleasure and the 'Frenzy of the Visible'*. Berkeley: University of California Press.

Wilson, P. R., and D. Chappell. 1969. 'Prostitution in Australia', *Australian Journal of Social Issues*, 4(2): 61–72.

Winter, M. 1976. *Prostitution in Australia: A Sociological Study Prepared by a Qualified Research Team under the Supervision of Marcel Winter*. Balgowlah, NSW: Purtaboi Publications.

Wodak, R., ed. 1989. *Language, Power and Ideology: Studies in Political Discourse*. Amsterdam and Philadelphia: John Bejamins.

Wotherspoon, G. 1990. *This Nest of Perverts: Policing Male Homosexuality in Cold War Australia*. London: Sir Robert Menzies Centre for Australian Studies, Institute of Commonwealth Studies, University of London.

Yeatman, A. 1990. *Bureaucrats, Technocrats, Femocrats*. Sydney: Allen and Unwin.

Zillman, D., and J. Bryant. 1989. *Pornography: Research Advances and Policy Considerations*. Hillsdale, NJ: Lawrence Erlbaum.

Index